Lexical Issues in Language Learning

LEXICAL ISSUES IN LANGUAGE LEARNING

Birgit Harley, Editor
Ontario Institute for Studies in Education

Language Learning/John Benjamins Publishing Company
Ann Arbor/Amsterdam/Philadelphia

Library of Congress Cataloging-in-Publication Data

Lexical issues in language learning / Birgit Harley, ed.
　　p.　cm. — (The best of Language Learning)
　Includes bibliographical references and index.
　　1. Second language acquisition. 2. Vocabulary. 3. Bilingualism in
children. 4. Language and languages—Study and teaching. I. Harley,
Birgit. II. Series.
P118.L44 1995
401'.93--dc20　　　　　　　　　　　　　　　　　　　　　　95–21039
　ISBN 90 272 2352 1 (Eur.) / 1–55619–715–2 (US) (alk. paper)　　CIP

Published by:
Research Club in Language Learning, 178 Henry S. Frieze Building, 105
South State Street, Ann Arbor, Michigan 48109–1285, USA.

Distributed by:
John Benjamins Publishing Co., Post Office Box 75577, 1070 AN Amsterdam,
The Netherlands
John Benjamins North America, 821 Bethlehem Pike, Philadelphia, Pennsyl-
vania 19118, USA

Contents

continued

Section III: Lexical Acquisition and Use in Communication Tasks

Sincere thanks are extended to Alister Cumming, Wendy Wang, and
Irene Zadonsky for their valuable assistance in preparing this volume for
publication.

Introduction:
The Lexicon in Second Language Research

Birgit Harley
Ontario Institute for Studies in Education

The lexicon is central to language use and acquisition. A sociolinguistic perspective sees the word as "the most central element in the social system of communication" (Labov, 1973, p. 340); psycholinguists have characterized the lexicon as "driving" speech production (Levelt, 1989) and standing "at the heart" of listening comprehension (Marslen-Wilson, Tyler, Waksler, & Older, 1994); studies of early child language have revealed the fundamentally lexical nature of the initial stage of acquisition (e.g., Clark, 1994; Radford, 1990), and the lexicon is said to offer a "unique window on the process of acquisition for language as a whole" (Clark, 1994, p. 1). In the educational domain, a consistently strong relationship between vocabulary knowledge and reading comprehension (e.g., Anderson & Freebody, 1981) has led to the conclusion that lexical development is also crucially implicated in educational success.

Emphasis on the importance of the lexicon in language acquisition, use, and education is growing in second language (L2) studies too. As documented by Meara (1987, 1992), the past decade has witnessed exponential growth in lexically oriented L2 research. However, Meara has also identified the fragmented

I am grateful to Razika Sanaoui, Mari Wesche, and an anonymous reviewer for their helpful comments on an earlier draft of this article.

nature of this research and the apparent lack of connection
between psycholinguistic studies investigating mental representation of the bilingual lexicon and pedagogically motivated
vocabulary studies. The present volume attempts to bridge this
gap. Bringing together nine empirical studies with a wide range
of research objectives—monitoring development of the bilingual
lexicon in children, examining psycholinguistic factors in lexical
learning and use, and assessing the impact of lexically oriented
classroom instruction—it shows how each type of study makes an
essential contribution to an overall understanding of lexical
acquisition and use among young bilinguals and older L2 learners. The nine studies are all drawn from issues of *Language
Learning* from 1990 to 1995. In this introductory survey of current
research trends, I consider each study's contribution in relation to
some major research themes.

Nature and Growth of the L2 Lexicon

Assessment of Lexical Proficiency

The number of words a learner knows provides a commonsense
indicator of vocabulary knowledge and growth—assuming that
we know what a word is, what it means to "know" a word, and how
to obtain a valid and reliable sample of that knowledge. These are
all complex issues that resist definitive solutions (Baumann &
Kameenui, 1991; Goulden, Nation, & Read, 1990). Learners do
not know words on an all-or-nothing basis, and even mature
native speakers may often be "in a state of partial knowledge"
(Drum & Konopak, 1987, p. 77). The L2 literature has long
emphasized that there are varying degrees and different kinds of
word knowledge (e.g., Carter, 1987; Nation, 1990; Richards,
1976). Different kinds of receptive and productive vocabulary
tasks place differing demands on the learner in terms of word
knowledge and access/retrieval (for discussion: see Meara, 1990;
Teichroew, 1982). The learner's knowledge may be more or less
firmly established with respect to word form (morphology, phonol-

ogy, orthography) or meaning (conceptual, syntactic, pragmatic, affective, etc.). Because "vocabularies are not jumbled heaps of words rattling loose" (Griffiths, 1986, p. 304), the L2 learner may also, like the L1 learner, have more or less organized knowledge of paradigmatic relationships between words that share features of meaning and/or form, and of syntagmatic relationships between words that co-occur in language use.

Although the above distinctions by no means exhaust the kinds of lexical knowledge that exist, they suffice to show that any measure of L2 vocabulary knowledge is bound to be only partial. Whereas measures of vocabulary size, or "breadth", cover a broad sample of words, and are often receptive in nature (e.g., Goulden et al., 1990; Meara & Buxton, 1987; Nation, 1990), measures of vocabulary "depth" (how well words are known) focus more narrowly on specific aspects of meaning, word associations, or use (e.g., Read, 1993, 1994; Verhallen & Schoonen, 1993; Wesche & Paribakht, 1995). Other kinds of measures include indices of vocabulary richness and variety based on oral or written L2 corpora (e.g., Broeder, Extra, van Hout, Strömqvist, & Voionmaa, 1988; Harley & King, 1989; Laufer & Nation, in press), as well as lexical decision tasks, where the time taken to decide whether a string of letters is a word or not serves as a measure of lexical access (e.g., Segalowitz's article in this volume). The range of techniques for assessing lexical proficiency has expanded considerably in recent years, but ultimately, as Curtis (1987, p. 49) has argued, "the value of vocabulary tests depends on the goals of the user". In the examples in the present volume, different research objectives give rise to a considerable variety of measurement techniques.

The Bilingual Lexicon: Size, Growth, and Educational Needs

Global assessment of vocabulary breadth, or size, provides an initial index of how well the learner is progressing in relation to educational needs. In Europe and North America, studies have repeatedly found low educational achievement among bilingual minority children, and limited lexical knowledge in the majority language of schooling has emerged as one of the major obstacles in these children's path (e.g., Hancin-Bhatt & Nagy, 1994; Verhallen & Schoonen, 1993; Vermeer, 1992). Assessment of these children's vocabulary size has revealed that, after starting school with a relatively small vocabulary in the majority language, they may continue to lag behind majority-monolingual children year by year, even if their rate of lexical growth is similar (Vermeer, 1992). This lexical gap may not be confined to vocabulary size. On the basis of word definition tasks (a measure of vocabulary depth), Verhallen and Schoonen (1993) found that even when bilingual children were using L2 words productively, their knowledge of the hierarchical, paradigmatic relations of these words to other words—knowledge that is of particular importance in formal education—also lagged behind that of majority-monolingual children. Whether children's difficulties in this type of situation are restricted to the school language or are evident in their minority language as well is an important, but unresolved, issue.

Most studies of minority children's lexical development have examined their progress in the majority language alone. In the present volume, two articles examine lexical development in *both* languages of simultaneous-bilingual children. Pearson, Fernández, and Oller measure rate of receptive and productive lexical growth in very young simultaneous-bilingual children (English-Spanish) in terms of two measures: Total Vocabulary in the children's two languages together, and Total Conceptual Vocabulary taking account of the overlap of lexicalized concepts in the two languages. Using these double-language measures (derived from parent report forms) to gauge overall lexical development, Pearson et al. establish that the range of lexical growth patterns among the simultaneous-bilingual children studied did not differ from that of monolingual children in a single language. This research team is now focusing on investigating the bilingual children's language development in greater depth (e.g., Pearson & Fernández, 1994). In the second article, Umbel and Oller assess the vocabulary knowledge in Spanish and English of older, middle-class Hispanic children in Miami, using complementary standardized tests of receptive vocabulary in each language. These children, with substantial exposure to Spanish in the home and living in a facilitating wider environment where both languages are valued, performed near monolingual norms in Spanish at each of three grade levels, and by Grade 6 were close to English language norms as well. This positive correlation between lexical knowledge in each language provides important clues concerning the sociolinguistic conditions that promote additive lexical growth in simultaneous-bilingual children.

The assessment of vocabulary size also relates to how much vocabulary adult L2 learners need to cope with academic studies in the L2 (Hazenberg & Hulstijn, 1995; Laufer, 1992; Nation, 1993). Hazenberg and Hulstijn, for example, constructed a multiple-choice test of receptive vocabulary in Dutch, using a dictionary and a large corpus of written Dutch to identify a representative sample of words of appropriate frequency. Nonnative university applicants were one of the groups tested, and their scores were related to performance on a Dutch reading comprehension test required for university entrance. Results pointed to a minimum threshold level of 10,000 words necessary to cope with academic reading requirements in L2 at the university level. This sobering figure reinforces the importance of lexical development for meeting educational needs in L2.

Lexical Retention / Attrition

Maintaining first language (L1) literacy skills in a bilingual community where much of one's schooling has taken place in the L2 is an issue of concern to many adult bilinguals. In the present volume, Segalowitz examines the relationship between advanced skill in L2 reading and automaticity of L1 word recognition skill. The two groups of adult Canadian French/English bilinguals he studied both had equally high L2 reading comprehension scores but differed in their reading rates: One of the groups read more slowly in L2 than in L1, whereas the other read at the same rate in both languages. On a visual lexical decision task in L1, the "same rate" bilinguals performed significantly more slowly than the other group, indicating a negative relationship between advanced L2 skill and speed of lexical access in L1 (see also Hakuta & D'Andrea, 1992; Mägiste, 1986). On the other hand, under priming conditions that required automatic (as opposed to controlled) processing of some of the L1 words, the same rate bilinguals showed greater relative facilitation than the other group, suggesting that there was no reduction in L1 automaticity. Segalowitz suggests a need for further investigations of the development of processing skill in L1 at younger ages as a function of different patterns of bilingual exposure, in order to determine how best to nurture advanced reading skills in both of the bilingual's languages.

Although the adults in Segalowitz's study were in an environment where continued exposure to their two languages could be assumed, other studies have focused on language retention/ attrition in contexts where the L2 has fallen into more or less complete disuse. Longitudinal studies have shown that receptive L2 vocabulary knowledge, once established, can remain remarkably robust over a period of years (Bahrick, 1984; Weltens, van Els, & Schils, 1989), although speed of access potentially declines and greater attrition in production typically occurs (for review: Weltens & Grendel, 1993). The linguistic characteristics of lexical attrition in production and the compensatory strategies (Poulisse & Schils, this volume) applied have received growing attention from researchers. Crosslinguistic influence, including incorporation of lexical items from the dominant language, for example, is a phenomenon observed in both L1 and L2 attrition (e.g., Boyd, 1993; Olshtain, 1989). The range of factors affecting long-term maintenance has important social and educational implications. Both Olshtain (1989) and Cohen (1989), for example, found that once both groups had left the L2 environment, lexical retention among older L2 speakers was superior to that of younger children who were unable to read in the language, leading the researchers to conclude that literacy may be a key factor in the long-term maintenance of vocabulary knowledge.

The issue of L2 lexical retention involves not only how long-term disuse of the L2 affects proficient L2 speakers but also how lasting is the impact of initial L2 lexical learning. Wang and Thomas, in this volume, deal with L2 retention in this sense, showing that an apparent immediate advantage of one lexical learning condition over another may dissipate a few days later. In this case, the learning of Chinese characters by novice English-speaking learners via an imagery-based technique was subject to just as much forgetting as a rote-learning condition, if not more. This study's methodological implications for further lexical research are clear: Delayed posttesting is essential to determine the long-term merits of different approaches to lexical learning.

Organization of the L2 Mental Lexicon

Research into the nature of the L2 learner's mental lexicon has asked a fundamental question: whether the L2 lexicon is organized in the learner's mind similarly to, or differently from, that of the native speaker. For example, referring to a series of word association experiments, Meara (1984) found that whereas native speakers responded in a stable, semantically motivated way to word stimuli, L2 learners' responses were much less predictable, appearing often to be influenced by the phonological or orthographic form of the stimulus word rather than by its meaning. Meara saw the apparently tenuous and loosely organized nature of learners' lexical networks as pointing to "major differences between native speakers and learners of a language in the way they store and handle words" (p. 235). Similarly, Laufer (1989) reported that deceptive formal similarities between words were a source of error among the adult EFL learners she studied, suggesting that in contrast to the mental lexicon in L1, the connections between L2 words are "primarily phonological" (p. 17). These views have since been challenged by Singleton and Little (1991), who argued that such findings suggest only that the learners did not know the words in question, not that the structure of the L2 lexicon is qualitatively different from the L1—particularly because "clang" associations are also characteristic of children in L1. From new data they collected, Singleton and Little claimed instead that the structure of the L2 lexicon, like that of the L1, is primarily semantic; however, Chapelle (1994) has questioned the appropriateness of the C-test they used to gather data, casting some doubt on their interpretation. Nonetheless, one can reasonably conclude from existing studies that growth in L2 word knowledge leads gradually from an initial focus on sound similarities to a more stable, semantically motivated type of lexical organization (cf. Henning, 1973). This pattern of development appears similar to that occurring in L1.

Related to the preceding issue, a much debated question among psycholinguists has been whether a bilingual's mental lexicon in L2 is stored independently from the L1 lexicon or whether the two are interdependent (for recent discussion, e.g., Lee, 1994; Schreuder & Weltens, 1993). Experiments with bilingual word association (i.e., translation) tasks, for example, have suggested that some areas of the mental lexicon in each language are more closely connected than others: Concrete words and cognates that have a high degree of meaning overlap may be represented by the fluent bilingual in a compound (interdependent) fashion, whereas abstract nouns and noncognates are more likely to be stored in coordinate (independent) form (e.g., de Groot, 1993). Green (1993), however, has argued that it is not necessary to propose different kinds of mental representation, but just that close translation equivalents such as cognates share "more of their representations in common" (p. 258). If these observations apply generally to advanced bilinguals, links between the L1 and L2 lexical systems could be at least as close for less proficient L2 learners, and L2 teaching approaches that avoid all reference to the L1 may need to be reconsidered.

Effects of L1 on L2 Learning

In studies of L2 acquisition, numerous findings demonstrate crosslinguistic influence from the L1 on the use of lexical items in L2, influence that may be overt or covert, negative or positive (Ringbom, 1987). Negative L1 influence can be attributed to a variety of psycholinguistic factors: for example, subtle differences between L1 and L2 in the categorization of nonprototypical vocabulary items or meanings, which may continue to affect advanced L2 speakers' L2 use (e.g., Aitchison, 1992; Ijaz, 1986); the misleading formal similarity of L1/L2 words, such as false cognates, which nonetheless differ partly or entirely in meaning (Holmes & Ramos, 1993); or lexicalization patterns, which differ from L1 to L2, such as the different way in which directional motion events are typically expressed in English and French (Harley, 1989) or the different syntactic frames associated with some English and French verbs (Adjemian, 1983; Harley, 1993). Perceptions of language distance may also affect transferability. Broeder et al. (1988) noted wholesale borrowing from Spanish on the part of one Spanish-speaking learner of French; on the other hand, Kellerman (1978, 1986) found Dutch learners unwilling to transfer peripheral meanings of Dutch words into English L2, in spite of equivalent meanings in the L1.

Although studies of crosslinguistic influence have tended more often to focus on negative aspects, there is growing evidence of the facilitative effect of L1/L2 relationships on L2 learning. Ringbom (1986, 1987) presented the example of Finnish students learning English L2; those with Swedish L1 (a Germanic language cognate with English) had a strong initial advantage over students with Finnish L1 (typologically unrelated to English). Even in languages that are typologically distinct, there may be specific lexical similarities that provide an advantage to the L2 learner. Thus, a similarity in the lexicalization of motion verbs in Chinese and English appears to give Chinese learners of English an advantage over Japanese learners in acquiring English motion verbs (Yu, 1995).

Other studies have demonstrated that cognate relationships play a positive role in supporting the L2 performance of learners. Meara, Lightbown, and Halter (1994), for example, found that an unduly high proportion of French/English cognates on a yes/no test of English vocabulary boosted the vocabulary scores of French-speaking learners. Ard and Homburg (1983) showed that on a vocabulary test in English, Spanish-speaking learners had an advantage over Arabic-speaking learners that was evident not only in their performance on items that were cognate in English and Spanish but also more generally on the test as a whole. Nagy, Garcia, Durgunoglu, and Hancin (1993) and Hancin-Bhatt and Nagy (1994) found that awareness by bilingual Hispanic children of cognate relationships between Spanish and English was re-lated to their comprehension of written English sentences containing these cognates and that their ability to translate cognates increased from Grade 4 to Grade 8. The older children also demonstrated somewhat greater awareness of systematic relationships between Spanish and English suffixes, although in keeping with developmental trends in L1 (Tyler & Nagy, 1989), this type of morphological awareness lagged behind their recogni-tion of cognate stems. These age-related findings among bilingual Hispanic children provide an interesting perspective on those of Umbel and Oller (this volume), who found that Hispanic children in Grade 6 were doing better in English vocabulary than younger children (relative to monolingual age norms) while also maintain-ing a high level of Spanish vocabulary knowledge. Competency in a Romance language may be a benefit in dealing with the "lexical bar" created by Greco-Latin words that Corson (in press) has identified as characteristic of academic English discourse and as a barrier to scholastic achievement among children whose out-side-school exposure to English may contain few such words.

In the present volume, several studies indicate further ways in which the L1 can serve to support L2 vocabulary learning. In a study of the psycholinguistic factors influencing the relative difficulty of L2 words, Ellis and Beaton, for example, provide evidence that L2 words that are acoustically and orthographically similar to the L1 are easier than dissimilar words for novice adult learners to recall, and that the reminding power of a mnemonic L1 keyword is also enhanced by greater acoustic similarity with its target L2 word. Danan shows that a video with "reversed" subtitles (L1 soundtrack and L2 subtitles) is particularly useful to adult beginners for the purpose of L2 vocabulary learning. She argues that as the L1 audio and visual images provide the global context, the written L2 subtitles give the learners more time for efficient processing, and the translation process involved establishes more paths for retrieval of the L2 words. Luppescu and Day's study of the use of bilingual dictionaries by Japanese university students learning English provides a further indication of the potential usefulness of reference to the L1 (cf. Knight, 1994). Although mean scores were low, learners who were permitted to use a bilingual dictionary while reading a short story in English scored slightly higher on a posttest of vocabulary knowledge than did other students who were not supplied with a dictionary. However, the dictionary group took longer to read the story and also made more errors on some items, suggesting that they were misled by some dictionary definitions (cf. Nesi & Meara, 1994). The overall conclusion, nonetheless, is that reference to the L1 provides useful support for L2 vocabulary learning.

Learnability and Developmental Patterns in L2 Lexis

A key issue in L2 lexical research is what makes some words easier than others to learn. This is the central theme of the article by Ellis and Beaton, who reviewed psycholinguistic factors found in experimental research to affect word learnability, including, for example: similarity to the L1 in terms of phonology, orthography, or semantics; the concreteness and imageability of the L2 word; the L2 word's part of speech; and its frequency (see also review by R. Ellis, 1994).

A further perspective on the learnability issue is provided by research investigating developmental patterns in the productive use of L2 vocabulary in learners' speech and writing. Studies that have examined the kinds of L2 words that beginning learners use have found that nouns and verbs appear to have particular significance. Dietrich (1990) found the early productive lexicon of adult immigrants in Germany to be a mainly nominal one, with growth in verbs occurring later in the acquisition process (cf. Yoshida, 1978). Interpretations of such findings have varied. Whereas for L1, Gentner (1982) attributed the initial preponderance of nouns to the greater perceptual salience and stability of concrete objects, Dietrich (1990) emphasized the pragmatic value of nominal reference for basic communication. A psycholinguistic explanation more in line with Gentner's is that nouns are easier to learn owing to their imageability. In their experiment involving the learning of written German words by English-speaking adults, Ellis and Beaton (this volume) found that nouns were much easier for novice learners to recall than verbs and that relative imageability of the concept to be learned was also a determinant of learnability. Aitchison (1987) provided a further interpretation: that verbs are more difficult in the sense that they tend to be more closely tied to syntactic constructions than nouns.

Although nouns may predominate in the speech of beginning learners of L2, verbs appear to be most centrally involved in lexical development. Broeder, Extra, van Hout, and Voionmaa (1993), who studied the L2 development of adult immigrants in Western Europe, found that an increase in the proportion of verbs relative to other word categories was positively associated with overall lexical richness, whereas the opposite was the case for nouns: The higher the proportion of nouns in a learner's lexicon, the lower the overall lexical richness tended to be. Broeder et al. (1993) suggested that: "An increase in the proportion of verbs corresponds to a development in the *structuring* of learners' utterances" (p. 159, emphasis in original), an observation that appears to concur with Aitchison's (1987) view (see above) concerning the relative difficulty of nouns and verbs.

Other studies have examined the nature of the lexical verbs that L2 learners produce in the early stages. For example, Harley and King (1989) and Harley (1993) found that elementary school children learning French in Canadian immersion programs made substantially greater use of general verbs of high coverage in writing and speaking French than did the same-aged native speakers, although they did not necessarily use these verbs in a full range of meanings. With increasing grade level, more specificity of verbs was observed. In a study of 6-year-old children learning Swedish, Viberg (1993) reported that they had a tendency to favor one or two typologically unmarked nuclear verbs in each of several semantic fields. Compared with native Swedish-speaking peers, the L2 learners overused these nuclear verbs, overextended their primary meanings, and underused their language-specific meanings. Viberg suggested that nuclear verbs serve as syntactic prototypes, providing entry points to L2 sentence structure. Ard and Gass (1987) have also proposed that lexical development is a cause and not an effect of syntactic development in L2.

As noted above, awareness of word morphology appears to be a relatively late development in L1 acquisition (Tyler & Nagy, 1989). There is corresponding evidence to suggest that the process of derivation is acquired late in L2 acquisition. Broeder, Extra, and van Hout (1989), for example, presented data from several adult learners indicating that semantically transparent composition, and in particular noun compounding, was a preferred word formation process in the early acquisition of Dutch L2, whereas the more opaque process of derivation was hardly used, if at all. Similarly, Harley (1993) noted that in oral L2 use, French immersion students in Canada generally produced few derived verbs (cf. Harley & King, 1989, on immersion students' writing). Olshtain (1987), on the other hand, found that intermediate L2 learners of Hebrew were more likely to use affixation than were advanced learners and native speakers. Olshtain (p. 229) attributed this unexpected finding to an instructional focus in the intermediate students' L2 classes, noting that affixation in Hebrew is formally simpler than blending, which was also used by the native speaker and advanced learner groups but was completely absent among the intermediate learners. Going beyond such descriptive analy-

ses, Robinson (1994) undertook an examination of L2 word formation from the perspective of language universals. He found that
an implicational hierarchy and Universal Grammar have some
tentative predictive value in explaining the acquisition of noun
incorporation processes in Samoan L2.

The acquisition of word formation processes in L2 has so far
received relatively little attention from researchers; however,
numerous recent studies of the acquisition and mental representation of morphologically complex words in L1 point to this area
as a promising one for further investigation of developmental
patterns in L2.

Processes in L2 Vocabulary Comprehension, Learning, and Use

Second language learners encounter L2 words under a great
variety of conditions: in oral or written form, with higher or lower
frequency, embedded or not in an L2 discourse context, with more
or less useful textual and/or extratextual (e.g., visual, L1 equivalents) cues to meaning, and involving reception only or production
and feedback as well. Learners also have a host of individual
differences: for example, in age, aptitude, motivation, prior knowledge, and language learning experience. Any understanding of
how L2 vocabulary learning proceeds has to take account of the
way in which such factors interact to promote learning.

Guessing and Learning Through Reading

Written text, less fleeting and typically providing exposure to
more vocabulary than oral conversation, is an important source of
vocabulary learning. Indeed, beyond an early stage of acquisition,
the growth of vocabulary knowledge in L1 or L2 is often closely
linked to the development of reading comprehension (e.g., Anderson & Freebody, 1981; Nation, 1993; Stanovich, 1986). Stanovich
has described the relationship as one of "reciprocal causation":
Reading comprehension is dependent on prior vocabulary knowl-

edge, but reading is also a major source of new vocabulary learning.

Researchers have recently directed a substantial amount of attention to describing how L2 learners approach unfamiliar words in a written text and the kinds of cues they use to infer word meaning (e.g., de Bot, Paribakht, & Wesche, 1995; Haastrup, 1991; Huckin & Bloch, 1993; Parry, 1991; Schouten-van Parreren, 1989). The effectiveness of the inferencing process in promoting successful guessing appears to depend on a variety of conditions: that the learner already has sufficient prior lexical knowledge to be able to make use of the context (Laufer, 1992; Nation, 1993); that the context itself is intrinsically useful (Beck, McKeown, & McCaslin, 1983; Li, 1988); and that the learner makes efficient use of different kinds of cues (Haastrup, 1991) rather than settling for the first "reckless guess" (Holmes & Ramos, 1993). Successful guessing of a word meaning in context is a prerequisite for learning it through reading; yet as Mondria and Wit-de Boer (1991) have shown, learners are not likely to retain words too easily guessed from context, perhaps because they have devoted too little mental effort to the inferencing task.

Elley and Manghubai (1983), Krashen (1989), Day, Omura, and Hiramatsu (1991), and Hulstijn (1992) have nonetheless all provided evidence that L2 learners, as well as native speakers, can acquire new vocabulary "incidentally" in the context of reading, apparently without any intention to learn. One or two encounters with unfamiliar words under these conditions generally produce only a meager amount of learning, however (Hulstijn, 1992). The process (in L1 at least) appears gradual and incremental, with more frequent exposure to specific words prompting better results (Jenkins, Stein, & Wysocki, 1984; Nagy, Anderson, & Herman, 1987). On the other hand, interest and emotional saliency can occasionally lead to the retention of L2 words encountered only once (Schouten-van Parreren, 1989).

The Role of Consciousness

The role of consciousness in learning word meaning from context is controversial. Krashen (1989), for example, has argued that incidental acquisition of vocabulary from context happens unconsciously, whereas N. Ellis (1994a, 1994b) has argued that any aspect of vocabulary learning having to do with meaning involves conscious, explicit learning, in contrast to the mainly implicit learning of surface word forms. Ellis' argument implies that success in learning word meaning will depend on the strategic use of mental effort or deep processing, whether in inferring word meaning from context, in using mnemonic techniques to remember words, or in engaging in any other activity that elaborates links between the new word and existing knowledge. This view further implies that knowledge of L2 word meanings will be positively related to academic success and that instruction that stimulates explicit learning will benefit vocabulary development.

As already noted, there are indications that mental effort does have a positive effect on the learning of word meaning via reading. Moreover, when added effort is promoted, for example by warning students of an impending test (Hulstijn, 1992), more learning is achieved. Other researchers, assuming an important role for consciousness, have recommended various ways of raising learners' awareness of inferencing strategies so as to improve their ability to comprehend words while reading (e.g., Haastrup, 1991; Nation, 1990; Oxford & Scarcella, 1994). So far, however, we lack research gauging the efficacy of these recommendations for L2, though there is evidence that adolescents can benefit from being taught how to infer word meaning from text in L1 (Buikema & Graves, 1993).

Reading is not the only context in which the learning of word meaning occurs, though it has received the lion's share of attention (cf. R. Ellis, 1994). Studies of oral learning suggest that consciousness is involved here too. One study of children acquiring English as an L2, for example, found a relationship between oral L2 vocabulary knowledge and academic success (Saville-

Troike, 1984). In the present volume, the classroom experiment
described by Ellis, Tanaka, and Yamasaki investigated the role of
student-initiated negotiation of meaning as a hypothesized prime
source of L2 comprehension and learning. Ellis et al. examined
the effects of different kinds of oral classroom input on Japanese
high school students' comprehension and learning of concrete
nouns in English. They found that not only comprehension but
also long-term retention of L2 vocabulary can be enhanced in
classes where students initiate negotiation of meaning, even for
students who are not directly involved in the negotiation. The
added time and opportunity afforded for focused recycling and
reviewing of the relevant lexical items apparently led these
learners (including the listeners) to process them more deeply.
Evidence that explicit, student-initiated vocabulary learning outside the L2 classroom is also beneficial comes from Sanaoui
(1995). She found that adult L2 learners who engaged in a wide
range of vocabulary-learning activities outside class retained
more words taught in class than did learners who undertook fewer
outside vocabulary-learning activities and spent less time at
them.

The relative merits of conscious mnemonic techniques for
vocabulary learning involving semantic and imagery mediation,
and in particular the keyword technique, are a matter of debate.
Some studies have shown that prompting explicit learning via
imagery-based mnemonic techniques effectively promotes vocabulary learning in both L1 and L2, though researchers have
noted limitations on such techniques' efficacy in nonlaboratory
settings (for review: Cohen, 1987; Pressley, Levin, & McDaniel,
1987). For example, cultural differences may affect the learners'
willingness to adopt specific techniques (O'Malley, 1987). Also, in
their experiment reported in this volume, Ellis and Beaton found
the keyword technique was useful only for receptive L2 vocabulary learning with words that were easily imageable. Implicit rote
learning involving phonological factors appears to have been more
heavily involved in production. Wang and Thomas (this volume),
who found no long-term advantage for imagery-based learning

over rote learning, doubt the value of imagery-based mnemonics, particularly when given to the learners by the experimenter. That mnemonic techniques may have a greater effect when learners are free to choose their own approach (cf. Cohen, 1990) concurs with the findings of those who have noted that simply giving learners information can lead to less mental effort on their part (e.g., Hulstijn, 1992; Tomasello & Herron, 1988). There is also evidence that a combination of techniques for remembering L2 words, even if experimenter-presented, works better than a single technique. In keeping with the "depth of processing" hypothesis, Brown and Perry (1991), for example, found that the keyword mnemonic technique together with a "semantic" approach (reading definitions of a word and answering a question) led to greater learning than use of a keyword alone. Similarly, Paribakht & Wesche (1993) have shown that more vocabulary learning can be achieved when reading is complemented by explicit, text-related vocabulary exercises.

Although inventing mental images in association with keywords and extracting images from Chinese ideographs (Wang & Thomas, this volume) have limitations in promoting L2 vocabulary learning, there is evidence that contextualized visual support in the form of television or video images can increase L2 vocabulary by encouraging deeper processing. Neumann & Koskinen (1992), for example, showed that watching captioned television was a more effective way for adolescent ESL students to learn science vocabulary than either reading along and listening to text or simply reading the textbook. Citing Paivio's (1986) dual coding hypothesis, Danan (this volume) argues that the video aspect of the input provided to learners in her study of different types of subtitling was an important factor in their learning, contributing to deeper processing.

Making associations within the L2 and between the L1 and L2 can also help in both comprehension and learning of L2 vocabulary (Cohen & Aphek, 1981), and cross-language associations are especially helpful when the L1 and L2 are cognate languages (see section above on L1/L2 relationships). Knight

(1994) found that instruction encouraging explicit reference to the L1 in interpreting L2 words in context can benefit low-level adult learners in particular. Tréville (1993) found that explicit instruction on the morphological relationships between cognates in English (L1) and French (L2) was helpful to beginning adult learners. It remains to be seen whether teaching relationships between Spanish and English derivational morphology would benefit younger bilingual Hispanic students as Hancin-Bhatt and Nagy (1994) have suggested.

In sum, evidence is growing that the process of learning L2 word meanings, at least by adults, is an explicit one, as N. Ellis (1994a, 1994b) has argued, and that various ways of encouraging increased strategic processing through instruction can be beneficial. More research is now needed to examine this issue in younger L2 learners and to investigate further the hypothesized dissociation between explicit learning of meaning aspects of L2 words and implicit learning of their surface forms. From an instructional perspective, there is also a need for more investigation of how L2 teachers generally approach vocabulary teaching in their classrooms (see e.g., Lapkin & Swain, 1995; Sanaoui, in press; Swain & Carroll, 1987). In her study of adult French L2 classes, Sanaoui, for example, argued that, as in Swain and Carroll's study of Grade 6 French immersion classes, not enough attention was paid to systematic teaching of many important aspects of L2 lexis.

Compensating for Lexical Gaps in L2 Production

Taking a different perspective on L2 lexical performance, a body of research has examined how learners (as well as "attriters") compensate for lexical gaps during oral production. For the past decade, much of this research has been descriptive, emphasizing the identification of communication strategies and the development of taxonomies of strategy types (for review: Bialystok, 1990; Poulisse, 1993). From different theoretical perspectives, Bialystok and Poulisse have been concerned with interpreting strategy use in terms of broader models of language use. Poulisse and Schils (in the present volume) make a process-oriented distinction be-tween conceptual and linguistic strategies and throw new light on the factors that influence strategy use, demonstrating that com-munication task has a substantial effect on strategy use, linked to aspects such as the availability of a supporting context and presence of an interlocutor.

The role of instruction in developing communication strate-gies to compensate for lexical gaps is unclear. Whereas raising awareness of inferencing strategies appears to help at least adolescent L1 readers, we lack strong evidence showing that teaching communication strategies is useful for oral L2 produc-tion.

Organization of This Volume

As this introductory overview of current research trends has shown, the articles in this volume contribute insights relevant to a wide variety of research issues in L2 lexical learning: issues in assessing lexical growth among bilinguals, language retention/attrition, the relevance of L1 in L2 learning, developmental patterns in L2 lexis and the factors that account for them, the processes involved in L2 learning, and the use of strategies to compensate for lexical problems in communication.

These studies are grouped under three headings reflecting the main shared emphases of the studies in each group. In the first section are the articles by Pearson et al., Umbel and Oller, and Segalowitz, concerned with the assessment of lexical develop-ment in bilinguals at different points in the life-span; the second section consists of the two experiments (by Ellis & Beaton and Wang & Thomas) dealing with psycholinguistic factors underly-ing the learnability and retention of L2 lexis; and the third section contains the articles by Ellis et al., Luppescu and Day, Danan, and Poulisse & Schils, emphasizing the conditions on communication tasks that promote classroom learning of L2 vocabulary or lead to different strategies for dealing with lexical problems in communi-cation.

References

Adjemian, C. (1983). The transferability of lexical properties. In S. M. Gass & L. Selinker (Eds.), *Language transfer in language learning* (pp. 250–268). Rowley, MA: Newbury House.

Aitchison, J. (1987). *Words in the mind: An introduction to the mental lexicon.* Oxford: Basil Blackwell.

Aitchison, J. (1992). Good birds, better birds, and amazing birds: The development of prototypes. In P. J. L. Arnaud & H. Béjoint (Eds.), *Vocabulary and applied linguistics* (pp. 71–84). Basingstoke, Hants: Macmillan.

Anderson, J. C., & Freebody, P. (1981). Vocabulary knowledge. In J. T. Guthrie (Ed.), *Comprehension and teaching* (pp. 77–117). Newark, DE: International Reading Association.

Ard, J., & Gass, S. M. (1987). Lexical constraints on syntactic acquisition. *Studies in Second Language Acquisition, 9,* 233–252.

Ard, J., & Homburg, T. (1983). Verification of language transfer. In S. M. Gass & L. Selinker (Eds.), *Language transfer in language learning* (pp. 157–176). Rowley, MA: Newbury House.

Bahrick, H. (1984). Fifty years of second language attrition: Implications for programmatic research. *Modern Language Journal, 68,* 105–118.

Baumann, J. F., & Kameenui, E. J. (1991). Research on vocabulary instruction: Ode to Voltaire. In J. Flood, J. Jensen, D. Lapp, & J. Squire (Eds.), *Handbook of research on teaching the English language arts* (pp. 604–632). New York: Macmillan.

Beck, I. L., McKeown, M. G., & McCaslin, E. S. (1983). Vocabulary development: All contexts are not created equal. *Elementary School Journal, 83,* 177–181.

Bialystok, E. (1990). *Communication strategies: A psychological analysis of second-language use.* Oxford: Basil Blackwell.

Boyd, S. (1993). Attrition or expansion? Changes in the lexicon of Finnish and American adult bilinguals in Sweden. In K. Hyltenstam & A. Viberg (Eds.), *Progression & regression in language: Sociocultural, neuropsychological & linguistic perspectives* (pp. 386–411). Cambridge: Cambridge University Press.

Broeder, P., Extra, G., & van Hout, R. (1989). Processes in the developing lexicon of adult immigrant learners. *AILA Review, 6,* 86–109.

Broeder, P., Extra, G., van Hout, R., & Voionmaa, K. (1993). Word formation processes in talking about entities. In C. Perdue (Ed.), *Adult language acquisition: Crosslinguistic perspectives: Vol. II. The results* (pp. 41–72). Cambridge: Cambridge University Press.

Broeder, P., Extra, G., van Hout, R., Strömqvist, S., & Voionmaa, K. (Eds.) (1988). *Processes in the developing lexicon.* Final report to the European

Science Foundation: Vol. 3. Strasbourg, Tilburg and Göteborg: European Science Foundation.

Brown, T. S., & Perry, F. L., Jr. (1991). A comparison of three learning strategies for ESL vocabulary acquisition. *TESOL Quarterly, 25*, 655–670.

Buikema, J. L., & Graves, M. F. (1993). Teaching students to use context cues to infer word meanings. *Journal of Reading, 36*, 450–457.

Carter, R. (1987). *Vocabulary: Applied linguistic perspectives*. London: Allen & Unwin.

Chapelle, C. A. (1994). Are C-tests valid measures for L2 vocabulary research? *Second Language Research, 10*, 157–187.

Clark, E. V. (1994). *The lexicon in acquisition*. Cambridge: CUP.

Cohen, A. D. (1987). The use of verbal and imagery mnemonics in second-language vocabulary learning. *Studies in Second Language Acquisition, 9*, 43–62.

Cohen, A. D. (1989). Attrition in the productive lexicon of two Portuguese third language speakers. *Studies in Second Language Acquisition, 11*, 135–149.

Cohen, A. D. (1990). *Language learning: Insights for learners, teachers, and researchers*. Boston, MA: Heinle & Heinle.

Cohen, A. D., & Aphek, E. (1981). Easifying second language learning. *Studies in Second Language Acquisition, 3*, 221–236.

Corson, D. (in press). *Using English words*. Boston: Kluwer Academic.

Curtis, M. E. (1987). Vocabulary testing and instruction. In M. A. McKeown & M. E. Curtis (Eds.), *The nature of vocabulary acquisition* (pp. 37–51). Hillsdale, NJ: Lawrence Erlbaum.

Day, R. R., Omura, C., & Hiramatsu, M. (1991). Incidental EFL vocabulary learning and reading. *Reading in a Foreign Language, 7*, 541–551.

de Bot, K., Paribakht, T. S., & Wesche, M. B. (1995, April). *Modelling lexical processing in a second language: Evidence from ESL reading*. Paper presented at the meeting of the American Association for Applied Linguistics, Long Beach, CA.

de Groot, A. M. B. (1993). Word-type effects in bilingual processing tasks: Support for a mixed-representational system. In R. Schreuder & B. Weltens (Eds.), *The bilingual lexicon* (pp. 27–51). Amsterdam: Benjamins.

Dietrich, R. (1990). Nouns and verbs in the learner's lexicon. In H. W. Dechert (Ed.), *Current trends in European second language acquisition research* (pp. 13–22). Clevedon, Avon: Multilingual Matters.

Drum, P., & Konopak, B. C. (1987). Learning word meanings from written context. In M. G. McKeown & M. E. Curtis (Eds.), *The nature of vocabulary acquisition* (pp. 73–87). Hillsdale, NJ: Lawrence Erlbaum.

Elley, W. B., & Manghubai, F. (1983). The impact of reading on second language learning. *Reading Research Quarterly, 19,* 53–67.

Ellis, N. C. (1994a). Consciousness in second language learning: Psychological perspectives on the role of conscious processes in vocabulary acquisition. *AILA Review, 11,* 37–56.

Ellis, N. C. (1994b). Vocabulary acquisition: The implicit ins and outs of explicit cognitive mediation. In N. C. Ellis (Ed.), *Implicit and explicit learning of languages* (pp. 211–282). London: Academic Press.

Ellis, R. (1994). Factors in the incidental acquisition of second language vocabulary from oral input: A review essay. *Applied Language Learning, 5,* 1–32.

Gentner, D. (1982). Why nouns are learned before verbs: Linguistic relativity versus natural partitioning. In S. A. Kucsaj II (Ed.), *Language development: Vol. 2. Language, thought and culture* (pp. 301–334). Hillsdale, NJ: Lawrence Erlbaum.

Goulden, R., Nation, P., & Read, J. (1990). How large can a receptive vocabulary be? *Applied Linguistics, 11,* 341–363.

Green, D. W. (1993). Towards a model of L2 comprehension and production. In R. Schreuder & B. Weltens (Eds.), *The bilingual lexicon* (pp. 249–277). Amsterdam: John Benjamins.

Griffiths, P. (1986). Early vocabulary. In P. Fletcher & M. Garman (Eds.), *Language acquisition,* (2nd ed., pp. 279–306). Cambridge: CUP.

Haastrup, K. (1991). *Lexical inferencing procedures or talking about words.* Tübingen, Germany: Gunter Narr.

Hakuta, K., & D'Andrea, D. (1992). Some properties of bilingual maintenance and loss in Mexican background high school students. *Applied Linguistics, 13,* 72–99.

Hancin-Bhatt, B., & Nagy, W. (1994). Lexical transfer and second language morphological development. *Applied Psycholinguistics, 15,* 289–310.

Harley, B. (1989). Transfer in the written compositions of French immersion students. In H. W. Dechert & M. Raupach (Eds.), *Transfer in language production* (pp. 3–19). New York: Ablex.

Harley, B. (1993). Patterns of second language development in French immersion. *French Language Studies, 2,* 159–183.

Harley, B., & King, M. L. (1989). Verb lexis in the written compositions of young L2 learners. *Studies in Second Language Acquisition, 11,* 415–439.

Hazenberg, S., & Hulstijn, J. (1995). *Defining a minimal receptive second-language vocabulary for non-native university students: An empirical investigation.* Manuscript submitted for publication.

Henning, G. H. (1973). Remembering foreign language vocabulary: Acoustic and semantic parameters. *Language Learning, 23,* 185–196.

Holmes, J., & Ramos, R. G. (1993). False friends and reckless guessers:

Observing cognate recognition strategies. In T. Huckin, M. Haynes, & J. Coady (Eds.), *Second language reading and vocabulary learning* (pp. 86–108). Norwood, NJ: Ablex.

Huckin, T., & Bloch, J. (1993). Strategies for inferring word-meanings in context: A cognitive model. In T. Huckin, M. Haynes, & J. Coady (Eds.), *Second language reading and vocabulary learning* (pp. 153–178). Norwood, NJ: Ablex.

Hulstijn, J. (1992). Retention of inferred and given word meanings: Experiments in incidental vocabulary learning. In P. L. Arnaud & H. Béjoint (Eds.), *Vocabulary and applied linguistics* (pp. 113–125). London: Macmillan.

Ijaz, I. H. (1986). Linguistic and cognitive determinants of lexical acquisition in a second language. *Language Learning, 36*, 401–451.

Jenkins, J. R., Stein, M. L., & Wysocki, K. (1984). Learning vocabulary through reading. *American Educational Research Journal, 21*, 767–787.

Kellerman, E. (1978). Giving learners a break: Native language intuitions as a source of predictions about transferability. *Working Papers on Bilingualism, 15*, 59–92.

Kellerman, E. (1986). An eye for an eye: Crosslinguistic constraints on the development of the L2 lexicon. In E. Kellerman & M. Sharwood Smith (Eds.), *Crosslinguistic influence in second language acquisition* (pp. 35–48). Oxford: Pergamon.

Knight, S. (1994). Dictionary use while reading: The effects on comprehension and vocabulary acquisition for students of different verbal abilities. *Modern Language Journal, 78*, 285–299.

Krashen, S. D. (1989). We acquire vocabulary and spelling by reading: Additional evidence for the input hypothesis. *Modern Language Journal, 73*, 440–464.

Labov, W. (1973). The boundaries of words and their meanings. In C.-J. N. Bailey & R. W. Shuy (Eds.), *New ways of analyzing variation in English* (pp. 340–373). Washington, DC: Georgetown University Press.

Lapkin, S., & Swain, M. (1995). *Vocabulary teaching in a grade 8 French immersion classroom: A descriptive case study.* Manuscript in preparation.

Laufer, B. (1989). A factor of difficulty in vocabulary learning: Deceptive transparency. *AILA Review, 6*, 10–20.

Laufer, B. (1992). How much lexis is necessary for reading comprehension? In P. L. Arnaud & H. Béjoint (Eds.), *Vocabulary and applied linguistics* (pp. 126–132). London: Macmillan.

Laufer, B., & Nation, P. (in press). Vocabulary size and use: Lexical richness in L2 written production. *Applied Linguistics, 16*, 307–322.

Lee, M. (1994). Functional architecture of the bilingual "lexicon". *Working Papers in English and Applied Linguistics, 1*, 1–13.

Levelt, W. J. M. (1989). *Speaking: From intention to articulation*. Cambridge, MA: MIT Press.

Li, X. (1988). Effects of contextual cues on inferring and remembering meanings of new words. *Applied Linguistics, 10*, 402–413.

Mägiste, E. (1986). Selected issues in second and third language learning. In J. Vaid (Ed.), *Language processing in bilinguals: Psycholinguistic and neuropsychological perspectives* (pp. 97–122). Hillsdale, NJ: Lawrence Erlbaum Associates.

Marslen-Wilson, W., Tyler, L. K., Waksler, R., & Older, L. (1994). Morphology and meaning in the English mental lexicon. *Psychological Review, 101*, 3–33.

Meara, P. (1984). The study of lexis in interlanguage. In A. Davies, C. Criper, & A. P. R. Howatt (Eds.), *Interlanguage* (pp. 225–235). Edinburgh: Edinburgh University Press.

Meara, P. (1987). *Vocabulary in a second language: Vol. 2*. London: Centre for Information on Language Teaching.

Meara, P. (1990). A note on passive vocabulary. *Second Language Research, 6*, 150–154.

Meara, P. (1992). Vocabulary in a second language: Vol. 3. *Reading in a Foreign Language, 9*, 761–837.

Meara, P., & Buxton, B. (1987). An alternative to multiple choice vocabulary tests. *Language Testing, 4*, 142–154.

Meara, P., Lightbown, P. M., & Halter, R. H. (1994). The effect of cognates on the applicability of yes/no vocabulary tests. *Canadian Modern Language Review, 50*, 296–311.

Mondria, J.-A., & Wit-de Boer, M. (1991). The effects of contextual richness on the guessability and retention of words in a foreign language. *Applied Linguistics, 12*, 249–267.

Nagy, W., Anderson, R. C., & Herman, P. A. (1987). Learning word meanings from context during normal reading. *American Educational Research Journal, 24*, 237–270.

Nagy, W., Garcia, G. E., Durgunoglu, A., & Hancin, B. (1993). Spanish-English bilingual students' use of cognates in English reading. *Journal of Reading Behaviour, 25*, 241–259.

Nation, I. S. P. (1990). *Teaching and learning vocabulary*. Boston: Heinle & Heinle.

Nation, P. (1993). Vocabulary size, growth, and use. In R. Schreuder & B. Weltens (Eds.), *The bilingual lexicon* (pp. 115–134). Amsterdam: John Benjamins.

Nesi, H., & Meara, P. (1994). Patterns of misinterpretation in the productive use of EFL dictionary definitions. *System, 22*, 1–15.

Neumann, S. B., & Koskinen, P. (1992). Captioned television as comprehensible input: Effects of incidental learning from context for language minority students. *Reading Research Quarterly, 27*, 94–106.

Olshtain, E. (1987). The acquisition of new word formation processes in second language acquisition. *Studies in Second Language Acquisition, 9*, 221–232.

Olshtain, E. (1989). Is second language attrition the reversal of second language acquisition? *Studies in Second Language Acquisition, 11*, 151–165.

O'Malley, J. M. (1987). The effects of training in the use of learning strategies on learning English as a second language. In A. Wenden & J. Rubin (Eds.), *Learner strategies in language learning* (pp. 133–143). Englewood Cliffs, NJ: Prentice-Hall International.

Oxford, R. L., & Scarcella, R. C. (1994). Second language vocabulary learning among adults: State of the art in vocabulary instruction. *System, 22*, 231–243.

Paivio, A. (1986). *Mental representation: A dual-coding approach.* New York: Oxford University Press.

Paribakht, T. S., & Wesche, M. B. (1993, August). *Vocabulary enhancement activities and reading for meaning in second language vocabulary acquisition.* Paper presented at the 10th World Congress of Applied Linguistics (AILA), Amsterdam.

Parry, K. (1991). Building a vocabulary through academic reading. *TESOL Quarterly, 25*, 629–653.

Pearson, B. Z., & Fernández, S. C. (1994). Patterns of interaction in the lexical growth in two languages of bilingual infants and toddlers. *Language Learning, 44*, 617–653.

Poulisse, N. (1993). A theoretical account of lexical communication strategies. In R. Schreuder & B. Weltens (Eds.), *The bilingual lexicon* (pp. 157–189). Amsterdam: John Benjamins.

Pressley, M., Levin, J. R., & McDaniel, M. A. (1987). Remembering versus inferring what a word means: Mnemonic and contextual approaches. In M. G. McKeown & M. E. Curtis (Eds.), *The nature of vocabulary acquisition* (pp. 107–127). Hillsdale, NJ: Lawrence Erlbaum.

Radford, A. (1990). *Syntactic theory and the acquisition of English syntax.* Oxford: Basil Blackwell.

Read, J. (1993). The development of a new measure of vocabulary knowledge. *Language Testing, 10*, 355–371.

Read, J. (1994, July). *Refining the word associates format as a measure of depth of vocabulary knowledge.* Paper presented at the 19th Annual Congress of the Applied Linguistics Association of Australia, Melbourne.

Richards, J. C. (1976). The role of vocabulary teaching. *TESOL Quarterly, 10*, 77–89.

Ringbom, H. (1986). Crosslinguistic influence and the foreign language learning process. In E. Kellerman & M. Sharwood Smith (Eds.), *Crosslinguistic influence in second language acquisition* (pp. 150–162). Oxford: Pergamon Press.

Ringbom, H. (1987). *The role of the first language in foreign language learning.* Clevedon, Avon: Multilingual Matters.

Robinson, P. (1994). Universals of word formation processes: Noun incorporation in the acquisition of Samoan as a second language. *Language Learning, 44,* 569–615.

Sanaoui, R. (1995). Adult learners' approaches to learning vocabulary in second languages. *Modern Language Journal, 79,* 15–28.

Sanaoui, R. (in press). Processes of vocabulary instruction in ten French as a second language classrooms. *Canadian Modern Language Review.*

Saville-Troike, M. (1984). What really matters in second language learning for academic achievement? *TESOL Quarterly, 18,* 199–219.

Schouten-van Parreren, C. (1989). Vocabulary learning through reading: Which conditions should be met when presenting words in texts? *AILA Review, 6,* 75–85.

Schreuder, R., & Weltens, B. (Eds.) (1993). *The bilingual lexicon.* Amsterdam: John Benjamins.

Singleton, D., & Little, D. (1991). The second language lexicon: Some evidence from university level learners of French and German. *Second Language Research, 7,* 61–81.

Stanovich, K. E. (1986). Matthew effects on reading. Some consequences of individual differences in the acquisition of literacy. *Reading Research Quarterly, 21,* 360–407.

Swain, M., & Carroll, S. (1987). Vocabulary instruction in immersion classes. In B. Harley, P. Allen, J. Cummins, & M. Swain (Eds.) *The development of bilingual proficiency: Final report: Vol. 2. Classroom treatment* (pp. 190–263). Toronto: Modern Language Centre, Ontatio Institute for Studies in Education.

Teichroew, F. J. (1982). Receptive versus productive vocabulary. *Interlanguage Studies Bulletin, 6,* 5–33.

Tomasello, M., & Herron, C. (1988). Down the garden path: Inducing and correcting overgeneralization errors in the foreign language classroom. *Applied Psycholinguistics, 9,* 237–246.

Tréville, M.-C. (1993). *Rôle des congénères interlinguaux dans le développement du vocabulaire réceptif: Application au français langue seconde* [The role of cognates in the development of receptive vocabulary: Application to French as a second language]. Quebec: Laval University, CIRAL.

Tyler, A., & Nagy, W. (1989). The acquisition of English derivational morphology. *Journal of Verbal Learning and Verbal Behavior, 14,* 638–647.

Verhallen, M., & Schoonen, R. (1993). Lexical knowledge of monolingual and bilingual children. *Applied Linguistics, 14,* 344–363.

Vermeer, A. (1992). Exploring the second language learner lexicon. In L. Verhoeven & J. H. A. L. de Jong (Eds.) *The construct of language proficiency* (pp. 147–162). Amsterdam: John Benjamins.

Viberg, Å. (1993). Crosslinguistic perspectives on lexical organization and lexical progression. In K. Hyltenstam & Å. Viberg (Eds.), *Progression and regression in language* (pp. 340–385) Cambridge: Cambridge University Press.

Weltens, B., & Grendel, M. (1993). Attrition of vocabulary knowledge. In R. Schreuder & B. Weltens (Eds.), *The bilingual lexicon* (pp. 135–156). Amsterdam: John Benjamins.

Weltens, B., van Els, T., & Schils, E. (1989). The long-term retention of French by Dutch students. *Studies in Second Language Acquisition, 11,* 205–216.

Wesche, M. B., & Paribakht, S. (1995). *Assessing vocabulary knowledge: Depth versus breadth.* Manuscript in preparation.

Yoshida, M. (1978). The acquisition of English vocabulary by a Japanese speaking child. In E. Hatch (Ed.), *Second language acquisition: A book of readings* (pp. 91–100). Rowley, MA: Newbury House.

Yu, L. (1995). *The role of L1 in the acquisition of motion verbs in English by Chinese and Japanese learners.* Manuscript in preparation.

SECTION I

DEVELOPMENTAL PERSPECTIVES ON THE BILINGUAL LEXICON

Lexical Development in Bilingual Infants and Toddlers: Comparison to Monolingual Norms

Barbara Zurer Pearson, Sylvia C. Fernández, and D. Kimbrough Oller
University of Miami

Author's Statement: *Until recently the field of bilingual studies has had mostly case studies of linguists' children from which to piece together a picture of early simultaneous acquisition. Whereas many of these have been exhaustive and excellent, indeed models of the case study model, it has been difficult to generalize their findings—to know what is typical and what is exceptional in bilingual children's development. It seemed to us time to make a systematic observation of a larger group of children. So we decided to follow 24 Spanish-and-English-learning children in the period from soon after birth to about 3 years of age within the context of a parent grant that provided monolingual controls.*

Our goal was first to provide basic descriptive information but also to test some widely held beliefs about bilingual development. One of our first targets was the belief that bilinguals develop language more slowly than do monolinguals. We were also eager to replicate Volterra and Taeschner's (1978) finding that young bilinguals moved

This research was supported by Grant 5 R01 DC00484, NIH NIDCD. Portions of this paper were presented at the Eighth International Conference on Infant Studies, 8 May 1992, Miami Beach, Florida.

We gratefully acknowledge the help of Donna Thal and Donna Jackson-Maldonado of the CRL in San Diego for the use of the Spanish forms and of Larry Fenson of San Diego and Bill LeBlanc of the University of Miami for their help in the evaluation of the children's scores.

*from an early stage with a single mixed lexicon, characterized by the
absence of translation equivalents in the child's two languages, to a
subsequent stage with a differentiated lexicon. By studying children
from a range of socioeconomic backgrounds, including especially
those from middle-class homes in a community with substantial
support for speaking two languages, we hoped to isolate bilingualism
per se from some of the confounding social factors that often hinder
quasi-experimental work such as this. The first work on these data
examined the canonical babbling of the bilinguals in relation to
milestones established with monolinguals. Next we turned our
attention to early lexical and phonetic development. The article
reprinted here is the first in a series of four on the early lexicon (see also
Pearson, Fernández, Lewedag, and Oller, 1994); we are currently
writing up our work on phonetic development (Oller, Pearson, 1991;
Oller, Lewedag, Umbel, & Basinger, 1992; Pearson, Navarro, &
Gathercole, 1994). Analyses of syntax and metalinguistic awareness
in these children have yet to begin.*

*The dominant impression from our work so far is that the
bilingual children have seemed to be learning similarly to
monolinguals. Differences between the groups have not been larger
than the wide range of differences between children in the same group.
When one frames the comparisons carefully, bilingual and monolingual children appear to achieve at equivalent rates. With respect to the
question of a single or double lexicon, few children were observed to
follow the path predicted by Volterra and Taeschner (1978). That is,
the single lexicon hypothesis was not upheld. Readers should recognize, however, that the methods we used were both laborious and
exploratory. There are not, to our knowledge, any convenient methods
available for meaningful comparisons of bilinguals. We hope our
work will help other researchers and practitioners look critically at
standards of assessment and recognize bilinguals as a special, not a
pathological, group—but one that requires a special set of standards
for single and double language achievements.*

Barbara Zurer Pearson, University of Miami, 1994

A knowledge of the advantages and disadvantages of bilingualism is of growing interest as the number of households in the
United States in which more than one language is spoken continues to rise (Veltman, 1988). Despite scanty and at times contradictory evidence, the view that bilingualism is a risk factor in

development seems to prevail. Anecdotal evidence suggesting that bilinguals develop language more slowly than do monolinguals is common, but the issue is far from resolved. We know of no controlled studies of large groups of children that show slow language-learning in bilinguals (Hakuta, 1986). Few studies have compared children learning one language with those learning two, especially at early ages. The research reported here compares bilingual and monolingual lexical development, as measured by the relative vocabulary sizes of very young simultaneous bilingual children and monolingual age-mates. A primary motive is to establish guidelines for identifying lexical delay in bilingual babies and toddlers.

Investigating lexical delay is particularly important, as several recent studies have confirmed that children with delayed language at 24 to 30 months are at risk for persisting difficulties (Dale, 1991). For example, Fischel, Whitehurst, Caulfield and DeBaryshe (1989) found that 65% of toddlers who were at least 2.5 standard deviations below the mean on the Expressive One-Word Picture Vocabulary Test remained delayed 5 months later. In another study, Rescorla (1989) identified 15 boys with specific expressive language delay at 24 to 30 months and found that at age 3 to 4 years 53% were still significantly delayed. Thus, a substantial proportion of late-talkers may not catch up, making it important to clarify factors that contribute to early language delay.

However, determining what constitutes "delay" in a bilingual child is not straightforward. There is no clearly appropriate measure of young bilingual children's language capabilities (American Psychological Association, 1985; Figueroa, 1990). No standardized measures are referenced to bilinguals directly, and single-language comparisons to monolinguals are problematic. Comparing performance in only one language at a time neglects the totality of the bilingual's abilities, especially the knowledge specific to the untested language. To sum measures in the two languages fails to correct for abilities, if any, that the child shares between the languages. Furthermore, there is no firm theoretical basis for choosing one comparison over another (Paivio & DesRochers, 1980; Hamers & Blanc, 1988).

The literature on early bilingual acquisition depends heavily on the case study method, a form in which systematic comparisons with other children are not generally attempted (McLaughlin, 1984; De Houwer, 1990). Group studies of older children have produced conflicting results. Some studies have found areas in which bilingualism seems advantageous. For example, research comparing the cognitive abilities of bilingual school-age children with those of monolinguals has shown that bilingual children may have greater adeptness at divergent and creative thinking, earlier and greater awareness of the arbitrary nature of word-meaning pairings, and greater linguistic creativity. Other studies show no difference or else disadvantage for bilinguals. (See Hakuta, 1986; Saunders, 1988; Hamers & Blanc, 1988 for reviews of this literature.)

Studies have generally reported negative effects of bilingualism on lexical measures. Several researchers have found that bilingual children show lower levels of receptive vocabulary than do their monolingual peers. Ben-Zeev (1977), for example, controlling for IQ, showed a 10-point deficit on the Peabody Picture Vocabulary Test (PPVT) for Hebrew-English bilingual 7-year-olds. Rosenblum and Pinker (1983) found bilingual 5-year-olds scored, on average, 26 points lower on the PPVT than did their monolingual counterparts, and Doyle, Champagne, and Segalowitz (1978) reported a similar disadvantage in French-English bilingual preschoolers. Umbel, Pearson, Fernández, and Oller (1992) found that bilingual first-graders matched for socioeconomic status were behind age-mates in English vocabulary and near, but slightly below, the mean on the Test de Vocabulario en Imagenes Peabody (TVIP), the Spanish version of the same test. A similar pattern on the PPVT and TVIP was found in English-Spanish bilingual preschoolers by Fernández, Pearson, Umbel, Oller, and Molinet-Molina (1992). These studies, which investigated bilingual children's vocabulary knowledge of both languages, have raised questions about the appropriateness of using monolingual vocabulary norms to evaluate bilinguals.

There is even less research on productive vocabulary development in younger, simultaneous-bilingual infants and toddlers. The only published records of lexical acquisition are from linguists who have studied their own children's development (Leopold, 1949; Volterra & Taeschner, 1978; Vihman, 1985; Saunders, 1988). (For reviews see McLaughlin, 1984; De Houwer, 1990.) Whereas their descriptions do not deal with norms, Volterra and Taeschner's (1978) widely cited claims, based on Taeschner's own children and Leopold's, highlight the lack of overlap in the lexicons of the children's two languages and therefore demonstrate the necessity of examining both the languages of a developing bilingual.

These authors have not generally noted bilingual lexical delay, but their participants are not considered typical. No studies of groups of infants have been reported. Perhaps the paucity of work derives from the fact that until recently there were no standardized lexical measures for infants in even one language (Dale, Bates, Reznick, & Morisett, 1989; Rescorla, 1989; Fenson et al., 1991). Now that such lexical measures are becoming available, there is still no standard form for measuring lexical knowledge in two languages at once.

This study adds to our knowledge of bilinguals' early vocabulary knowledge by reporting on lexical development, both receptive and productive, in a sample of 25 English-Spanish bilingual children for whom semilongitudinal data were available from 8 to 30 months. Data from an average of 9 bilingual children at each of six age groups were obtained using a standard instrument in English and Spanish that allows comparison to a norming sample as well as to other groups of infants. In addition, we outline a balanced approach to assessing children's vocabulary in two languages. We both describe a system to document the degree of overlap between the children's lexical knowledge in one language and their knowledge in the other and explore how such information could be used to make meaningful comparisons among bilinguals and between bilinguals and monolinguals.

The major questions to be answered are (a) In what ways can

the vocabularies of bilingual and monolingual children be meaningfully compared, (b) What can such comparisons tell us about
the nature of vocabulary acquisition in general, and (c) What
evidence can be brought to bear on the claim that early bilingualism hinders vocabulary acquisition? This paper differs from previous work on lexical development from first words to 30 months
of age in that it (a) uses a recently standardized vocabulary
measure in English, with an adaptation in Spanish; (b) proposes
a variety of measures for assessing the bilingual lexicons; and (c)
provides data on more participants than previous studies have.

Method

Participants

The participants were selected from those recruited for a
larger longitudinal study on vocal development. We used 25
children being reared in English-Spanish bilingual homes (9
females & 16 males) and 35 children being reared in monolingual
homes (14 females & 21 males) as the sample for the present
study. The data on them were those collected for the larger study.
However, the goals of the larger study were not identical to those
of the present research, so the same data had not been consistently collected for all the children. The number of observations
on file ranged from 1 to 7 per child, made at approximately 2- to
3-month intervals. The age ranges evaluated were for the bilingual children, 8 to 30 months with a mean of 20.6 months; and for
the monolinguals, 9 to 30 months with an average age at observation of 21.9 months. The average socioeconomic status of the
bilingual children's families, as determined from a modified
Hollingshead scale (1 to 5, 1 high), was 2.2 whereas the
monolingual's average socioeconomic status score was 2.5. The
children were all of normal intelligence; the average Bayley (1969)
score at 18 months of the bilingual group was 112 (SD=11.4) and
the monolingual group was 110 (SD=12.7). Four bilingual and 8
monolingual children were approximately 5 weeks premature

with no other health problems. Thirty-two of the monolinguals were from English-speaking homes; 3 were from Spanish-speaking homes.

All of the bilingual participants had significant exposure on a regular basis to both English and Spanish through their various caretakers, who are native speakers of one or the other or both languages. Although all parents of bilinguals expressed a desire to provide an environment equally balanced between the languages, and the conditions of their households appeared to support that desire, only 4 of the children appear to have had equal exposure to both languages. Parent estimates of language exposure, updated at regular intervals, averaged between 60–65% of one language and 35–40% of the other; 11% had an exposure less balanced than 75:25. Spanish predominated for slightly over half (13:25) of the children. Fourteen of the 21 children observed more than once experienced a relatively consistent language environment throughout the data collection period, whereas 7 children experienced changes in the percentage of time they were exposed to each language, including changes in the predominant language.

Materials

Normed parent report instruments, the MacArthur Communicative Development Inventory (CDI) Toddler and Infant forms (1989) and their Spanish adaptations, the Toddler and Infant Inventario del Desarrollo de las Habilidades Comunicativas (Jackson-Maldonado & Bates, 1988), were used to assess the participants' vocabulary sizes. The Infant English form, used to assess words frequently produced and understood by infants between 8 and 15 months of age, contains 395 words arranged in 22 semantic categories. The Toddler English form, for use with children between 15 and 30 months, contains 679 words. Instructions on the Toddler form tell the parents to mark the words that their child spontaneously produces whereas the Infant form instructs parents to mark words their child produces and comprehends as well as words only comprehended. The vocabulary scores for Infants are the number of words marked by the parent, one number for comprehension, another for production; for Toddlers, only production is tallied. Percentile norms for girls and boys, based on CDIs from 1,600 children, are available at one-month intervals, comprehension up to 16 months, production up to 30 months.

The Spanish version of the CDI has 428 words on the Infant form and 732 words on the Toddler form. It was developed by adopting the format of the English (and Italian and Japanese) Inventories, but using Spanish word-lists and research studies to dictate the items included. The version of the Spanish CDI used in our study was modified slightly to reflect lexical items used by the Cuban and Cuban-American population of Miami (Fernández & Umbel, 1991). Median values for the Spanish CDI, calculated on a sample of 328 monolingual Spanish children (Jackson-Maldonado, Marchman, Thal, Bates, & Gutierrez-Clellen, 1991) provide a rough standard of comparison for the Spanish vocabulary scores.

The CDI is more appealing than previous parent report measures because it relies on recognition rather than recall in assessing vocabulary size. Additionally, the two forms of this inventory focus on "emerging behaviors" at times when these behaviors are current (not retrospective) and limited in number. Its upper boundary at 30 months reflects the fact that most typically developing children know so many words at that age that parents can no longer keep track of them. After 30 months, other assessment instruments are more appropriate.

Evidence of the CDI's reliability and validity is reported in Fenson et al. (1991). The CDI has shown high internal consistency, producing Cronbach's alpha values of .95 for Infant Comprehension and .96 for Infant and Toddler Production. Test-retest reliability is also high yielding Pearson coefficient values in the .8 to .9 range for Infant Comprehension and Production and values exceeding .9 for Toddler Production (Fenson et al., 1991). In addition to demonstrating high reliability, the CDI has shown high concurrent and predictive validity (Dale et al., 1989; Dale, 1991). Dale tests concurrent validity correlations between CDI expressive vocabulary and performance on the Expressive One-Word Picture Vocabulary Test (EOWPVT), the Index of Productive Syntax (IPSyn), and information obtained from language samples. Correlations to lexical and syntactic measures ranged between .68 and .78, $p < .01$; to the number of types (different words) in a 100-utterance sample, .74; to the IPSyn, .78; to the EOWPVT raw scores, .73; and to Mean Length of Utterance, .68. Similar correlations for our sample for measures from 24-month laboratory samples to 2-year CDI production percentiles yielded the following values: to number of types in a 50-utterance sample, $r(29) = .66, p < .001$; and to the PPVT-R (Dunn & Dunn, 1981) at 30 months, $r(20) = .77, p < .001$.

Additionally, vocabulary scores from 228 children tested at two different times (Time 1 at 16–24 months, Time 2 at 22–30 months) were correlated at .71 ($p < .0001$), indicating relatively high stability, but allowing for differential growth over that period. Throughout the age range measured by the CDI/Toddler, correlations between successive ages are substantial and reasonably stable (Fenson et al., 1991). The CDI vocabulary list for a given child is close to being a true inventory; however, to the extent that the form does not exhaust the list of possible words children might say, it—like vocabulary tests at later ages—requires an extrapolation of the total vocabulary based on a controlled sample.

Procedure

The children's parents filled out a language background questionnaire that they updated each time they filled out the CDIs. In instructing the parents, we emphasized that these were measures of spontaneous vocabulary production rather than prompted repetition. The strict emphasis on marking only spontaneously-produced words may have made the instructions given to the parents in this study, more conservative than those given to the parents of the children in the norming sample, but all other procedures were standard (L. Fenson, personal communication, 8 May 1992). As indicated in the CDI instructions, the parents were told to mark words that their child said, even if the pronunciation was incorrect. Thus the consistent pairing of a certain sound with a particular meaning was sufficient for the parents to mark that word, even if their child's production of the word was very different from the adult pronunciation. Word-forms that were used for more than one concept within a language, such as *ba* for *ball* and *ba* for *baby* were counted separately because they reflected two sound-meaning pairings.

We should caution that the information provided by the CDI is approximate in that, although the words on the form are grouped by semantic category to aid recall, the parent is not asked to specify the referent of a word, or even to indicate whether the word is used referentially. At these ages, children's meanings for words are often either overextended or underextended, as compared to the adult definition. *Ball*, for example, may overextend to *anything round* or *anything one throws*, whereas a word like *zapatos* may underextend to refer only to one particular pair of sandals. No claims are made in the use of the CDI that the children's words have identical meanings to adults', just that the children have begun to use them meaningfully. This caution applies to both monolinguals and bilinguals.

The vocabulary size of the monolingual children was determined by counting the number of words that the parents had checked off on the form at a given age. This score, referred to as English or Spanish vocabulary, corresponds to the number of sound-meaning pairings the child has made at the given age, which for monolinguals is also a rough measure of the number of concepts for which the child has a lexical representation. To determine how the children's lexicons compared in size to those of other children of the same age and sex, percentile scores were obtained based on norms for the English CDI (Fenson et al., 1991). In arriving at the percentile scores for premature participants, corrected ages were used.

To analyze the vocabulary size of the bilingual participants, four measures were taken: two measures (English and Spanish Vocabulary) were taken directly from the respective CDIs; and two double-language measures (Total Vocabulary and Total Conceptual Vocabulary) were constructed from the comparison of the single-language forms. The first two, the single-language measures, were like the monolingual measures except that each bilingual participant had two "monolingual" assessments. The two double-language measures encompassed the bilingual child's abilities in both languages summed together and then corrected for knowledge shared between them. Unlike the monolingual child for whom the number of sound-meaning pairings (Total Vocabulary) and lexicalized concepts (Total Conceptual Vocabulary) is roughly equal to the number of words, in the bilingual child it is more difficult to assess overall knowledge of words and concepts. To the extent that words may be coded in one *or* both languages, the number of sound-meaning pairings is generally higher than is the number of concepts with lexical representations. To compute the double-language measures, it is necessary to determine how many words a child has coded in only one language and how many are coded in both.

For this study, to know when a word checked on the form for one language was similarly checked on the other, one form had to be mapped onto the other to the extent possible (Pearson, 1992). The first step in the mapping process was to compare the English and Spanish versions of the CDI and determine which words could be termed Translation Equivalents, or *doublets*. For the most part, this was fairly straightforward. The English and Spanish words in each pair were both assigned a *pair number*. For instance, *dog* and *perro* were both given the number 214, *table* and *mesa* were assigned number 927, and so forth. However, due to cultural and linguistic differences between Spanish and English and, in some cases, simple gaps on one form or the other, not all words could be paired. About 80% of the words could be matched with a translation equivalent on the other form. In the children examined here, unpaired words rarely made up more than 15% of a child's vocabulary; therefore, we could conduct an analysis of translation equivalents on at least 85% of each child's reported vocabulary.

In most cases, translation equivalents represent two sound-meaning pairings for one lexical concept, but some of the paired words are phonetically similar in the two languages, especially in baby talk. These words, such as *mama* and *choo choo*, are not clearly distinguishable as either English or Spanish. Because a child who says *choo choo* in English and *choo choo* in Spanish essentially has only one sound-meaning pairing, we counted phonetically-similar doublets such as these only once in arriving at a child's Total Vocabulary. In other words, a child's Total Vocabulary was calculated by summing all the English words the parent had checked off on the English CDI and all the Spanish words checked off on the Spanish CDI, then subtracting the number of phonetically-similar doublets, so they were counted only once in the tally.

Another measure, the Total Conceptual Vocabulary measure was designed to take account of the number of concepts lexicalized by the child, whether the words were coded in one or both languages. In effect, the measure includes all the words in one language plus the singlets of the other language (i.e., all the words from the other language that represent concepts or linguistic functions not lexicalized in the first language). Thus, a single concept known by different labels in English and Spanish was counted only once in the Total Conceptual Vocabulary (as opposed to Total Vocabulary). Calculating Total Conceptual Vocabulary in this manner, cross-language synonyms (e.g., *dog* and *perro*) were counted once whereas within-language synonyms (e.g., *hi* and *hello*) were counted twice, just as they were in the monolingual vocabulary size calculation.

We compared these four measures of vocabulary size— English, Spanish, Total, and Total Conceptual—to norms for monolingual English children (Fenson et al., 1991) to determine how the bilingual children's vocabulary sizes compared to those of monolingual children of the same age and sex. (Preliminary figures from Jackson-Maldonado et al., 1991, indicate that Spanish monolingual children's vocabulary sizes, as measured by the Spanish CDI, are roughly equal to those of their English monolingual counterparts throughout the age range in question. However, complete Spanish norms are not currently available, so percentiles were derived from the tables for the English form.) Similarly, the double-language scores were compared to the monolingual English norms to derive percentile scores. As the double-language measures have no normative baselines, the percentiles derived were for purposes of illustration and comparison only.

For each child at each age, a number-of-words score was associated with a percentile score. To compare the average performance of bilingual and monolingual participants over different time points, global mean percentiles were calculated for the percentile scores associated with each of the four measures of vocabulary for the bilingual participants and with English (or Spanish) Vocabulary for the monolinguals. In calculating the average percentiles in production and comprehension for those children observed more than once, we first calculated a mean percentile value from different ages. We then averaged the individual means to arrive at the global mean percentile by language group for each of the measures of vocabulary, treating comprehension and production separately.

Comprehension was measured between 8 and 16 months. The production figures were taken from observations between 14 and 30 months. For the analyses, only production data after 14 months were used, because more data were available for both language groups after that point and because most children had enough words—about 10 in Production and 100 in Comprehension—that small increments in the number of words known produced less drastic differences in percentile scores.

However, combining all the bilingual children's English and Spanish scores yielded a potentially confusing average in each language for this group, because some of the bilinguals were English-dominant whereas others were Spanish-dominant. There-

fore, we calculated the single-language percentile scores separately for English-dominant and Spanish-dominant children.
Especially important, this prevented making single-language
normative comparisons without knowing whether the comparison was to the children's dominant or nondominant language. The
language-dominance assignment was based on the language in
which the child had more words. All time points for which data
were available were examined in determining the higher-scoring
language. When the child had more words in one language at one
time point and more words in the other at another observation, we
could not determine language dominance and these children's
data were not considered in the single-language measures. There
were two such cases for comprehension and four for production.

Global mean percentiles, covering all the ages, for production
and comprehension in the monolinguals versus the bilinguals
were compared statistically. Because the double-language measures, Total Vocabulary and Total Conceptual Vocabulary, counted
all production—in dominant and nondominant languages—the
dominance differences were not an issue. For these measures, the
bilingual subgroups could be treated together, and the comparison to monolinguals was statistically tested. For the single-
language measures, only the Spanish-dominant children's Spanish and the English-dominant children's English were compared
statistically to the monolingual children's measures.

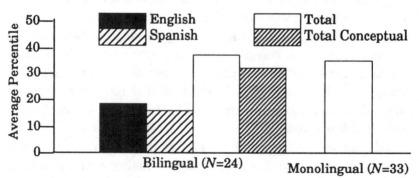

Figure 1. Bilingual and monolingual percentiles averaged across ages
(Production)

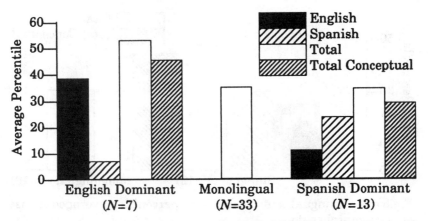

Figure 2. Average percentiles (Production): Monolinguals compared with bilinguals by dominant language group

Results

Figure 1 compares the mean production measures of the bilingual and monolingual children by depicting the global mean percentiles collapsed across time for the measures described above. Because the single-language measures in Figure 1 do not differentiate between children whose dominant language was English versus those who were Spanish-dominant, single-language comparisons were not analyzed statistically for the whole bilingual group together. Figure 2 compares average percentiles for production, with the bilingual group split according to language dominance.

Because the double-language measures take into account both the dominant and nondominant language, the data were analyzed for the whole bilingual group together. For production, the bilingual group's double-language measures were very close to the monolingual children's average, (BL M=36.9, SD=29.8 and ML M=34.8, SD=26.2, t(51)=−1.04, *n.s.* for bilingual Total Vocabulary; BL M=32.1, SD=25.6 vs. ML M=34.8, t(51)=−.34, *n.s.* for Total Conceptual Vocabulary).

Figure 2 reveals that in production the English-dominant

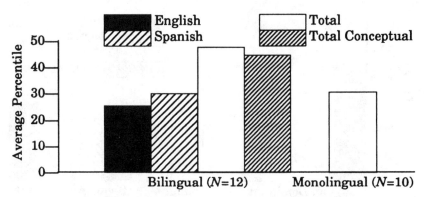

Figure 3. Bilingual and monolingual percentiles averaged across ages (Comprehension)

children, except in the case of their weaker language, Spanish, performed comparably to the monolingual children. A *t*-test comparing the mean for the English-dominant children's English production to the mean for the monolinguals' production revealed this difference was not significant, (ML *M*=34.8, *SD*=26.2 vs. BL *M*=38.4, *SD*=25.9), *t*(38)=−.33, *n.s.* Similarly, a *t*-test comparing the Spanish-dominant children's Spanish performance to the monolingual children's performance (BL *M*=23.6, *SD*=20.6 and ML *M*=34.8) was not significant, *t*(44)=1.38, *n.s.*

Analogous figures for comprehension are represented in Figures 3 and 4. With respect to comprehension, both double-language measures of bilingual vocabulary were higher than the monolingual average percentile, although these differences were not significant (BL *M*=47.9, *SD*=27.9 vs. ML *M*=30.3, *SD*=27.0, *t*(18)=−1.78, *n.s.* for bilingual Total Vocabulary and BL *M*=44.3, *SD*=26.1 vs. 30.3, *t*(18)=−1.51, *n.s.* for Total Conceptual Vocabulary).

As seen in Figure 4, in comprehension both groups of bilingual participants performed better than did their monolingual counterparts in all but their weaker language. Due to the very small sample sizes involved in these comparisons, we did not do statistical tests of significance for the single-language compre-

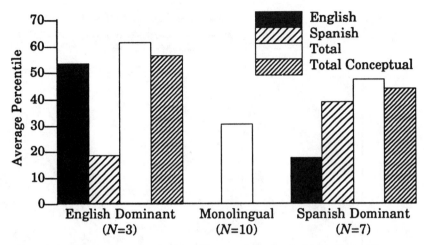

Figure 4. Average percentiles (Comprehension): Monolinguals compared with bilinguals by dominant language group

hension measures. Further, a cautionary note may be advisable: It is conceivable, especially for those families in which a single individual filled out both the English and Spanish forms, that bilingual parents' responses to the CDI for comprehension may have been somewhat overestimated compared to monolinguals'. Indeed, bilingual parents sometimes reported difficulty knowing in which language an interchange was taking place, so understanding in both languages may have been credited on the basis of comprehension in only one.

To evaluate further the two groups' similarity in vocabulary production throughout the age range, we plotted the average number of words produced by the bilingual and monolingual children between 16 and 27 months, the ages for which we had at least 7 participants in each group. (See Fig. 5.) To smooth the curve and increase the number of observations at each point, these data were collapsed into two-month groupings (but no child contributed more than one score to any one time point). The double-language measures—Total Vocabulary and Total Conceptual Vocabulary—were used for the bilingual group. Standard deviations associated with these means are given in Table 1.

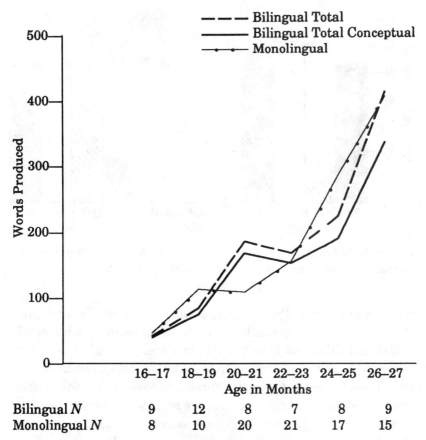

Bilingual *N*   9   12   8   7   8   9
Monolingual *N*   8   10   20   21   17   15

Figure 5. Bilingual and monolingual production

Table 1
Descriptive Statistics for Bilingual and Monolingual Production

	Bilingual					Monolingual		
	Total			Total Conceptual				
Ages	*N*	*M*	*SD*	*M*	*SD*	*N*	*M*	*SD*
16–17 months	9	42	32	39	31	8	44	35
18–19 months	12	82	66	73	59	10	113	103
20–21 months	8	186	135	168	118	20	109	71
22–23 months	7	168	151	154	141	21	155	114
24–25 months	8	224	169	190	136	17	286	170
26–27 months	9	414	264	337	203	15	406	172

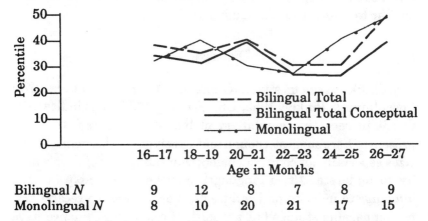

Figure 6. Bilingual and monolingual production (percentiles)

This comparison of the monolingual and bilingual children reveals that differences in average vocabulary size across the age range tested were relatively small. Neither group was consistently higher or lower than the other. Both groups seemed to follow the same general upward trend; both groups have large variability around their means, with standard deviations in most cases approximately three-quarters the size of the mean. Considering the small sample sizes and the large standard deviations, any apparent between-group differences should be interpreted with caution.

The same graph was next plotted using the means of the children's percentile scores for monolingual production, bilingual Total Vocabulary production and bilingual Total Conceptual Vocabulary production at these same ages. Figure 6 reveals that the average percentiles for both the bilinguals and the monolingual comparison group fell in the third quartile at all 6 time points. As mentioned above, this may indicate that the instructions given to these parents were more stringent and thus encouraged more conservative judgment criteria than did those given to the norming group parents. That the curves were fairly horizontal indicates that both language groups showed vocabulary acquisition rates similar to those of the norming sample.

Discussion

Unlike previous studies (Ben-Zeev, 1977; Doyle et al., 1978; Rosenblum & Pinker, 1983; Umbel et al., 1992) that indicated a deficit in receptive vocabulary of bilingual children, the data presented here suggest, though tentatively given the small sample sizes especially for comprehension, that bilingual children's ability to understand two languages may be comparable *in each language* to monolingual children's. For productive vocabulary, no comparable studies but a wealth of anecdotal evidence have been reported to help predict how the bilingual children's performance would compare to monolinguals'. Given that vocabulary production requires an additional performance from the child (one must understand a word to produce it appropriately, but the reverse is not true), bilingual children's productive vocabularies might have been expected to show a greater deficit with respect to monolinguals' than their comprehension vocabularies. In our data, the bilingual children's productive capabilities seemed more evenly split between the languages, and although each individual language showed fewer words than in the monolingual children, measures of the bilingual child's production *in the two languages together* indicated comparable vocabularies for bilingual and monolingual children.

The present work suggests that the type of vocabulary information needed when comparing bilingual children to monolingual children will depend on the purpose of the comparison. There are diverse uses for single-language and double-language measures of bilingual children's abilities. Often, the comparison of bilinguals' skills to those of monolingual controls is framed with reference to one or the other of the bilinguals' languages. It may be important, for example, to know how well a child controls the majority language, the one in which school instruction will take place. Or, to assess the more general relationship of linguistic knowledge to cognitive growth, one may focus on how well the child commands *any* language, regardless of which one is the majority language. In such cases, comparing bilinguals' single-language performance with monolinguals' may be justifiable.

However, if one's goal in investigating bilingual vocabulary is to provide an estimate of educational potential, to screen for language delay, or to provide the basis for comparison with monolingual vocabulary size in terms of lexicalized concepts, then measures that evaluate the bilingual child's ability in both languages would seem more revealing and appropriate. Two such double-language measures are the Total Vocabulary (TV) and Total Conceptual Vocabulary (TCV) discussed in this paper. As it happens, both measures show empirical values that are very close to monolingual production values throughout the age range of the study (Fig. 5).

The mapping of one language form of the CDI onto the other allows us to approximate how much of a bilingual child's lexicon is represented in each language uniquely, and how much in both languages. If there were no words known in the second language that were not already known in the first, there might be no need for a Total Language measure. The child's dominant language would be adequate for comparison of lexical concepts to monolinguals. Our observations, however, show that this is rarely the case. Even children who are very weak in a second language generally have some singlets in that language (Pearson & Fernández, 1992; Umbel et al., 1992). Therefore, any language measure based on only one language will fail to credit the child with knowledge unique to the "other" language. Additionally, that the bilingual double-language measures are so similar to monolingual production may suggest that either the number of sound-meaning pairings (TV) or the number of lexicalized concepts (TCV) may be the factor guiding the rate of expressive vocabulary acquisition.

Whereas either Total Vocabulary or Total Conceptual Vocabulary may be an appropriate measure in some situations, it is still not always clear how to choose between these measures.

Deciding which is more appropriate at a given age will hinge on what counts as a word. For every phonetic shape that the child produces consistently enough for the observer to recognize it as an instance of a given word, the child has established a sound-meaning pairing. Whatever the reason, within-language synonyms and hyponyms (like *dog* and *Rover* for the same pet) are rare in early child speech (Clark, 1983). Generally, a count of the number of words a monolingual child responds to and uses will correspond fairly closely to the number of concepts for which the child has a lexical representation.

But, for a bilingual child who knows, say, 10 words in English and 15 words in Spanish, one has several candidates for which number to use in the comparison. The count of the sound-meaning pairings and the count of the number of lexicalized concepts, which yielded approximately the same number for a monolingual lexicon, now yield different numbers. If one is to count sound-meaning pairings, this will be the Total Vocabulary. On the other hand, if one is interested in the number of lexicalized concepts, Total Conceptual Vocabulary is more appropriate.

The more conservative estimate of the bilingual child's lexicon is the Total Conceptual Vocabulary. However, this measure may mislead in that some apparent translation equivalent pairs, matched on the basis of their meanings for adults, may *not* be semantically equivalent for the child. Volterra and Taeschner (1978) present examples in which German and Italian potential doublets were used by the child to talk about different referents. Several of the parents in our study also have related such examples: *barco* being used for sailboats (triangles actually) and *boat* being used for all other boats, or *zapatos* being reserved for one special pair of sneakers and *shoes* being used for all the others. On the other hand, this may not always be the case. In our lab, we observe many examples of the child treating adult doublets as equivalents, asking for *keys* and *llaves*, playing one day with the *martillo* and another day with the same yellow plastic *hammer*. The most accurate estimate of a bilingual child's real conceptual vocabulary is probably somewhere between the Total Conceptual

Vocabulary and Total Vocabulary as measured here. Our analyses consider both. Thus far, no statistical outcomes have been different for one measure or the other, but our samples have been of limited size.

The striking similarity of Total Vocabulary and Total Conceptual Vocabulary to the monolingual patterns suggests that these double-language measures may share a similar cognitive underpinning and react to the same constraints on the child's knowledge—be they limits on memory, on perceptual categorization, or perhaps on motor programming and control of the vocal tract. At a very concrete level, the bilingual child's exposure to a given language is divided in a way that a monolingual's is not. The double-language measures correspond to the bilinguals' response to *all* of their language experience, rather than just one piece of it. To equate time of exposure to a given language for both a bilingual and a monolingual child, even in a thought experiment, the monolingual infant would have to be one who was not receiving any language stimulation for a portion of the day, corresponding to the time the bilingual was interacting with speakers of the other language. Or, stimulation in one language would have to be seen to give rise to vocabulary in the other, a situation not generally observed (Pearson & Fernández, in progress). For a bilingual toddler to have two lexicons each equivalent in size to a monolingual's would mean somehow overcoming the memory constraints that operate on young children's lexicons and being in a situation in which the needs for given words in the two language environments did not differ. To the extent that lexical development provides a window into the child's conceptual development, it is important to determine empirically how much lexical knowledge in one language overlaps with the lexical knowledge in the other and how much is encompassed by the two languages together. The comparison between Total Vocabulary and Total Conceptual Vocabulary provides an indication of the extent of that overlap.

Of the various language measures described here, single-language measures may be of more interest to educators, whereas a child's total language ability may be of more interest to clinicians. Indeed, there is as yet little agreement as to the criteria for language delay in monolinguals in this age range. Vocabulary production is only one measure that has been proposed, and it is generally seen as a screening device (Rescorla, 1989). When delay is suspected, other language behaviors are examined. Assessments of comprehension appear to be as important as assessing production (Thal, Tobias, & Morrison, 1991).

Furthermore, the effectiveness of the norms used here continues to improve. Separate norms are currently being developed for Spanish-speaking children (D. Thal, personal communication, 9 May 1992), and these will improve our percentile analyses of Spanish vocabulary. However, to our knowledge there are still no norms referenced to bilingual development on the horizon. It will be an empirical question whether monolingual norms can be used as a reliable substitute for genuine bilingual ones. That bilinguals' pattern of Total Conceptual Vocabulary and Total Vocabulary growth closely corresponds to the lexical development of monolingual control groups encourages us to think that bilingual norms for this skill at these ages, if they existed, would be very similar to monolingual norms. Therefore, current norms and guidelines for identifying delay should be adequate for bilinguals—provided the bilinguals' performance in two languages is taken into account.

Using the range of measures presented here, there is no statistical basis for concluding that the bilingual children in this study were slower to develop vocabulary before the age of 30 months than were the monolinguals. Indeed, bilinguals' comprehension may have been superior to monolinguals'. Further research is necessary to verify patterns identified here. In production, the bilinguals' mean percentile for a single language appeared to be lower than the monolinguals' but the differences were not statistically significant. Productive vocabulary for the two languages summed together in bilingual children was comparable to productive vocabularies of monolingual age-mates. The wide range of vocabulary sizes observed at these ages in normally developing children (Fenson et al., 1991) was observed in these bilingual children as well.

References

American Psychological Association Staff. (1985). *Standards for educational and psychological tests.* Washington, DC: Author.

Bayley, N. (1969). *Bayley Scales of Infant Development.* New York: New York Psychological Corporation.

Ben-Zeev, S. (1977). The influence of bilingualism on cognitive strategy and cognitive development. *Child Development, 48,* 1009–1018.

Clark, E. (1983). Convention and contrast in acquiring the lexicon. In T. B. Seiler & N. Wannenmacher (Eds.), *Concept development and the development of word meaning* (pp. 67–89). New York: Springer Verlag.

Dale, P. S. (1991). The validity of a parent report measure on vocabulary and syntax at 24 months. *Journal of Speech & Hearing Research, 34,* 565–571.

Dale, P. S., Bates, E., Reznick, J. S., & Morisett, C. (1989). The validity of a parent report instrument of child language at twenty months. *Journal of Child Language, 16,* 239–249.

De Houwer, A. (1990). *Bilingual first language acquisition: A case study.* Cambridge: Cambridge University Press.

Doyle, A., Champagne, M., & Segalowitz, N. (1978). Some issues in the assessment of linguistic consequences of early bilingualism. In M. Paradis (Ed.), *Aspects of bilingualism* (pp. 13–21). Columbia, SC: Hornbeam Press.

Dunn, L. & Dunn, L. (1981). *Peabody Picture Vocabulary Test—Revised.* Circle Pines, MN: American Guidance Service.

Fenson, L., Dale, P. S., Reznick, J. S., Thal, D., Bates, E., Hartung, J. P., Pethick, S., & Reilly, J. S., (1991). *Technical manual for the MacArthur Communicative Development Inventories.* San Diego, CA: San Diego State University.

Fernández, M. C., Pearson, B. Z., Umbel, V. M., & Oller, D. K., & Molinet-Molina, M. (1992). Bilingual receptive vocabulary in Hispanic preschool children. *Hispanic Journal of the Behavioral Sciences, 14,* 268–276.

Fernández, M. C. & Umbel, V. M. (1991). *Inventario del Desarrollo de las Habilidades Comunicativas: Adaptación Cubana* [Communicative Development Skills Inventory, Cuban adaptation]. Miami, FL: University of Miami, Mailman Center for Child Development.

Figueroa, R. A. (1990). Best practices in the assessment of bilingual children. In A. Thomas & J. Grimes (Eds.), *Best practices in school psychology*

II (pp. 93–106). Washington, DC: National Association of School Psychologists.

Fischel, J., Whitehurst, G., Caulfield, M., & DeBaryshe, B. (1989). Language growth in children with expressive language delay. *Pediatrics, 82,* 218–227.

Hakuta, K. (1986). *Mirror of language: The debate on bilingualism.* New York: Basic Books.

Hamers, J. F. & Blanc, M. H. A. (1988). *Bilinguality and bilingualism.* Cambridge: Cambridge University Press.

Jackson-Maldonado, D., & Bates, E. (1988). *Inventario del Desarrollo de las Habilidades Comunicativas* [Communicative Development Skills Inventory]. San Diego, California: University of California, Center for Research on Language.

Jackson-Maldonado, D., Marchman, V., Thal, D., Bates, E., & Gutierrez-Clellen, V. (1991). *Early lexical acquisition in Spanish-speaking infants and toddlers.* Unpublished manuscript, University of California, San Diego.

Leopold, W. F. (1949). *Speech development of a bilingual child: A linguist's record: Vol. 3. Grammar and general problems in the first two years.* Evanston, IL: Northwestern University Press.

MacArthur Communicative Development Inventory. (1989). San Diego: University of California, Center for Research in Language.

McLaughlin, B. (1984). *Second language acquisition in childhood: Vol. 1. Preschool children.* Hillsdale, NJ: Lawrence Erlbaum Associates.

Oller, D. K., Lewedag, V., Umbel, V. M., & Basinger, D. L. (1992, May). *The onset of rhythmic babbling in infants exposed to bilingual and monolingual environments.* Paper presented at International Conference on Infant Studies, Miami Beach, FL.

Oller, D. K., Pearson, B. Z. (1991, January). *Phonological differentiation in a simultaneous bilingual infant.* Paper presented at the Conference on Spanish and Portuguese Bilingualism, Miami, FL.

Paivio, A., & DesRochers, A. (1980). A dual-coding approach to bilingual memory. *Canadian Journal of Psychology, 34,* 388–399.

Pearson, B. Z. (1992). *Rationale for English-Spanish CDI mapping.* Unpublished manuscript, University of Miami, Mailman Center for Child Development, Miami, FL.

Pearson, B. Z., & Fernández, S. C. (1992, May). *Lexical development and organization in bilingual infants: Are bilinguals slower? more diverse?* Paper presented at the International Conference on Infant Studies, Miami Beach, FL.

Pearson, B. Z., Fernández, S. C., Lewedag, V., & Oller, D. K. (1994, October). Input factors in lexical learning of bilingual infants (ages 10 to 30 months). Paper presented at the Second Language Research Forum, Montreal, Quebec, Canada.

Pearson, B. Z., & Fernández, S. C. (1994). Patterns of interaction in the lexical growth in two languages of bilingual infants and toddlers. *Language Learning, 44,* 617–653.

Pearson, B. Z., & Fernández, S. C. (in progress). *Lexical organization in bilingual infants.* Unpublished manuscript, University of Miami, Mailman Center for Child Development, Miami, FL.

Pearson, B. Z., Fernández, S. C., & Oller, D. K. (in press). Cross-language synonyms in the lexicons of bilingual infants: One language or two? *Journal of Child Language.*

Pearson, B. Z., Navarro, A., & Gathercole, V. M. (1994, November). *Assessment of phonetic differentiation in bilingual learning infants.* Paper presented at the Conference of Child Language Development, Boston University.

Rescorla, L. (1989). The language development survey: A screening tool for delayed language in toddlers. *Journal of Speech and Hearing Disorders, 54,* 587–599.

Rosenblum, T. & Pinker, S. A. (1983). Word magic revisited: Monolingual and bilingual children's understanding of the word-object relationship. *Child Development, 54,* 773–780.

Saunders, G. (1988). *Bilingual children: From birth to teens.* Clevedon, Avon: Multilingual Matters.

Thal, D. J., Tobias, S., & Morrison, D. (1991). Language and gesture in late talkers: A 1-year follow-up. *Journal of Speech & Hearing Research, 34,* 604–612.

Umbel, V. M., Pearson, B. Z., Fernández, M. C., & Oller, D. K. (1992). Measuring bilingual children's receptive vocabularies. *Child Development, 63,* 1012–1020.

Veltman, C. (1988). *The future of the Spanish language in the United States.* Washington, DC: Hispanic Policy Development Project.

Vihman, M. M. (1985). Language differentiation by the bilingual infant. *Journal of Child Language, 12,* 297–324.

Volterra, V. & Taeschner, T. (1978). The acquisition and development of language by bilingual children. *Journal of Child Language, 5,* 311–326.

Developmental Changes in Receptive Vocabulary in Hispanic Bilingual School Children

Vivian M. Umbel and D. K. Oller
University of Miami

Author's Statement: *Concern has been expressed about whether exposure to two languages induces delay in language acquisition. School-age language minority children in the United States have been found to score below their English speaking peers when tested in their second language. These children also achieve at lower levels than do their English-speaking peers, differences in performance increasing with grade level. Sociolinguistic conditions can play important roles in language and literacy outcomes. In particular, to be considered are the nature and schedule of the exposure to multiple languages and socioeconomic status. These factors, however, are seldom given the consideration they merit. With respect to the nature of language learning, detailed information about knowledge of both languages over time is required. Although language experience is considered an important factor in bilingual language development, the nature and schedule of exposure to both languages is often not taken into consideration. Furthermore, social attitudes about language may influence learning in bilingual children. If the bilinguality experienced is based on an appreciation of and openness toward both cultures and languages, a bilingual advantage is more likely. Also to be considered is the role socioeconomic status plays in language and literacy outcomes—specifically, years of schooling and occupational level. Research has shown these variables to be related to various aspects of children's performance.*

This work was supported by NIH/NIDCD Grant 5 R01 DC00484, D. K. Oller, P.I.

This study furthers our understanding of the linguistic knowledge of bilinguals by assessing the receptive vocabulary skills of Hispanic children growing up in a facilitating environment. The study was conducted in the Miami metropolitan area, which differs from other areas of the country with large Hispanic populations, in that assimilation to English does not appear to be accompanied by loss of Spanish. This pattern of commitment to Spanish includes exposure of children to Spanish and English in different proportions across a wide variety of age levels, making possible the comparison of children whose home environments differ in the extent of English use over time. Miami also provides a unique setting within which the whole range of socioeconomic levels is found in substantial numbers. The Hispanic children who were the participants compared favorably in income and educational opportunity with mainstream America, offering a rare opportunity to evaluate bilingual linguistic skill with children who may be expected to be similar in environmental support and linguistic talent to monolingual comparison groups.

Vivian M. Umbel, University of Miami, 1994

Studies considering the effects of early home environment on child development have expressed concern about whether exposure to two languages may induce delay in language acquisition. School-age language minority children in the United States often score below the native English-speaking norm group on standardized measures when tested in their second language (cf. Skutnabb-Kangas & Toukomaa, 1976). This lack of success is of particular concern as regards Hispanics, the US's second largest minority (Arias, 1986). Linguistic and literacy achievement among Spanish-speaking children is an area of continuing national concern (Goldenberg & Gallimore, 1991) because of the long-term implications for educational outcomes and employability. Children whose native language is Spanish consistently achieve at lower levels than do their nonminority English-speaking peers, the gap widening with grade level (De La Rosa & Maw, 1990; Goldenberg & Gallimore, 1991; Orfield, 1986).

Although there is concern about possible effects of bilingualism, it is not at all certain that bilingualism per se is the culprit in the low achievement of many Hispanic school children.

Sociolinguistic conditions may play important roles, and the impact of bilingualism may be different in different circumstances. In particular, it is important to consider both the nature and schedule of the exposure to multiple languages and socioeconomic status (SES).

First, contemplate the nature of language learning—how knowledge is instilled and maintained in native and nonnative languages. Bilingual learning is extremely varied in Hispanic American culture (Laosa, 1984). Some takes place sequentially, with Spanish learned in the home and with English introduced at entry to school. In other circumstances, there is simultaneous learning of English and Spanish from the first year of life. In addition, simultaneous language learning circumstances can involve exposure to English and Spanish in different proportions. These different language learning experiences not only may be distinguishably related to linguistic outcomes in the two languages, but also may interact differently with educational success. One possibility suggested by previous research on vocabulary acquisition (Umbel, Pearson, Fernández, & Oller, 1992) is that simultaneous learners, particularly those with greater exposure to English at home, have stronger English skills at entry to the school system than sequential learners and thus may be more able to benefit from English instruction with formal schooling.

Furthermore, social attitudes about language may influence learning in bilingual children. Lambert (1977) has emphasized the potential importance of attitude toward language in language and literacy outcomes. He has characterized two forms of sequential bilingualism, *additive* and *subtractive*. In the additive form, positive values are attributed to both languages, and the learning of the second language in no way threatens to replace the first. Subtractive bilinguality occurs when one of the languages is not sufficiently valued outside the home. In this case, the language of the economically and culturally more prestigious group tends to replace the minority language. The first language of children whose bilingualism is subtractive regresses while they are acquiring the second language. Thus, a subtractive learning experience may inculcate negative feelings whereas additive bilingualism or simultaneous learning of both languages may foster positive ones.

Such reasoning suggests that the social environment may influence linguistic and educational outcomes in bilingual children. But not only parents' attitudes and the amount of Spanish/English in the home appear to be relevant. Such factors as parental educational level and occupational status may also be important. These factors are commonly subsumed under the heading SES. On average, Hispanic and non-Hispanic White parents differ along salient SES dimensions known to be related to differences in children's performance in both Hispanic and non-Hispanic ethnic groups (Laosa, 1984). Although there is tremendous diversity within Hispanic America (Orfield, 1986), Hispanic parents on average have fewer years of schooling and lower status occupations. Research has shown these variables are related to various aspects of children's performance in school and at home (White, 1982).

Olson (1976) described a presumable mechanism of effect of SES. Distinguishing language's interpersonal functions from its cognitive or logical functions, Olson proposed that children must be exposed to decontextualized language in order to be prepared to master the academic language tasks encountered in school. He assumed that mid-SES parents are more likely to communicate the explicit logical structure found in printed texts, both through their own abstract language and also through reading printed stories to their children, thus preparing them for the context-reduced tasks encountered in school. Success on these decontextualized tasks should, in turn, facilitate the continued development of language and literacy skills.

It is important to note that the presumed influence of SES on decontextualized knowledge may interact with bilingualism. We posit the following scenario as one possibility: Mid-SES bilingual children may have frequent opportunities to interpret decontextualized information in both languages, providing them a head start toward educational success. Low-SES bilingual children might be doubly handicapped—by less exposure to academically stimulating speech, and by the fact that when decontextualized speech is presented, it may be presented in a language they do not yet command extensively. In this scenario, mid-SES bilingual children might show special benefits compared to monolingual peers, whereas low-SES bilingual children might show special deficits.

Cummins (1979, 1984) introduced the *interdependence* hypothesis to account for another possible sociolinguistic effect in bilingualism. He suggested that sequential bilingualism is most likely to succeed if the first language is both well-established and systematically maintained. Under these circumstances, knowledge of the first language would support the learning of the second, through common underlying linguistic structures and through the fact that solid knowledge of a first language gives children access to information from teachers and parents that might otherwise be unavailable to them, thus providing cognitive foundations for further learning. One prediction of the interdependence hypothesis is that sequentially bilingual Hispanic children who are relatively knowledgeable in Spanish should possess more ability to become relatively knowledgeable in English than children who have less command of Spanish.

Assessing the role of social factors such as SES or amount of exposure to two languages in the home on the bilingual child's educational or linguistic success requires detailed information about knowledge of both languages over time. Surprisingly few empirical data are available on the nature of bilingual knowledge in varying social circumstances. Even the measurement of bilingual acquisition is problematic. Instruments developed for one language translate inconsistently to another, and it is rare to find an instrument that can be used equally well in two languages (Wilen & Sweeting, 1986). Results from nonstandardized tests are difficult to interpret, and few standardized complementary measures are available (Figueroa, 1990). Analyses of available psychometric tests by Radencich (1984) and Wilen and Sweeting (1986) catalog most entries as "available in Spanish, no separate norms". The American Psychological Association's guidelines for testing linguistic minorities (American Educational Research Association, American Psychological Association, American Council on Measurement, 1985) cast doubt on almost all current practices in this field.

Vocabulary is one area of language development where crosslinguistic standardization has recently been achieved. The Peabody Picture Vocabulary Test (PPVT) (Dunn, 1965) has been revised and restandardized as well as translated and standardized in Spanish. Independent studies have established the concurrent validity and reliability of the Peabody Picture Vocabulary Test-Revised (PPVT-R) with the Language Assessment Scales (Hakuta, 1987) and other language measures (Beck, Black, & Doles, 1985; D'Amato, Gray, & Dean, 1987). The Spanish version of the PPVT-R, the Test de Vocabulario en Imágenes Peabody-Adaptacion Hispanoamericana (TVIP-H) (Dunn, Padilla, Lugo, & Dunn, 1986), is a carefully constructed instrument standardized on a large number of children.

The existence of these complementary standardized vocabulary tests, the PPVT-R and the TVIP-H, affords new investigative opportunities. We can now evaluate the vocabulary knowledge of Hispanic bilingual children in both of their languages, with relative comparability of results. Previous research using the PPVT (Argulewicz & Abel, 1984; Ben-Zeev, 1977; Serapiglia, 1978) showed young Hispanic bilingual children scoring in the low average range in English, their second and generally weaker language. In this pre-TVIP-H work, only homegrown test translations without age norms (Ben-Zeev, 1977) were used, and consequently it was impossible to provide adequate assessment of the bilingual children's ability in Spanish.

More recently, Umbel et al. (1992) used the PPVT-R and the TVIP-H to evaluate both the English and the Spanish receptive vocabulary knowledge of Hispanic children. The results contradicted the prevailing view of bilingualism as a risk factor in vocabulary development. Although the English vocabulary performance of first graders exposed to both English and Spanish at home was in the low-average range, their Spanish vocabulary performance was comparable to that of the monolingual Spanish-speaking TVIP-H norming sample, suggesting that extensive exposure to the second, majority language does not inhibit normal growth in the first language. Home language experience was of course found to be an important variable in bilingual vocabulary acquisition. Even though the Spanish vocabulary performance of children exposed to English and Spanish at home was similar to that of children exposed to only Spanish at home, their English vocabulary scores were significantly better than those of the latter group.

To our knowledge, only one study has used standardized tests to assess the linguistic knowledge of Hispanic bilingual children in both languages at different age levels. Using the Prueba del Desarrollo Inicial del Lenguaje (PDIL) (Hresko, Reid, & Hammill, 1982), which measures expressive and receptive language ability, Dunn (1987) reported that the Spanish language scores for Hispanic children in the United States were comparable to scores of children in Mexico and Puerto Rico only during the early school years. After the age of 6½, the US children scored progressively worse. These results, accompanied by evidence of low scores in English receptive vocabulary as measured by the PPVT-R, led Dunn to conclude that US Hispanics were "inadequate bilinguals," displaying a wide range of linguistic disabilities in both English and Spanish.

However, the performance curves for Hispanic-American children were not based on data from all the ages of interest, but rather represented extrapolations from fragmentary data. Dunn's (1987) conclusions were, thus, highly speculative. Additionally, as Dunn noted, the PDIL does not constitute a full evaluation, but is merely a screening test, and is inadequately standardized with regard to SES. Not only were small numbers of children tested at each level, but samples were far from randomly selected from the population of Hispanic children. Consequently, it is unclear how lack of decontexualized linguistic experience may have interacted with language learning in producing the Spanish outcomes. Dunn also failed to take account of the possible effects of language exposure at home. We know neither whether the children tested had learned English simultaneously or sequentially nor what extent of exposure to English and Spanish the simultaneous learners had had. If language learning took place in a sequential circumstance, the experience could have been subtractive rather than additive (Lambert, 1977), a pattern that might explain the progressive decline in Spanish scores over time.

The present work is an attempt to further our understanding of linguistic knowledge in Hispanic bilingual children by: (a) evaluating both the English and Spanish vocabulary knowledge of simultaneous bilinguals across three grade levels (first, third, and sixth) using standardized tests in each language, and (b) assessing the relationship between performance in the two languages, as well as the roles of sociolinguistic variables (extent of exposure to English, and SES) in vocabulary acquisition, by comparing simultaneous bilingual children whose home environments differ in the extent of English use and the presumed environmental support contributed by socioeconomic conditions.

The Miami metropolitan area provides a unique setting within which such an effort can be pursued. Unlike Hispanic bilingual populations in other parts of the United States, the whole range of socioeconomic levels is found in substantial numbers among the Miami Hispanic community. In particular, the main strata of Hispanic society in Miami compare favorably in income and educational opportunity with mainstream America (Boswell & Curtis, 1983; Pérez, 1986). Miami also appears to differ markedly from other areas of the country with large Hispanic populations in that the assimilation to English in Miami does not appear to be accompanied by loss of Spanish—put another way, the Miami Hispanic child appears to learn English additively, maintaining a strong command of Spanish to pass on to yet another generation. This pattern of commitment to Spanish includes exposure of children to Spanish and English in different proportions across a wide variety of age levels. Many children begin learning Spanish only, and shift to more English exposure at school age, whereas others show simultaneous learning from the earliest ages.

Method

Participants

We recruited 102 (34 at each grade level) English-Spanish bilingual first, third, and sixth graders satisfying the requirements of the study from two Dade County public schools in predominantly middle-class communities. They ranged in age from 6 to 8 ($M=6.7$), 8 to 10 ($M=8.87$), and 11 to 13 ($M=11.56$), respectively. Boys and girls were distributed almost equally across the three levels; 41, 44, and 41% of first, third, and sixth graders, respectively, were boys. The extent to which English was spoken in the home, occupational level of the family, and educational level of the mother were closely matched across grade levels.

The extent to which English was spoken in the home (EEH) was determined by parental report via questionnaire. Possible choices for language exposure at home were: only Spanish, mostly Spanish, English and Spanish equally, mostly English, and only English. We selected children only from families where either mostly Spanish or English and Spanish equally were spoken. Parents were also asked how long the indicated home language environment had been maintained. All the selected children had been exposed to English since birth, and degree of exposure to the two languages at home was for the most part constant over the child's lifetime. Approximately 50% of parents at each grade level reported mostly Spanish was spoken at home and that this pattern of exposure had been maintained since the child's birth. Of those parents reporting English and Spanish were spoken equally at home, only 6 (3 third grade and 3 sixth grade) reported that there had been a switch from mostly Spanish to equally English and Spanish. In all cases the switch occurred before the child's third birthday.

We classified the children according to the educational level of the mother (ELM): Group 1 consisted of children whose mothers had completed between 6 and 8 years of formal education; Group

2, of children whose mothers had completed between 9 and 11 years of formal education; Group 3, of children whose mothers had completed between 12 and 15 years of formal education; and Group 4, of children whose mothers had completed between 16 and 21 years of formal education. Although all educational levels were represented, 94, 94, and 91% of first, third, and sixth grade mothers, respectively, were high-school educated or better; 24, 21, and 26% were college educated.

We classified families according to the occupation of the major wage earner, using the Occupational Levels (OL) set out by Dunn and Dunn (1981) in the PPVT-R standardization. Occupational levels were: Level 1—operatives, including transport; plus service workers. Level 2—craftsmen, foremen, and kindred workers. Level 3—sales workers; plus clerical and kindred workers. Level 4—professionals, technical, and kindred workers; plus managers and administrators. Although all occupational levels were represented, 79, 79, and 82% of first, third, and sixth grade parents, respectively, held Level 3 or 4 occupations. Forty-four, 47, and 47% of these parents held Level 4 occupations.

Procedure

All students in the targeted public schools at the selected grade levels were given a questionnaire printed in both English and Spanish to be taken home, completed by parents, and returned to the classroom teacher. The questionnaire provided information regarding the extent to which English was spoken in the home and SES. Virtually all the questionnaires were returned. Participation exceeded 90% of the students satisfying the requirements of the study.

We tested each child individually in a quiet room at the school on the PPVT-R and the TVIP-H (order of presentation balanced across the sample with respect to grade level and EEH). Both tests were administered by the same bilingual examiner in a single testing session lasting about 20 minutes. All the children were tested late in the school year in April or May.

Measures

Peabody Picture Vocabulary Test-Revised (PPVT-R) (Dunn & Dunn, 1981): The PPVT-R, normed on American English speakers, is a multiple-choice test designed to evaluate receptive vocabulary knowledge. The PPVT-R consists of 175 plates, each containing four pictures. The child is asked to point to the picture that corresponds to the word pronounced by the examiner. Items are arranged in increasing levels of difficulty.

Test de Vocabulario en Imágenes Peabody-Adaptación Hispanoamericana (TVIP-H) (Dunn et al., 1986): The TVIP-H is a Spanish adaptation of the PPVT-R, normed on Spanish speakers in Puerto Rico and Mexico. Dunn and his associates attempted to make the test as universal as possible for the different groups that comprise what is considered "Hispanic". The TVIP-H has 125 plates arranged in increasing levels of difficulty. For both the PPVT-R and the TVIP-H, raw scores are converted into standard scores (M=100, SD=15).

Results

PPVT-R and TVIP-H scores were examined to determine any effects of grade level (GL) on the children's receptive vocabulary performance. Analysis of Variance (ANOVA) conducted for each test revealed a significant effect of grade level, $F(2, 101)=3.48$, $p=.035$, for the PPVT-R (Table 1). English receptive vocabulary performance increased with grade level, first graders functioning approximately one standard deviation below the mean for the norming sample and sixth graders near the mean. Scheffé's multiple comparison procedure was used for pairwise comparisons of means. Although first and third graders did not differ significantly with respect to their English receptive vocabulary skills, sixth graders outperformed first graders by a significant margin, $p<.05$. In contrast, ANOVA on Spanish receptive vocabulary performance revealed no effect of grade level on TVIP-H performance, $F(2, 101)=1.11$, n.s. Spanish scores were near the value for the norming sample at first and sixth grade.

Table 1
PPVT-R and TVIP-H Scores of Bilingual School Children

	First Graders (n=34)		Third Graders (n=34)		Sixth Graders (n=34)		F
	M	*SD*	*M*	*SD*	*M*	*SD*	*F*
PPVT-R	87.7	15.4	92.4	18.3	98.9	14.6	3.48*
TVIP-H	97.7	15.3	92.5	15.3	97.8	19.4	1.11

df=2, 101
*p<.05

ANOVA was also conducted to determine any effects of extent to which English was spoken in the home (EEH) on the children's receptive vocabulary scores. There was a significant effect of EEH, $F(1, 101)=4.45$, $p=.037$, for the PPVT-R (Table 2). Increased exposure to English at home was related to increased English receptive vocabulary development. In counterpoint, ANOVA on TVIP-H scores revealed no effect of EEH on Spanish receptive vocabulary development, $F(1, 101)=.03$, n.s. Spanish scores were near mean values regardless of extent of English exposure at home.

Because both tests were given at the same sitting and the one

Table 2
PPVT-R and TVIP-H Scores of Bilinguals Exposed to Mostly Spanish at Home (MSH) and Equally English and Spanish at Home (ESH)

	MSH (n=50)		ESH (n=52)		F
	M	*SD*	*M*	*SD*	*F*
PPVT-R	89.75	15.00	96.57	17.37	4.45*
TVIP-H	95.71	14.76	96.30	18.64	.03

df=1,101
*p<.05

test is an adaptation of the other, sharing most of the same picture sets, it was of interest to determine whether scores on the second test were being inflated by the children remembering answers from the first test on those items based on shared pictures. Such an effect would be most pronounced, we reasoned, in cases where the target words were cognates. Owing to their common roots, cognates have similar pronunciation and meaning in both languages; hence, when the second item of a cognate pair is presented, it may tend to remind the child that the item has been seen before. Consequently, if the results were affected by the child's remembering answers from the first test during administration of the second, then the tendency should be strongest for cognate items. Analysis of the percentage correct in English and Spanish performance for approximately 15% of the sample revealed that cognates were not "automatic doublets" for the children. The cognates were right in both languages about 60% of the time, compared to 65% of the time for all words. The difference in favor of all words suggests that the phonological similarity of cognates did not play a major role in test performance, and likewise that remembering of items was not a major factor in performance on the second test.

Stepwise multiple regression procedures were performed to determine which variables best predicted PPVT-R and TVIP-H performance. A backward solution was applied first, so as to include in the stepwise solution just those variables making a unique contribution to the variance in performance. TVIP-H (or PPVT-R in the case of TVIP-H regression analysis), grade level (GL), English exposure at home (EEH), occupational level (OL), and educational level of the mother (ELM) were entered as independent variables.

Only TVIP-H, GL, and EEH were found to make a unique contribution to the variance in PPVT-R performance. Together, these variables accounted for approximately 36% of the variance in the English receptive vocabulary scores of the children (Table 3). Stepwise regression procedures revealed TVIP-H performance had the highest zero-order correlation with PPVT-R performance, accounting for approximately 27% of the variance in English

Table 3
Stepwise Multiple Regression Analysis

	Order of Entry	R^2	R^2Ch	F FCh	df	Sig F FCh
PPVT-R	TVIP-H	.265		36.09	1, 100	<.001
	GL	.328	.064	9.38	2, 99	<.005
	EEH	.363	.034	5.30	3, 98	<.05
TVIP-H	PPVT-R	.265		36.09	1,100	<.001

PPVT-R= Peabody Picture Vocabulary Test-Revised; TVIP-H=Test de Vocabulario en Imágenes Peabody-Adaptación Hispanoamericana; GL=Grade Level; EEH=English Exposure at Home

receptive vocabulary scores. The relationship was positive, increases in PPVT-R performance being related to increases in TVIP-H scores. The increment in the proportion of variance accounted for by GL was also meaningful, PPVT-R performance increasing with grade level. A significant contribution was also made by EEH; increased exposure to English at home was related to increased PPVT-R performance. Only PPVT-R was found to make a unique contribution to the variance in TVIP-H performance, accounting for approximately 27% of the variance.

Discussion

Our evaluation of Hispanic bilingual children's receptive vocabulary development indicates that learning two languages at once does not harm development in the first language and lays the groundwork for improved performance in the second, majority language with grade level. Not only was the Spanish receptive vocabulary performance of first, third, and sixth graders comparable and in the average range, but their English receptive vocabulary scores increased with grade level, first and sixth graders functioning in the low average and average ranges, respectively. The observed maintenance of Spanish skills, coupled with demonstrated increases in English vocabulary development with grade level, highlights the importance of evaluating bilinguals in both their languages over time. However, these results are based on cross-sectional data; it would be advantageous to pursue longitudinal research in order to support a developmental interpretation.

In addition, Spanish receptive vocabulary development was the strongest predictor of English receptive vocabulary scores. This finding is consistent with Cummins' (1979, 1984) interdependence hypothesis, which postulates that a strong foundation in one language facilitates second language development. The first graders in our study had age-appropriate Spanish receptive vocabulary skills. Possibly this proficiency in Spanish, coupled with instruction in English with formal schooling, provided for the maintenance of Spanish receptive vocabulary development, while offering a firm foundation for the development of English receptive vocabulary skills. There is evidence supporting a "reverse" interdependence hypothesis, from the study of effects of systematic training in a second language on maintenance of competence in the first language. Holmstrand (1979), for example, found that elementary-school children who already have high proficiency in their mother tongue and who start to learn a foreign language at an early age improve their competence in the mother tongue more than peers who do not have exposure to a foreign language. Our results, indicating a reliable correlation of TVIP-H and PPVT-R scores, suggest interdependence—although it is uncertain whether the effect is unidirectional, bidirectional, or the product of some third factor.

The simultaneous learning of English and Spanish from the first year of life may have played a role in the English receptive vocabulary development of many of these Hispanic children. Even first graders functioned within one standard deviation of the mean on the PPVT-R; this suggests that as a group they had fairly strong English receptive vocabulary skills at the point of entry to the school system. They may have, thus, been relatively well-equipped to benefit from English instruction at entry to school, providing the possibility of age-appropriate majority language functioning by the sixth grade. Although Dunn (1987) reported increases in PPVT-R performance with age, the English vocabulary performance of the children in our study was superior to that of their age-mates in Dunn's study. The disparity increased with grade level, reaching nine points by the sixth grade. The differences between our results and Dunn's may, at least in part, be a function of language exposure, a variable for which Dunn failed to control. Another possibility is that the superior PPVT-R performance of our Hispanic students was due to higher SES. Most of the children in our study were of mid SES. Approximately 93% of their mothers were high-school educated or better. Similarly, approximately 80% of the parents' reported occupational levels were semiprofessional or professional. Although Dunn's data were obtained by administering the PPVT-R to all children participating in American Guidance Service standardizations of three individualized tests, suggesting SES was normally distributed, the children in our study were primarily from relatively higher SES groups.

The middle-class status of the children in our study may also account for the Spanish-language performance differences between our results and Dunn's (1987). Although the disparity in performance is not clear-cut, due to differences in the domains tapped by the TVIP-H and the PDIL, the decrements in Spanish language skills with age that Dunn reported were not corroborated by our study. Because the PDIL is inadequately standardized, the decrement reported by Dunn could at least partly be due to relatively low SES in his Hispanic sample. Whether children who enter school with relatively limited English proficiency overcome the risk imposed by their disadvantage in English may depend on how their home environment helps them adapt. Mid-SES bilinguals may thus become better prepared for the decontextualized tasks encountered in school and more readily benefit from the academic English to which they are exposed there. Mid-SES simultaneous bilinguals may be doubly advantaged, having stronger English language skills at entry to school than their sequentially bilingual peers.

Although neither mother's educational level nor parental occupational level reliably predicted the children's vocabulary performance in our study, our sample's homogeneity on these variables was probably a limiting factor. As mentioned above, the vast majority of the children were of mid SES. This restricting of range may have attenuated correlations.

Our sample's English and Spanish vocabulary performance may also be related to the sociocultural context in which bilingual experience occurs in metropolitan Miami. Spanish is the first language of 49% of the population (*Metro-Dade County Planning Department 1990 Hispanic Profile*, Miami, Florida Office of Latin Affairs Research Division); Spanish-language media compete with English newspapers, radio and TV. All socioeconomic levels are represented, people of Hispanic background participating at high levels of government, banking, law, medicine, and industry. Thus, the bilinguality experienced by Miami Hispanics is for the most part based on an appreciation of, and openness toward, both cultures and languages. Lambert (1977) proposed that in such (additive) circumstances the learning of the majority language does not encroach on the home language. The Canadian experience provides empirical support for this notion, showing bilingual students outperforming monolingual peers on various language measures (Hakuta, 1986; Lambert & Tucker, 1972; Peal & Lambert, 1962). By the sixth grade, the children in our study had native-like receptive vocabulary skills in both their languages, suggesting they did not suffer subtractive bilingualism and its hypothesized negative effects (Lambert, 1977).

Within the simultaneous language-learning circumstance of the children in our study, increased exposure to English at home was unrelated to Spanish receptive vocabulary performance. Children receiving comparable exposure to English and Spanish at home compared favorably with those receiving mostly Spanish at home on the TVIP-H. However, children receiving increased exposure to English at home did significantly better on the PPVT-R. These results are generally consistent with those reported by Umbel et al. (1992). In their study, the Spanish receptive vocabulary performance of children receiving exposure to English and Spanish at home was comparable to that of those exposed to only Spanish at home. However, their PPVT-R performance was significantly better than that of the latter. Thus, exposure to English and Spanish at home appears sufficient both to maintain Spanish receptive vocabulary skills and lay the groundwork for improvement in English receptive vocabulary development.

One might still question whether the children in our study did not sacrifice some proficiency in Spanish as a result of learning English. Although middle-class children growing up in a facilitating environment might be expected to score above the norming mean, these children did not. However, their Spanish vocabulary knowledge may have been greater than their TVIP-H scores indicated.

First, the children in our study were of a different dialect (primarily Cuban) from the TVIP-H norming sample (Mexican and Puerto Rican). Fernández, Pearson, Umbel, Oller, and Molinet-Molina (1992), studying Hispanic children in Miami, found evidence that the order of difficulty on the TVIP-H items was substantially different from that derived from the norming sample by Dunn et al. (1986). In administration of the test, a ceiling is established when the child misses six of the last eight items tested. Thus, children are at a disadvantage on the TVIP-H if harder words precede easier ones because of a lack of equivalence across dialects.

Furthermore, given the interruption in Spanish language development that often corresponds to the beginning of formal schooling in the United States, one might have expected a decline in the Spanish receptive vocabulary skills of the children in our sample. The monolingual TVIP-H norming sample in Mexico and Puerto Rico would have had more consistent instruction in Spanish throughout elementary school. Thus, the children in our study were at a disadvantage on the TVIP-H that could only be made up by age-appropriate formal instruction in Spanish. Reading, in particular, has been found to be an important source of vocabulary growth (Eldredge, Quinn, & Butterfield, 1990; Elley, 1989;

Stanovich & Cunningham, 1992; West & Stanovich, 1991); education in English only may have limited the Spanish vocabulary growth of these children. For example, González (1986) compared Mexican-born students who were schooled for at least two years in Mexico before emigrating to the United States with Mexican-born students who emigrated to the US before beginning school. The Mexican-schooled group performed significantly better on Spanish reading tasks than did the group schooled entirely in the US. It appears, then, that an educational program that maintained the development of Spanish could very well have improved the Spanish scores of the children in our sample.

In addition, the scores in both English and Spanish in our study may underestimate the number of lexicalized concepts available to the children. Many bilingual children know some words without knowing their translation equivalents (Umbel et al., 1992). To the extent that vocabulary in the two languages covers distinguishable semantic domains, then scores in either language alone underestimate the bilingual child's total lexicalization of concepts.

In the Miami schools investigated here, Hispanic children were educated in an English immersion approach (i.e., very little support for Spanish in school). Bilingual education, including instruction in Spanish throughout elementary school, might have resulted in enhanced Spanish skills compared to instruction through English immersion.

Although results cannot be generalized to other populations, our findings suggest that English immersion programs provide sufficient conditions for the maintenance of Spanish receptive vocabulary skills (at least through the sixth grade) and allow for improved English receptive vocabulary development with grade level, at least in the case of mid-SES simultaneous bilinguals growing up in an additive environment. However, these results constitute only a small piece of a large and complex picture. Although empirical studies have found vocabulary tests are fairly sensitive indicators of more general language growth (Doyle, Champagne, & Segalowitz, 1978; Hakuta, 1987), whether bilinguals can maintain Spanish and concomitantly develop English in domains other than vocabulary, without the benefit of bilingual instruction, remains to be clearly demonstrated. Our results are consistent with the possibility that vocabulary production, syntax, and academics are positively affected by bilingual instruction and that age-appropriate functioning in these domains requires instruction in the stronger language at entry to school. However, additional studies must be conducted to more definitively demonstrate this position.

References

American Educational Research Association, American Psychological Association, American Council on Measurement. (1985). *Standards for educational and psychological tests*. Washington, DC: American Psychological Association.

Argulewicz, E. N., & Abel, R. R. (1984). Internal evidence of bias in the PPVT-R for Anglo-American and Mexican-American children. *Journal of School Psychology, 22*, 299–303.

Arias, M. B. (1986). The context of education for Hispanic students: An overview. *American Journal of Education, 95*, 26–57.

Beck, F. N., Black, F. L., & Doles, J. (1985). The concurrent validity of the Peabody Picture Vocabulary Test-Revised relative to the Comprehensive Tests of Basic Skills. *Educational & Psychological Measurement, 45*, 705–710.

Ben-Zeev, S. (1977). The effect of Spanish-English bilingualism in children from less privileged neighborhoods on cognitive development and cognitive strategy. *Working Papers on Bilingualism, 14*, 83–122.

Boswell, T. D., & Curtis, J. R. (1983). *The Cuban-American experience: Culture, images, and perspectives*. Totowa, NJ: Rowman & Allanheld.

Cummins, J. (1979). Linguistic interdependence and the educational development of bilingual children. *Review of Educational Research, 49*, 222–251.

Cummins, J. (1984). *Bilingualism and special education: Issues in assessment and pedagogy*. Clevedon, Avon: Multilingual Matters.

D'Amato, R. C., Gray, J. W., & Dean, R. S. (1987). Concurrent validity of the PPVT-R with K-ABC for learning problem children. *Psychology in the Schools, 24*, 35–39.

De La Rosa, D., & Maw, C. (1990). Hispanic education: A statistical portrait. Washington, DC: National Council of La Raza.

Doyle, A., Champagne, M., & Segalowitz, N. (1978). Some issues in the assessment of linguistic consequences of early bilingualism. In M. Paradis (Ed.), *Aspects of bilingualism* (pp. 13–21). Columbia, SC: Hornbeam Press.

Dunn, L. (1965). *Peabody Picture Vocabulary Test*. Circle Pines, MN: American Guidance Service.

Dunn, L. (1987). *Bilingual Hispanic children on the U.S. Mainland: A review of research on their cognitive, linguistic, and scholastic development*. Circle Pines, MN: American Guidance Service.

Dunn, L., & Dunn, L. (1981). *Peabody Picture Vocabulary Test-Revised*. Circle Pines, MN: American Guidance Service.

Dunn, L., Padilla, E., Lugo, D., & Dunn, L. (1986). *Test de Vocabulario en Imágenes Peabody*. Circle Pines, MN: American Guidance Service.

Eldredge, J. L., Quinn, B., & Butterfield, D. D. (1990). Causal relationships between phonics, reading comprehension, and vocabulary achievement in the second grade. *Journal of Educational Research, 83*, 201–214.

Elley, W. B. (1989). Vocabulary acquisition from listening to stories. *Reading Research Quarterly, 24*, 174–187.

Fernández, M. C., Pearson, B. Z., Umbel, V. M., Oller, D. K., & Molinet-Molina, M. (1992). Bilingual receptive vocabulary in Hispanic preschool children. *Hispanic Journal of the Behavioral Sciences, 14*, 268–276.

Figueroa, R. A. (1990). Best practices in the assessment of bilingual children. In A. Thomas & J. Grimes (Eds.), *Best practices in school psychology* (Vol. 2, pp. 93–106). Washington, DC: National Association of School Psychologists.

Goldenberg, C., & Gallimore, R. (1991). Local knowledge, research knowledge, and educational change: A case study of early Spanish reading improvement. *Educational Researcher, 20*, 2–14.

González, L. A. (1986). *The effects of first language education on the second language and academic achievement of Mexican immigrant elementary school children in the United States*. Unpublished doctoral dissertation, University of Illinois, Urbana-Champaign.

Hakuta, K. (1986). *Mirror of language: The debate on bilingualism*. New York: Basic.

Hakuta, K. (1987). Degree of bilingualism and cognitive ability in mainland Puerto Rican children. *Child Development, 58*, 1372–1388.

Holmstrand, L. E. (1979). The effects on general school achievement of early commencement of English instruction. *Uppsala Reports on Education, 4*, 1–45.

Hresko, W. P., Reid, D. K., & Hammill, D. D. (1982). *La prueba del desarrollo inicial del lenguaje*. Austin, TX: Pro-ed.

Lambert, W. E. (1977). Effects of bilingualism on the individual. In P. A.

Hornby (Ed.), *Bilingualism: Psychological, social and educational implications* (pp. 15–28). New York: Academic Press.

Lambert, W. E., & Tucker, G. R. (1972). Bilingual education of children: The Saint Lambert Experiment. Rowley, MA: Newbury House.

Laosa, L. M. (1984). Ethnic, socioeconomic, and home language influences upon early performance on measures of ability. *Journal of Educational Psychology, 76,* 1178–1198.

Metro-Dade County Planning Department 1990 Hispanic Profile, Miami, FL: Office of Latin Affairs Research Division.

Olson, D. R. (1976). Culture, technology and intellect. In L. B. Resnick (Ed.), *The nature of intelligence.* Hillsdale, NJ: Lawrence Erlbaum.

Orfield, G. (1986). Hispanic education: Challenges, research, and policies. *American Journal of Education, 95,* 1–25.

Peal, E., & Lambert, W. E. (1962). The relation of bilingualism to intelligence. *Psychological Monographs, 76,* 1–23.

Pérez, L. (1986). Cubans in the United States. *Annals of the American Academy of Political and Social Sciences, 487,* 126–137.

Radencich, M. (1984). *Intelligence and process tests for non-English speaking children and adults.* Unpublished manuscript, University of Miami, National Origin Desegregation Center, Coral Gables, FL.

Serapiglia, T. (1978). Comparison of the syntax and vocabulary of bilingual Spanish, Indian, and monolingual Anglo-American children. *Working Papers in Bilingualism, 16,* 75–91. (ERIC Document Reproduction Service No. ED 165 477)

Skutnabb-Kangas, T., & Toukomaa, P. (1976). *Teaching migrant children's mother tongue and learning the language of the host country in the context of the socio-cultural situation of the migrant family.* Tampere, Finland: University of Tampere, Department of Sociology and Social Psychology.

Stanovich, K. E., & Cunningham, A. E. (1992). Studying the consequences of literacy within a literate society: The cognitive correlates of print exposure. *Memory & Cognition, 20,* 51–68.

Umbel, V. M., Pearson, B. Z., Fernández, M. C., & Oller, D. K. (1992). Measuring bilingual children's receptive vocabularies. *Child Development, 63,* 1012–1020.

West, R. F., & Stanovich, K. E. (1991). The incidental acquisition of information from reading. *Psychological Science, 2,* 325–330.

White, K. R. (1982). The relation between socioeconomic status and academic achievement. *Psychological Bulletin, 91,* 461–481.

Wilen, D. K., & Sweeting, C. (1986). Assessment of limited English proficient Hispanic students. *School Psychology Review, 15,* 59–75.

Does Advanced Skill in a Second Language Reduce Automaticity in the First Language?

Norman Segalowitz
Concordia University

Author's Statement: *This study addressed a question that is often asked by concerned parents and educators, but seldom systematically researched in the laboratory. The general form of the question is: What effect, if any, does mastery of a second language have on one's first language skill? Here, the question was formulated more narrowly, taking a cue from the frequent observation that when a second language user spends less and less time in the medium of the first language, functioning in the first language slows down. In this study the question was formulated in terms of whether there is a loss of "automaticity" in the first language as a function of mastery of the second language.*

Up to the time of publication of this paper, all discussion about loss of automaticity in the first language had been formulated solely in terms of speed of response, wherein slowed first language responding was assumed to indicate loss of automaticity. Automaticity, however, has a specific meaning—indeed, several specific meanings— in cognitive psychology. And although automatic responses are held to be faster than nonautomatic responses by all accounts of automaticity, speed is never the sole defining characteristic. Thus, an important aim of this study was to examine automaticity effects in the first language using an operational definition that takes account of factors beyond speed of response.

This research was funded by a grant from the Quebec Ministry of Education (FCAR). The author thanks Claire Carrière, Johanne Courte, Elizabeth Gatbonton, Mel Komoda, Diane Poulin-Dubois and Vivien Watson for their comments on earlier versions of this manuscript.

The study revealed, interestingly, that whereas response time was slower in the first language as a function of more advanced second language skill, automaticity as such was not reduced. This conclusion is important and interesting for two reasons. First, it indicates that claims about the impact of one language on skill in another need to be carefully nuanced by taking into account processing factors that go beyond consideration of mere speed. Second, it may have implications for efforts to reverse such effects on first language skill. For example, we would expect it to be easier to train or practice one's first language in order to speed up nonautomatic processing than to actually reestablish automaticity: the present study suggests that reestablishing automaticity may not be necessary. It was hoped that this study would encourage future researchers to focus on the generalizability of the issues. This should involve not only testing other populations, languages, and language situations in both longitudinal and cross-sectional designs, but should also employ other operational definitions of automatic and nonautomatic processing

Norman Segalowitz, Concordia University, 1994

This paper addresses an issue that might broadly be considered an aspect of language loss: performance decrements in one's first language (L1) that are attributable to the possession of a second language (L2). The loss of a first language due to sociocultural pressures from a second language has been the object of some discussion in the literature on languages in contact (Weinreich, 1953; Dorian, 1981, 1982; Sharwood Smith, 1983). Overall, however, it appears that there is little in the *psycholinguistic* literature to document performance decrements in L1 associated with advanced skills in L2, and even less consideration of the processes that might be involved in such effects (see Sharwood Smith, 1983, for a discussion of hypotheses regarding the way structural similarities and differences between L1 and L2 might operate to affect L1 performance).

The specific focus of this paper is whether advanced skill in L2 is associated with reduced performance in L1 and, if so, what processing changes may be responsible for this reduced performance. Our concern here will be with a relatively simple, but fundamental, aspect of language functioning: speed of visual word recognition.

Word recognition is, of course, a basic component of skilled use of language. One basic issue regarding the way changes may occur in the psychological processes underlying a given skill, such as visual word recognition, concerns the distinction between automatic and controlled processes (Posner & Snyder, 1975; Shiffrin & Dumais, 1981). Controlled processes are those that generally require attention, reflect strategic considerations (i.e., reflect intentions based on expectations), and take considerable time. Automatic processes are those that require little or no attentional effort, do not reflect strategic considerations (e.g., they operate independently of the user's intentions or conscious expectations) and take relatively little time. Every skilled performance, of course, includes some components that can be characterized as automatic as well as those that can be characterized as controlled. The development of skill is presumed to involve, among other things, both the increased automatization of underlying processes and increased effectiveness of strategic processing (Laberge & Samuels, 1974; Ackerman, 1987; see Segalowitz (1986) and Gatbonton & Segalowitz (1988) for discussions with respect to L2 development). With reading, the advantage of automatic word recognition is that it reduces the demand made on attentional resources that might be used for other aspects of the reading task, such as integrating words across syntactic structures or updating one's story schema.

Now, practice that involves dealing with information in a consistent manner (and not mere repetition) has been demonstrated to be a major factor in determining the development of high levels of skill, because it is just such extensive consistent practice that leads to automatization (Schneider & Fisk, 1982; Shiffrin & Schneider, 1977). Thus, for example, extensive use of L2 might be expected to promote automatic word recognition in that language to the extent that repeated encounters with a given word require similar interpretation of that word (consistent practice) (see Favreau & Segalowitz, 1983). Given this skills perspective, one can raise the following question: might the time spent reading in L2 be considered, in effect, time taken away from just this sort of consistent practice with L1, and does this produce adverse results such as reduced speed of processing (less automaticity and/or reduced effectiveness of strategic processing) in L1 reading?

Evidence of Costs in Speed of L1 Processing

Among the most clearly documented claims of decrements in L1 performance associated with extensive L2 experience come from studies by Magiste (see Magiste, 1986, for a summary). She studied German-speaking individuals living in Sweden who used German at home and in school (the Bilingual School in Stockholm) but Swedish elsewhere. Magiste attempted to relate speed of word naming, picture naming, reading two-digit numbers and performance in bilingual Stroop color tasks in German (L1) and Swedish (L2) to length of residence in Sweden (i.e., exposure to L2). In general, she reported that with the newly arrived immigrant, performance was faster in L1 than in L2, but that performance rates in the two languages converged as the stay in Sweden lengthened. For bilinguals who had lived about five to seven years in the L2 environment, performance was faster in L2 than in L1.

In our laboratory we have obtained data consistent with this general picture. For example, in Favreau and Segalowitz (1982) we tested English-French bilinguals who were all skilled in L2 according to a reading test used for assessment purposes (they could read standardized English and French stories with equally high levels of comprehension). For half, English was L1, and for half, French was. Some of these bilinguals were identified as having high level reading skill in L2 (native-like) because they could read their L2 at the same rate as their L1 (referred to here as Same Rate bilinguals). Others were identified as less skilled because they read their L2 more slowly than their L1 (Different Rate bilinguals). The Same Rate bilinguals reported that they had spent at least five years of their preuniversity education in the medium of L2 whereas the Different Rate bilinguals had spent less than two years. Thus the Same Rate bilinguals would appear to have had more extensive and intensive exposure to L2 and less to L1 than did the Different Rate bilinguals, and possibly during a critical time of development. We noticed that, as a group, the Same Rate bilinguals were significantly *slower* readers of L1 compared to the Different Rate bilinguals (262 vs. 318 wpm; but of course, they were significantly faster in L2: 275 vs. 234 wpm). Thus it would seem, as Magiste (1986) had found, that the relatively slower performance in L1 may be related to extensive exposure to L2.

In subsequent studies we found similar patterns. For example, in Segalowitz & Hébert (1990) new groups of Same Rate and Different Rate bilinguals (half with English L1, half with

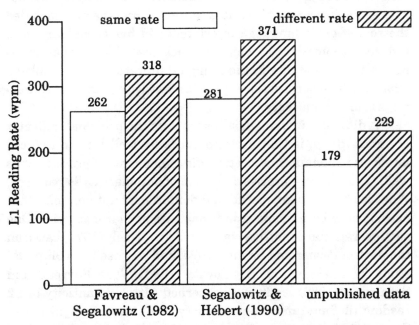

Figure 1. Reading rate in L1 for same rate and different rate bilinguals in three independent samples of students. Sample sizes in the unpublished data were 26 Same Rate and 24 Different Rate bilinguals.

French L1) were tested in lexical decision and sentence verification tasks (this study focused on phonological recoding). Students had to meet a minimum reading rate criterion for L1 (275 wpm) to participate in the study. Again, the Same Rate bilinguals exhibited slower reading rates in L1 (313 wpm) compared to the Different Rate bilinguals (375 wpm) and this L1 pattern difference was also reflected in their response latencies to the various tasks. We have again found similar results for another, independently tested sample of bilinguals (see Fig. 1).

Reduced Automaticity in L1?

Magiste (1986) attributed the slower latencies in L1 to reduced automaticity (p. 105) in terms that generally accept fast response time as indicating automaticity and slowed response rate as an indication of reduced automaticity (she also included the role of cross language interference in her consideration of reduced automaticity). This approach resembles earlier treatments of automaticity in the bilingual literature (e.g., Lambert, 1955) in which performance speed is regarded as the chief characteristic of automaticity.

A difficulty in using fast response as the principal indicator of automaticity, is that practice may very well lead to reduced latencies in *non*automatic, strategic components of processing as well. Thus, a more precise definition of automaticity is required. What is needed is an operational definition of automaticity that encompasses both its speed and nonstrategic characteristics. One such operational definition was provided by Neely (1977) based on the work of Posner and Snyder (1975) and was used in a bilingual study by Favreau and Segalowitz (1983). The Favreau and Segalowitz (1983) study was concerned with automaticity in L2 reading (it found more automaticity of L2 word recognition in Same Rate bilinguals). The study did not report on the issue of costs to L1 performance. However, the L1 data in that study can, in fact, shed light on the effects that advanced L2 skill may have on L1 automaticity. Therefore, an analysis of the L1 data from that study will be the focus of the discussion that follows. The advantage of that study is that its design permits one to distinguish the operation of automatic from strategic (controlled) processing.

The basic logic of the design of the Favreau and Segalowitz (1983) study followed that of Neely (1977). Students were required to perform a lexical decision task in which they had to decide whether a target string of letters constituted a real word (e.g., *ROBIN*) or not (*SOBIN*). This task may be considered to require access to the semantic mental representation of the target word and so performance on this task provides an index of word recognition skill (e.g., see den Heyer, Goring, Gorgichuk, Richards, & Landry, 1988).

We used a *primed* lexical decision task in which each target letter string, always in uppercase letters, was preceded by a string of lowercase letters that served as a prime that could potentially affect the response latency to the target. Sometimes the prime was semantically related to the target (*bird-ROBIN*), sometimes it was unrelated (*flower-ROBIN*) and sometimes the prime was neutral, that is, it had no meaning (always *ooooo*). In addition, we manipulated the interval between the onset of the prime and the onset of the target (stimulus onset asynchrony-SOA). Sometimes the interval was long (1150 msec) and sometimes it was short (200 msec).

Finally, we manipulated the student's expectancies. Sometimes the student was set to expect the prime to name the category of the target (Expect-Related condition: e.g., *bird-ROBIN*, *bird-SPARROW*, etc.), and sometimes the student was set to expect the target to come from a specifically different category from the one named by the prime (Expect-Unrelated; e.g., *bird-CHAIR*, *bird-TABLE*, *bird-COUCH*, etc.). Students were told that the expected relationship would hold throughout the session and for the vast majority of trials the relationship was indeed respected. The expected relationship was maintained for 83% of the positive trials (when the target was a real word) in a given block of trials. On 17% of the positive trials, however, a surprise trial was introduced in which the expectation was violated. In the case of the Expect-Related block of trials, the surprise trial would involve a semantically unrelated target, such as *bird-CARROT* instead of *bird-NAME OF BIRD*. In the Expect-Unrelated block of trials, the surprise trial would involve a semantically related target, such as *bird-ROBIN* instead of *bird-NAME OF A PIECE OF FURNITURE*.

Consider first the case when the SOA is long and the student has enough time to think about the expected target after seeing the prime. Normally, one would expect faster lexical decision latencies to targets preceded by a semantically related prime (*bird-ROBIN*) compared to a control trial with a neutral prime (*ooooo-ROBIN*). That is, semantically related primes should cause facilitation of a lexical decision. In contrast, one would normally expect a semantically unrelated prime (*flower-ROBIN*) to result in inhibition or a slowing of lexical decision latencies (again, compared to the latencies obtained with a neutral prime). This is what has been found when the student is set to expect primes to be related to the target or when there are no particular expectancies at all (Neely, 1977; Favreau & Segalowitz, 1983; Burke, White, & Diaz, 1987; see Jonides & Mack, 1984, for a discussion of issues related to the use of such techniques). Figure 2 (Long SOA, Expect-Related) illustrates this with an idealized pattern of results.

An interesting situation obtains when students are instructed to expect primes to be unrelated to the target as, for example, when the student is instructed to expect *flower* to be followed by the name of a bird. Here we obtain the reverse pattern to the one described above if the SOA is relatively long. That is, there is facilitation when the prime-target relation conforms to expectancy (as in *flower-ROBIN*) and inhibition when it does not (a surprise trial with *bird-ROBIN*) (See Fig. 2, Long SOA, Expect-Unrelated.) Such effects have been reported by Favreau and Segalowitz (1983) and Neely (1977). This condition is the most difficult because the student must remember the arbitrary pairing of prime category names with unrelated category sources for

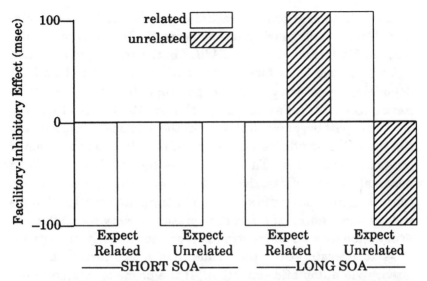

Figure 2. Idealized patterns of facilitory (RT to primed trials faster than to neutral trials) and inhibitory effects (RT to primed trials slower than to neutral trials) in lexical decision as a function of SOA, semantic relation between prime and target, and expectancy. (See text for explanation.)

targets. This clearly requires strategic processing for there to be facilitation for the expected but semantically unrelated targets. Thus, in the long SOA condition the magnitude of facilitation for expected (unrelated) targets and the magnitude of inhibition for unexpected (related) targets on surprise trials can provide an indication of the operation of controlled or strategic processes.

Consider now the case in which the SOA is too short for expectancies to exert their influence. Here the pattern of facilitation and inhibition changes dramatically and reflects the semantic relatedness of the prime and target, not the student's expectation. Thus, there is facilitation on trials like *bird-ROBIN*, even on a surprise trial when the student expects bird to be followed by the name of a piece of furniture (Fig. 2, Short SOA). However, when the prime is not related to the target, as in a trial like *bird-TABLE*, there is no inhibition (i.e., latencies do not differ significantly from trials with neutral primes) regardless of the student's expectation. Thus, students will show no priming effect (neither inhibition nor facilitation) for *bird-TABLE* in the short SOA condition but will indeed show facilitation or inhibition in the long SOA depending upon what kind of expectancy they were trained to have (Neely, 1977; Favreau & Segalowitz, 1983). (See Fig. 2).

This pattern of facilitation with the absence of inhibition in the short SOA condition is interpreted to reflect the operation of automatic processes. That is, because the student has a long personal history of associating "bird" with the names of birds, there is rapid, automatic activation by the prime of related items in long-term store. If a target is presented very soon after the prime—too soon for the controlled processes underlying expectations to operate—then the prime may affect lexical decision latency via automatic activation. If the prime is related to the target, then the prime will initiate activation of the representation of that target and related items before the target actually appears on the screen (e.g., *bird* will automatically initiate activation of *ROBIN, SPARROW,* etc.). The student will be more "prepared" to see it than if the prime had been the neutral *ooooo* and hence, there will be a facilitation effect (faster response). If the prime is semantically unrelated to the target (e.g., *bird-TABLE*), inappropriate items will be activated (e.g., again, *bird* will automatically initiate activation of *ROBIN, SPARROW,* etc.), but the resting activation level of potential target items (*TABLE, CHAIR,* etc.) will remain unchanged. Hence there will be no inhibition effects from the semantically unrelated primes.

To summarize, with a long SOA, priming effects will reflect the student's expectancy, yielding facilitation for expected targets and inhibition for unexpected targets, regardless of the semantic relatedness of prime to target. Because the priming effect reflects conscious expectancies it can be used as an index of controlled processing. In contrast, with a short SOA, priming effects will reflect the semantic relationship between the prime and the target, regardless of the student's expectancies. The effect will be confined to facilitation for semantically related targets. Because this priming effect reflects relatedness and not expectancy it can be used as an index of automaticity.

In the study presented below, such indices of controlled and automatic processing in L1 were analyzed across Same Rate and Different Rate bilinguals who differed in their L1 reading rates. In this way, one can examine if costs to L1 processing reflect changes in automatic or controlled processing or both in L1. If high level skill in L2 (a level that equals L1 performance) reduces L1 automaticity, then one would expect to see significantly less facilitation on related trials in the short SOA condition for the Same Rate bilinguals than for the Different Rate bilinguals. Similarly, if high level skill in L2 reduces the effectiveness of controlled processing in L1, then one would expect to see significantly less priming effect (facilitation, inhibition, or combined effects) in the long SOA condition for the Same Rate bilinguals than for the Different Rate bilinguals. Put another way, for the Same Rate bilinguals, attentional processing of the prime might be less effective, and so in the interval between prime onset and target, there will be less opportunity for facilitation and/or inhibition of activation of the target to occur.

Method

Because this paper reports a reanalysis of data collected in an already published study (Favreau & Segalowitz, 1983), only those aspects of the original study that are relevant to the present discussion will be highlighted. For example, there is neither discussion here of the L2 data nor of the data from negative trials. The reader is invited to consult the original paper for more detail.

Participants

The bilinguals whose data are reported here comprise two groups of 20 selected from the two original groups of 30 tested in Favreau and Segalowitz (1983). One group, the Different Rate bilinguals, read their L1 at least 10% faster than their L2 according to the test procedures of Favreau and Segalowitz (1982). The other group, the Same Rate bilinguals, read their two languages at approximately the same rate (less than 10% difference). In the original study, the Different Rate bilinguals read L1 significantly faster than did the Same Rate bilinguals, but there was considerable overlap in reading rates of the two groups. For purposes of the present reanalysis of the Favreau and Segalowitz (1983) study, data from the 10 slowest L1 readers in the Different Rate group and the 10 fastest L1 readers in the Same Rate group were eliminated to yield two groups of 20 students with no overlap whatever in their L1 reading rates (Same Rate group: M=218 wpm, range 160 to 269 wpm; Different Rate group: M=364 wpm, range 272 to 543 wpm). In the reconstituted Same Rate group, 8 students had English as L1 and 12 had French as L1; in the Different group 9 and 11 had English and French as L1, respectively. The mean age of each group was 23 years.

Materials

The materials are fully described in Favreau and Segalowitz (1983). Four English and four French sets of 96 prime-target letter-string pairs were used. In each set the *primes* were of two types: 48 primes were words (name of a category) and 48 were a string of five *o*'s (neutral prime). These neutral primes served to provide base line control data to compare with performance on trials with word primes. In each set the *targets* were also of two types: 48 of the targets were words and 48 were pronounceable nonwords formed by changing one letter of the corresponding real word. Thus each experimental set was made up of 24 word prime-word target, 24 word prime-nonword target, 24 neutral prime-word target, and 24 neutral prime-nonword target pairs.

In each language there were two sets prepared for the Expect-Related condition and two sets for the Expect-Unrelated condition. Word primes were the names of four categories. In each of the Expect-Related sets, 20 of the 24 word targets were members of the category named by the prime (five different members for each category) (e.g., *bird-ROBIN*). The remaining four pairs were used for surprise trials and contained target words drawn from a fifth category, one target word used once with each of the four category names. Finally, in a given Expect-Related set, 24 target words were drawn from the four categories named by each of the word primes and paired with the neutral control primes.

In the Expect-Unrelated sets, 20 of the 24 word targets were members of four categories other than the ones named by the primes. Thus each set contained 20 word-word prime-target pairings in which the target was semantically unrelated to the prime (e.g., *bird-CARROT*). In these pairs the targets always came from the same category (e.g., *bird-NAME OF VEGETABLE*). The four remaining word-word pairs were used for surprise trials and contained targets from the category named by the prime. In addition, in a given Expect-Unrelated set, 24 target words were drawn from the four main categories used as sources for targets and paired with the neutral control primes.

Nonwords were formed from each target word by replacing one of the letters (occasionally two letters when necessary) to form a pronounceable nonword (position of the changed letter varied randomly and orthographic shape of the word was preserved).

Practice sets consisting of 48 trials were constructed using the same primes as in the experimental sets but different target words. The practice sets corresponded in structure to the sets described above, except that there were no surprise trials.

All materials consisted of black letters on white background. Stimuli were presented in a four channel Gerbrands tachistoscope. The average six-letter target's height and width subtended visual angles of approximately 0.5 and 2.4 degrees, respectively. An *X* was used for the fixation point.

Design

Each student took part in eight blocks spread over four sessions of approximately 40 minutes each. The blocks were formed by crossing the various combinations of Expect-Related and Expect-Unrelated, L1 and L2, Long SOA (stimulus onset asynchrony between prime and target=1150 msec) and short SOA (200 msec). Order of sessions was counterbalanced across students. Only the L1 conditions are relevant to the issues discussed here (the L2 data are thoroughly discussed in Favreau & Segalowitz, 1983).

Prime and target words were rotated through the experiment across students so that a given word appeared in all possible conditions (e.g., across the experiment as a whole, *ROBIN* appeared in an Expect-Related trial and in an Expect-Unrelated trial in each SOA condition). For each student a given prime appeared in only one Expect context.

Procedure

Students were individually tested in four sessions over four different days. The general instructions emphasized that (A) the student should fixate the X at the beginning of each trial; (b) a lowercase string consisting of either a category name or *ooooo* would immediately replace the X; (c) an uppercase string consisting of a word or nonword would appear next; (d) the students should press one of the response keys to indicate their decision about the lexical status of the uppercase string; and (e) each trial would require full attention.

Each session consisted of two blocks of trials. First the student received the instructions in the language of the upcoming block of trials. Next the student received 24 practice trials with feedback. Then the student received 24 more practice trials without feedback, followed by the experimental trials. Students always had advance knowledge of the four category names that would serve as primes in that block and the type of target word to expect with them. In the case of the Expect-Unrelated condition, students were required to show that they had correctly memorized the prime category and the unrelated target category pairings.

Trials began with a verbal *ready* (*prêt*) signal, followed by a

1500 msec fixation X and then the prime for 150 msec. Following the onset of the prime, there was either a 200 msec (short SOA) or 1150 msec (long SOA) interval to the onset of the target. The target remained in view until the student pressed a reaction time panel. There was a four-second intertrial interval. There was a 20-minute rest period between blocks within a given session.

Results

Only data from trials with correct responses were analyzed (error rate <3% for each reading rate group). For purposes of the present discussion only data from the L1 conditions in which the target was a word are relevant. The facilitation and inhibition effects in the Expect-Unrelated and Expect-Related conditions are illustrated in Figures 3 and 4, respectively.

Automaticity in L1

The measure of automaticity used in this study was the facilitation effect in the short SOA condition, that is, the degree to which latencies were faster for targets on Related trials than on Control trials.

Now, the effect of most interest to us will be facilitation to a related target in the Expect-Unrelated condition, because this effect will have to occur in a direction opposite to any influence from the student's conscious strategy. The data from the short SOA Expect-Unrelated condition were submitted to a 2×2 analysis of variance, where the factors were Group (Same Rate vs. Different Rate bilinguals), and Condition (Control vs. Related trials) with repeated measures over Condition. In this analysis, there was a significant group effect indicating that the Different Rate bilinguals were responding faster overall (564 msec) than were the Same Rate bilinguals (611 msec) ($F[1, 38]$=4.18, MSE=10,168.44, p<.05). There was a Condition effect indicating that both the Same Rate and Different Rate groups showed significant facilitation (RT on Control trials=637 msec, RT on

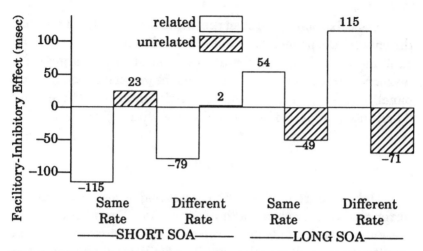

Figure 3. Patterns of facilitory (RT to primed trials faster than to neutral trials) and inhibitory effects (RT to primed trials slower than to neutral trials) in lexical decision as a function of SOA (short, long), semantic relation between prime and target (related, unrelated) for Same Rate and Different Rate bilinguals in the Expect-Unrelated condition.

Related trials=538 msec; $F(1, 38)$=188.73, MSE=1,021.93, p<.0001). The interaction between Group and Condition was significant, indicating that the groups differed significantly in the extent to which there was facilitation; however, the direction of the difference indicated greater, not lesser, automaticity for the slower reading Same Rate group (Control and Related trial RTs for the Same Rate group were 668 and 553 msec, respectively reflecting a facilitation effect of 115 msec; for the Different Rate group, they were 605 and 523 msec, respectively, reflecting a facilitation effect of 82 msec; $F(1, 38)$=5.14, MSE=1,021.93, p<.05) (see Fig. 3).

A similar analysis of the data from the Expect-Related revealed a significant facilitation effect across groups (Control and Related trial RTs were 642 and 562 msec, respectively). There were no other significant effects or interactions in this analysis (see Fig. 4).

Finally, as can be seen in Figures 3 and 4, there was the expected absence of inhibition in the Short SOA condition.

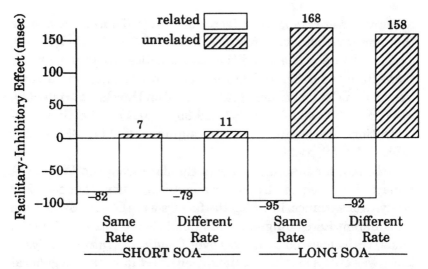

Figure 4. Patterns of facilitory (RT to primed trials faster than to neutral trials) and inhibitory effects (RT to primed trials slower than to neutral trials) in lexical decision as a function of SOA (short, long), semantic relation between prime and target (related, unrelated) for Same Rate and Different Rate bilinguals in the Expect-Related condition.

Controlled Processing in L1

The measure of controlled processing used in this study was the facilitation and inhibition effects found in the Long SOA condition, because these effects reflect the degree to which the students' expectations affected their RT. Again, the data from the Expect-Unrelated condition are the most pertinent because facilitation and inhibition effects reflecting strategic expectations should be in the opposite direction from those due to semantic relatedness.

To test for facilitation effects, the data from the Long SOA Expect-Unrelated condition were submitted to a 2×2 analysis of variance, where the factors were Group (Same Rate vs. Different Rate bilinguals), and Condition (Control vs. Unrelated trials) with repeated measures over Condition. In this analysis, there was a significant Group effect indicating that the Different Rate bilinguals were responding faster overall (567 msec) than were the Same Rate bilinguals (622 msec) ($F[1, 38]=8.75$, MSE= 7,079.49, $p<.01$). There was a Condition effect indicating that both the Same Rate and Different Rate groups showed significant facilitation (RT on Control trials=624 msec, RT on Unrelated trials=564 msec; $F(1, 38)=48.90$, MSE=1,469.89, $p<.001$). The Group-by-Condition interaction was not significant ($F[1, 38] =1.57$, MSE=1,469.89, $p>.20$).

To test for inhibition effects the data from the Long SOA Expect-Unrelated condition were similarly submitted to a 2×2 analysis of variance, in which the factors were Group (Same Rate vs. Different Rate bilinguals), and Condition (Control vs. Related trials) with repeated measures over Condition. In this analysis, there was only a significant Condition effect indicating a general inhibition effect across all students (RT to Control trials=624 msec, Related trials=709 msec; $F(1, 38)=23.831$, MSE=6,020.9, $p<.001$). Finally, the Same Rate bilinguals had a smaller inhibition effect than did the Different Rate bilinguals (54 vs. 115 msec), but this Group-by-Condition interaction was not significant ($F[1, 38]=3.182$, MSE=6,020.9, $p<.09$).

To further test for the possibility that the two groups differed in terms of the effectiveness with which they experienced expectancy effects, the facilitation and inhibition scores were combined to produce a single, overall Primed trial effect for each student. This was carried out as follows. The data reflecting inhibition effects (RT from the Related trial minus the RT from the Control trial) were first averaged with the data reflecting facilitation effects (RT from the Control trials minus the RT from the Unrelated trials). This yielded an overall priming effect measure reflecting the magnitude of deviation in RT on Primed trials from the RT on Control trials. Each student's Priming Effect measure was added onto his or her mean RT from Control trials to yield a Primed trial RT. These data were submitted to a two-way analysis of variance with the factors Group (Same Rate vs. Different Rate bilinguals) and Condition (Control, Primed) with repeated measures over Condition. The results yielded a significant Condition effect (RT for Control and Primed trials were 624 and 696 msec, respectively; $F[1, 38]=47.37$, $MSE=2,208.39$, $p<.001$). In addition, there was a nearly significant Group-by-Condition interaction effect ($F[1, 38]=3.94$, $MSE=2,208.39$, $p=.054$) reflecting a greater priming effect for Different Rate bilinguals than for Same Rate bilinguals (93 vs. 52 msec).

Similar analyses were conducted with the data from the Expect-Related conditions. One analysis revealed an overall significant facilitation effect (Control and Related RTs were 672 and 578 msec, respectively; $F[1, 38]=118.47$, $MSE=1,492.47$, $p<.001$) and the other analysis revealed an overall inhibition effect (Control and Unrelated RTs were 672 and 838 msec, respectively; $F[1, 38]=46.45$, $p<.001$). Neither analysis revealed Group-by-Condition interaction effects (all Fs <1).

Discussion

These results indicate that slowed L1 processing speed can indeed be associated with advanced skills in L2: Same Rate bilinguals read L1 more slowly than do Different Rate bilinguals. However, they show that in the present case the effect does not reflect a reduction of automaticity in L1 word recognition, as operationally defined here. In fact, the data indicated, if anything, that automatic processing was more effective for the slower reading Same Rate bilinguals than for the Different Rate bilinguals. In contrast, there was a nearly significant interaction in the Long SOA Expect-Unrelated analysis ($p=.054$) reflecting a weaker expectancy effect for the Same Rate bilinguals than for the Different Rate bilinguals. This suggests that if the achievement of very high levels of L2 skill is associated with slower L1 reading then it may involve reduced effectiveness of strategic processing (expectancy effects).

In retrospect, perhaps the lack of a reduced L1 automaticity effect in the Same Rate group is not surprising after all. Presumably, both groups of students had mastered L1 to the point of achieving normal automatic word recognition skills in reading

(Laberge & Samuels, 1974). Following Shiffrin and Dumais (1981) we might expect that once such skills had been developed, they would not easily be lost. Their studies showed that once an automatic detection skill had been developed for specific targets, students could not ignore these targets in subsequent tasks. Such automaticity of detection arose in their study from extensive exposure (thousands of trials) to consistent training (target items never or seldom served as distracter items; Schneider & Fisk, 1982). In the case of L1 reading, readers probably frequently encounter words under conditions that would consistently encourage them to form semantically based associations between them (fruit-apple; furniture-table, etc). Such extensive and consistent association of words is likely to give rise to the automatic processing observed in L1 in the present data.

In the Long SOA controlled processing condition, both groups showed a significant expectancy effect; however, the Same Rate bilinguals showed a nearly significant slower effect. One must, of course, view this result with caution ($p=.054$), but it may indicate that strategic processes operated less effectively or more slowly for them in L1 than it did for the faster reading Different Rate bilinguals. Why might this be so? From a skills perspective, it might be that the Same Rate bilinguals had less frequent exposure to L1 print than did the Different Rate bilinguals, and that their exposure to print involved less consistent word-concept mapping because experience with a given concept would sometimes be associated with words in one language and sometimes with the other. These conclusions are consistent with what we know about the language histories of the two groups; the Same Rate bilinguals had many fewer years of schooling at the primary and secondary levels in their L1 than did the Different Rate bilinguals (hence less exposure to L1 reading situations and less consistent mapping between a concept and the written representation of it).

One interesting aspect of the data deserves further comment. The Same Rate bilinguals read L1 more slowly than did the Different Rate bilinguals but evidenced more, not less, automaticity. This result is interesting because normally one associates slower reading skill with reduced automaticity. However, it is important to remember that reading a text involves much more than single word recognition; a great deal of controlled processing in syntax parsing, schema building, text integration, and so on is also involved. Thus, the Same Rate bilinguals' slower reading rate with stories may reflect the (nearly significant) finding in the Long SOA Expect-Unrelated condition that they were less effective in their controlled processing than were the Different Rate bilinguals. Thus, in the present case the factor of less effective controlled processing may have more than offset any advantage to reading speed that might come from automaticity of word recognition.

Given these results, one can raise several interesting questions for further investigation. One is whether the automaticity eventually achieved in L1 is delayed when there is concurrent, extensive exposure to L2. Testing of younger students at various ages might provide an answer to this. The present data (together with the results of Schneider & Dumais, 1981) suggest that once L1 word recognition automaticity is achieved, such automaticity is fairly secure. In terms of the time course and stability of this automaticity, however, it would be useful to know if automaticity in L1 should be consolidated before undertaking extensive L2 practice or if it can be achieved just as easily concurrently with such practice.

A second question concerns the development of controlled processes. Are the weaker L1 expectancy effects observed in the Same Rate bilinguals long lasting or can they be modified? Schneider and Fisk (1982) found that once performance with controlled processes (their varied mapping condition) had levelled off, additional extensive training resulted in little change in performance. A related question is whether a process can become automatic through training after long experience in which it has been nonautomatic.

Clearly, at this stage we have very few answers to questions about how exposure to L2 may affect speed of processing in L1.

More work needs to be done with attention to the operation of automatic and controlled processes, and not simply with a focus on global measures of speed of processing. Focus on reading skills is especially relevant to practical concerns because many bilinguals will encounter the L2 primarily in written form, particularly if the L2 is a minority language of the region. Ideally we would like to create learning conditions that will optimize L2 reading skills while minimizing possible adverse effects on L1 reading skills. The data reviewed here suggest some of the factors that may be involved. If we are careful to devise research techniques that can distinguish automatic from nonautomatic processes, we may be more successful in pinpointing the mechanisms affected by L2 exposure in different situations. In this way we can hope to draw useful conclusions about how training in one language may affect performance in the other.

References

Ackerman, P. L. (1987). Individual differences in skill learning: An integration of psychometric and information processing perspectives. *Psychological Bulletin, 102*, 3–27.

Burke, D., White, H., & Diaz, D. (1987). Semantic priming in young and older adults: Evidence for age constancy in automatic and attentional processes. *Journal of Experimental Psychology: Human Perception and Performance, 13*, 79–88.

den Heyer, K., Goring, A., Gorgichuk, S., Richards, L., & Landry, M. (1988). Are lexical decisions a good measure of lexical access? Repetition blocking suggests the affirmative. *Canadian Journal of Psychology, 42*, 274–296.

Dorian, N. (1981). *Language death*. Philadelphia: University of Pennsylvania Press.

Dorian, N. (1982). Language loss and maintenance in language contact situations. In R. D. Lambert & B. F. Freed (Eds.), *The loss of language skills* (pp. 44–59). Rowley, MA: Newbury House Publishers.

Favreau, M., & Segalowitz, N. (1982). Second language reading in fluent bilinguals. *Applied Psycholinguistics, 3*, 329–341.

Favreau, M., & Segalowitz, N. (1983). Automatic and controlled processing in reading a second language. *Memory & Cognition, 11*, 565–574.

Gatbonton, E., & Segalowitz, N. (1988). Creative automatization: Principles for promoting fluency within a communicative framework. *TESOL Quarterly, 22,* 473–492.

Jonides, J., & Mack, R. (1984). On the cost and benefit of cost and benefit. *Psychological Bulletin, 96,* 29–44.

Laberge, D., & Samuels, S. (1974). Toward a theory of automatic information processing in reading. *Cognitive Psychology, 6,* 293–323.

Lambert, W. E. (1955). Measurement of linguistic dominance in bilinguals. *Journal of Abnormal and Social Psychology, 50,* 197–200.

Magiste, E. (1986). Selected issues in second and third language learning. In J. Vaid (Ed.), *Language processing in bilinguals: Psycholinguistic and neuropsychological perspectives* (pp. 97–122). Hillsdale, NJ: Lawrence Erlbaum Associates.

Neely, J. (1977). Semantic priming and retrieval from lexical memory: Roles of the inhibitionless spreading activation and limited capacity attention. *Journal of Experimental Psychology: General, 106,* 226–254.

Posner, M., & Snyder, C. (1975). Attention and cognitive control. In R. C. Solso (Ed.), *Information processing and cognition: The Loyola Symposium* (pp. 55–85). Hillsdale, NJ: Lawrence Erlbaum Associates.

Schneider, W., & Fisk, A. (1982). Degree of consistent training: Improvements in search performance and automatic process development. *Perception & Psychophysics, 31,* 160–168.

Segalowitz, N. (1986). Second language reading. In J. Vaid (Ed.), *Language processing in bilinguals: Psycholinguistic and neuropsychological perspectives* (pp. 3–19). Hillsdale, NJ: Lawrence Erlbaum Associates.

Segalowitz, N., & Hébert, M. (1990). Phonological recoding in the first and second language reading of skilled bilinguals. *Language Learning, 40,* 503–538.

Sharwood Smith, M. (1983). On explaining language loss. In S. W. Felix & H. Wode (Eds.), *Language development at the crossroads* (pp. 49–59). Tübingen, Germany: Narr.

Shiffrin, R., & Dumais, S. T. (1981). The development of automatism. In J. R. Anderson (Ed.), *Cognitive skills and their acquisition* (pp. 111–140). Hillsdale, NJ: Lawrence Erlbaum Associates.

Shiffrin, R., & Schneider, W. (1977). Controlled and automatic human information processing: II: Perceptual learning, automatic attending and a general theory. *Psychological Review, 84,* 127–190.

Weinreich, U. (1953). *Languages in contact.* The Hague, The Netherlands: Mouton.

SECTION II

PSYCHOLINGUISTIC FACTORS IN VOCABULARY LEARNING

Psycholinguistic Determinants of Foreign Language Vocabulary Learning

Nick C. Ellis
University College of North Wales

Alan Beaton
University College of Swansea

Author's Statement: *This article reviewed the many psycholinguistic factors that affect ease of learning of foreign language (FL) vocabulary, and described an experiment demonstrating that: (a) productive (native to foreign) learning of foreign words depends on the degree to which they conform to the phonological and orthographic patterns of the native language, thus implicating phonological short-term memory in FL vocabulary learning; (b) the part of speech and the imageability of the concept are also strong determinants of learnability, suggesting an important influence of meaningfulness; and (c) keyword effectiveness, particularly in the case of receptive learning, is influenced by the part of speech and imageability of the keyword. Keywords must also share considerable acoustic similarity with their foreign words in order to be effective in productive learning. Otherwise learners must practice these novel phonotactic and orthographic patterns in order to acquire them.*

In retrospect we consider the main merits of this paper to be as follows: First, it furthers the bridge between psychological theory and applied linguistics, areas that still need bringing together. Too much psychology prides itself on its pure theoretic nature. Yet we believe that psychological theory can be usefully extended at the same time as useful applied questions are addressed. Too much educational practice is based on lore, is used by tradition, and is never evaluated for its effectiveness. Second, it strengthens the position that there is no one process of "acquiring a new word". Rather there are many facets of "knowing a word", these facets are dissociable, and their

---

We thank Sue Sinclair for gathering the pronunciation latency data.

107

representations are dealt with in different "departments" of our cognitive architecture and different parts of the brain. This paper shows, for example, clearly separate effects of the surface structure of words (word length, phonological regularity, etc.) and word meaning (in terms of perceptual / imaginal conceptual correlates). More recent publications of ours take these themes further (Ellis, 1994a, 1994b, in press; Beaton, Gruneberg, & Ellis, in press).

Nick Ellis, University College of North Wales, 1994

Why are some foreign language (FL) vocabulary items so much easier to learn than others? Why is it easy to learn that the German word *Friseur* means *hairdresser* yet much harder to learn that *Zahlen* means *to pay*? Why is it easy to remember that the German for trousers is *Hose*, and to forget that *to rent* is *Mieten*?

Many factors might affect the ease of FL vocabulary acquisition (see Higa, 1965 for an early review). In essence, the process of learning a FL word is to map a novel sound pattern (which will be variable across speakers, dialects, emphases, etc.) to a particular semantic field that may (or may not) have an exact equivalent in the native language. Even this rudimentary description implicates a range of relevant variables: pronounceableness, familiarity with semantic content, and clear labeling of that meaning in the native language. We will briefly review established findings concerning such psycholinguistic variables before describing a study that assesses their effects on vocabulary learning.

Phonological Factors

Familiarity of Features

Clearly, novice language learners are bound up in the orthographic and phonological aspects of vocabulary. While native speakers' lexical entries are clustered semantically (as evidenced by free associations of the type *top—>snow—>hill—>valley*, etc., learners often make associations driven by orthographic or phonological confusion, for example, *béton—>stupide* (confusion with *bête*) or *orchestre* (confusion with *bâton*) or *téléphoner* (confusion with *jeton*) or *Normandie* (confusion with *breton*), etc. (Meara, 1984). Similarly, Henning (1973) demonstrated that in a vocabulary recognition task, more-advanced learners and native speakers made errors indicating semantic clustering of lexical items whereas less-advanced learners showed evidence of a predominance of acoustic rather than semantic clustering.

Three or four dozen different independent gestures of the articulatory apparatus play distinctive roles in human speech (Wang, 1971). Different languages make use of different ranges of articulatory features. Thus difficulty arises when the FL learner is faced with features not exploited in the native language. For example, the contrast between /u/ and /y/ in French pronunciation differentiates between utterances of *au-dessous=below* and *au-dessus=above*. This contrast is not exploited in English and thus English learners of French must (a) learn to identify these unfamiliar features to perceive speech and (b) develop new motor patterns to accurately reproduce these in their own speech (Desrochers & Begg, 1987). This leads to predictions at both language and word levels:

1. The less the overlap between the feature set of the native and the foreign language, the harder it will be for the FL learner to learn to speak that language. This is exemplified by the great difficulty that native speakers of English have with the tonal differences that distinguish the meaning of Mandarin characters. The following five characters are all pronounced as *ma*, but with five distinctive tones. The tone marks over the vowel *a* visually capture the contour of each pitch pattern: " ˉ " for the First, High and Level Tone, " ´ " for the Second or Rising Tone, " ˇ " for the Third or Low Tone, " ˋ " for the Fourth or Falling Tone, and no marking for the Neutral Tone:

mā	má	mǎ	mà	ma
mother	*hemp*	*horse*	*to scold*	*a particle*

2. The less the overlap between the feature set of the native and the foreign word, the harder it will be for the FL learner to learn that word. Thus, for example, a Chinese student of English has much more difficulty with the words *rice, regular,* and *eighth* (which exploit contrasts not found in Chinese) than with *pen, see,* and *sun* (Nation, 1987).

Combinations of Features: Phonotactic Regularity

The pronounceableness of a word is determined not only by its phonemes and their articulatory features, but also by their position in a spoken word. Both absolute and relative position are important. An example of absolute position is /ŋ/ (the *ng* sound), which is common in English at the end of words but never occurs at the beginning. In many languages such as Hopi, Eskimo, or Samoan, *ng* is a common beginning for a word. "Our patterns set up a terrific resistance to articulation of these foreign words beginning with /ŋ/" (Whorf, cited in Carroll, 1956, p. 227). With regard to relative position, just as each language has its own set of phonemes so also does it have its characteristic sequential phoneme probabilities—the sequences that constitute phonotactic regularity. Rodgers (1969) demonstrated that Russian words that were more difficult for an English speaker to pronounce were learned more slowly than were those that were easier to pronounce, even if they did not have to be spoken. However, such pronounceableness effects can be countered if the learner has had practice with the sounds, sound combinations, and spelling used in these words (Faust & Anderson, 1967). Similarly, Seibert (1927) showed that for productive learning of French vocabulary, saying the words aloud led to faster learning with better retention than did silent rote repetition of vocabulary lists. She emphasized that learning the novel pronunciation of FL words is as much a matter of motor skill as of auditory perceptual memory, that "it is impossible to memorize speech material without articulating it in some form or another" (p. 309), and that this must be practiced "since the golden rule of sensorimotor learning is much repetition" (p. 309).

Recent work in cognitive psychology suggests that individual differences in ability to repeat novel phonological patterns (phonological short-term memory span) play a part in determining long-term vocabulary acquisition. Gathercole and Baddeley (1989) demonstrated in a longitudinal study that 5-year-old children's native receptive vocabulary acquisition was predicted by their short-term phonological memory ability (assessed by nonword repetition) one year earlier. In a recent reanalysis of the Gathercole and Baddeley (1989) corpus, Gathercole, Willis, Emslie, and Baddeley (1991) demonstrated that the "wordlikeness" of nonwords (e.g., *defermication* is high in English wordlikeness compared to *loddenapish*) predicted 11% of the variance in children's nonword repetitions even when word length was controlled. They concluded that not only word length but also phonological structure are important determinants of ease of repetition of novel words. This is a "linguistic hypothesis," whereby the familiarity of a novel word's phonological structure determines its repetition accuracy, with phonological frames constructed from similar vocabulary entries in the learner's lexicon being used to support the temporary phonological representation. Whereas these conclusions accord with our theoretical perspective, it is unfortunate that they go beyond their data—the method used by Gathercole et al. (1991) to assess phonological familiarity was to have undergraduates rate the wordlikeness of the nonwords on a dimension of *very like a word* to *not like a word at all*, a task that potentially confounds many dimensions of similarity, with the raters' judgments open to a variety of orthographic, phonological, and semantic factors. One purpose of the experiment that we will report will be to disentangle these aspects.

This review suggests that the overall similarity between sequential phoneme probabilities in the foreign and native languages will determine the ease of learning that foreign language. Specifically, the degree to which a particular FL word accords with the phonotactic patterns of the native language will affect the ease of learning that particular word.

Semantic Content

Items of experience are classified differently by different languages. The class corresponding to one word and one thought in Language A may be represented by Language B as two or more classes corresponding to two or more words and thoughts (Whorf, cited in Carroll, 1956). Thus, for example, Desrochers and Begg (1987) refer to the French distinction between *balle*—a spherical object that can be caught with one hand, and *ballon*—that requiring both hands; the English translation *ball* is insufficient to represent and distinguish these meanings. Terms for color, temperature, divisions of the day, kinship, and parts of the body are all semantic fields that are divided up in different ways in different languages (Carter & McCarthy, 1988). Navajo has a fourth person singular and plural, which is used to address someone in the room or within earshot without naming him or her directly, and many African languages have inclusive and exclusive forms of the first person plural (we, including you to whom I am speaking vs. we, not including you to whom I am speaking). Hopi has one noun that covers every thing that flies, with the exception of birds—Hopi Indians call insect, plane, and aviator all by the same word and feel no difficulty about it. These few examples demonstrate the phenomenon of linguistic relativity (Whorf, cited in Carroll, 1956). Learning a new FL word is going to be easy if there is a 1:1 mapping of meanings represented by the native and foreign words. It is going to be harder if the same conceptual fields are covered by different lexical fields in different languages (Carter & McCarthy, 1988). Ijaz (1986) demonstrated that even advanced adult ESL learners differed substantially from native speakers in the semantic boundaries that they ascribed to English spatial prepositions, with word usage being heavily influenced by native language transfer. She concluded

the second language learners essentially relied on a *semantic equivalence hypothesis*. This hypothesis facilitates the acquisition of lexical meanings in the L2 in that it reduces it to the relabelling of concepts already learned in

the L1. It confounds and complicates vocabulary acquisition in the L2 by ignoring crosslingual differences in
conceptual classification and differences in the semantic
boundaries of seemingly corresponding words in the L1
and L2. (p. 443)

The implications for FL learners are clear: When the native
language does not encourage the distinction between concepts,
then students necessarily will have an additional conceptual
chore in learning the FL that relies on these very distinctions. The
greater the mismatch, the greater the problem: Two French balls
present less difficulty than 22 (or however many it is—Whorf,
cited in Carroll, 1956; Lakoff, 1987) forms of Eskimo's snow.

Word Class

The part of speech of a word affects its learning: Nouns are
the easiest to learn, adjectives next, whereas verbs and adverbs
are the most difficult to learn in FL vocabulary list-learning
experiments (Rodgers, 1969). These word-class effects are also
found in other psycholinguistic performance measures; for example, Broca's aphasics have more difficulty in producing function
words and inflections in their speech than they do substantives
(agrammatism—Ellis & Young, 1988, chap. 9); deep dyslexic
patients also have greater difficulty reading function words,
including auxiliary verbs, adverbs, and pronouns (Morton &
Patterson, 1980; Patterson, 1981); meaningful nouns produce
substantially more interference in Stroop tasks than do relatively
meaningless function words (Ehri, 1977; Davelaar & Besner,
1988); children acquire nouns before they do other parts of speech
(Gentner, 1982). These effects may directly reflect grammatical
word-class or they may stem from imageability (in general, nouns
are more imageable than verbs—Davelaar & Besner, 1988; Ellis
& Beaton, 1993) or meaningfulness (imageable items are more
meaningful—Paivio, Yuille, & Madigan, 1968; Ellis, 1991).

Imageability of Concept

When people are asked to learn lists of words, the greater the imageability of a word—that is the degree to which it arouses a mental image—the more likely it is to be recalled. This is a robust effect in free recall experiments (Paivio, 1971). It is even more reliable in paired-associate learning (PAL), a laboratory analog of vocabulary learning, in which the student has to learn a novel association of a stimulus word experimentally paired with a response word (Paivio, 1971; Rubin, 1980). This effect has withstood many attempts to demonstrate that its association with recall is spurious and attributable to *tertium quid* psycholinguistic attributes such as meaningfulness (Dukes & Bastian, 1966; Paivio, Yuille, & Smythe, 1966; Christian, Bickley, Tarka, & Clayton, 1978; Rubin, 1983), concreteness (Christian et al., 1978), familiarity (Frincke, 1968; Paivio, 1968) or age-of-acquisition (Gilhooly & Gilhooly, 1979).

In the particular case of FL vocabulary learning, Carter (1987) notes that concrete FL words are generally learned earlier and more easily than are abstract words, but he cautions that this may be confounded by frequency, familiarity, and word class effects. We cannot find any reference to imageability effects when students are using their own strategies of FL vocabulary learning. However, many experimental studies (e.g., Wimer & Lambert, 1959; Kellog & Howe, 1971) have compared native language words with pictures or objects as stimuli for learning word responses in the FL. The results have consistently shown that FL vocabulary items are learned in fewer trials and with fewer errors if nonverbal referents rather than native language words serve as stimuli.

Word Frequency

Vocabulary learning may be affected by the frequency of the concept. This is certainly true in naturalistic learning situations because frequency determines exposure. It is less likely in controlled experimental situations that ensure equal exposure to all the vocabulary. However, in free recall experiments word frequency has a small but significant positive effect (Christian et al., 1978; Rubin, 1983). In PAL, a closer analog of vocabulary learning, there is in general a facilitative effect of the frequency of the response word (Postman, 1962; Shapiro, 1969; Paivio, 1971, pp. 262–266), a result which suggests that higher frequency responses are more available. The effects of stimulus frequency are more variable and may even be negative (Paivio, 1971).

Word Meaningfulness

In PAL experiments, speed of learning varies directly with the meaningfulness of both the stimulus and the response word, but this relationship is considerably more pronounced for the response word (Underwood & Schulz, 1960; Postman, 1962). The major determinant of success in PAL is the degree to which the stimulus and response words are strongly yet uniquely associated. When both stimulus and response are more meaningful, there is a greater chance of forging associations between them. However, the PAL of FL vocabulary is rather different in that the student is essentially learning a nonsense sound—word association and thus extrapolation from these findings is questionable.

Orthographic Factors

Orthographic Regularity and Different Alphabets

A native speaker of a language using the Roman alphabet transfers more easily to another of the same script than to one that uses different orthographic units or frames such as the Cyrillic alphabet or the logographs of Kanji (Carroll & Sapon, 1955). Similarly transfer is easier if both scripts contain frames that move in the same way (e.g., in rows from left to right vs. the reverse, or vertically in columns. See Desrochers & Begg, 1987; Nation, 1987).

Sequential Letter Probabilities

The argument concerning orthographic regularity parallels that of phonotactic regularity: Different languages have different sequential letter probabilities; for example, *ll* is common at the beginning of a Welsh word but never introduces an English word. Thus, the learning of the orthography of FL words may be determined by the degree to which the sequential letter probabilities match those of the native language. The same holds at the individual word level: The degree to which a particular FL word accords with the orthographic patterns of the native language may affect its ease of learning.

Word Length

The longer the FL word, the more to be remembered, the more scope for phonotactic and orthographic variation and thus the more room for error. This is also likely to be confounded and reinforced by frequency because Zipf's law (1935) holds that more frequent words evolve a shorter form.

Familiarity of Grapheme to Phoneme Mappings

For Reading

In studies of the repetition and learning of nonwords, experimenters and participants alike assume that the spelling-sound correspondences operate just as in the L1. Unfortunately, different languages do not work in the same way in this respect. The L2 student has to learn how FL orthography maps onto FL pronunciation.

Scripts based on alphabetic writing systems reflect to a lesser (e.g., English) or greater (e.g., Korean, Serbo-Croatian, Welsh) degree the pronunciation of language units. There are rules of correspondence between graphemes and phonemes (e.g., see Venezky, 1970, for the English "rules"). If the FL is regular in this respect, then it is easier to learn to read. An English learner of Maori can read sentences in Maori aloud, without understanding them, after only a few minutes study because Maori uses the same letters as English and the relationship between spelling to sound is very regular (Nation, 1987). Yet these rules of correspondence can differ markedly between languages sharing the same script (*pace* the naïve English learner of Welsh who continues to pronounce *f* as /f/ rather than /v/. There are further difficulties of a different type if the script is logographic (e.g., Kanji) and contains no such cues for assembling phonology from script. It may be predicted for language and word levels that (a) the less the overlap between the grapheme-phoneme correspondence rules of the native and the foreign language, the harder it will be for the FL learner to learn to read or write that language; and (b) the less the overlap between the grapheme-phoneme correspondence rules for the graphemes of the native and the foreign word, the harder it will be for the FL learner to learn to read or write that word.

For Spelling

Phoneme-grapheme correspondence rules are not invariably the simple reverse of grapheme-phoneme correspondences. For example, in English the phoneme /O/ is only rarely ($p=.15$) spelled *au* (as in *auction*), yet the graphemic option *au* is almost always ($p=0.95$) pronounced /O/ (Berndt, Reggia, & Mitchum, 1987). Yet the learner must acquire these correspondences to spell an alphabetic FL using a phonological strategy.

Similarity of FL and Native Words

Sometimes FL words just remind us of the native word, a factor that usually stems from the languages' common origins or from language borrowing. Thus the German *Hund* (dog) may be more easily retained than the French *chien* because of its etymological and sound similarity with the English *hound* (Nation, 1982). Such reminding, whether based on orthography, phonology, etymology, or "borrowing" (e.g., *le hot-dog*) typically facilitates the learning of that FL word (Anderson & Jordan, 1928) and students who are instructed to look for such inter- and intralingual mnemonic associations generally retain new words with greater efficacy (Cohen & Aphek, 1980). There can, of course, be interference when such reminding is inappropriate (For example, the Englishman mentally groping for a French hug might be happily surprised to get more than he bargained for if he lunged at *embrasser.*)

Using Keyword Mediation

Atkinson and Raugh (1975) reported an experiment in which they compared learning of FL vocabulary by means of mnemonics with a control condition in which participants used their own strategies.   In the experimental condition, participants were presented with a Russian word and its English translation together with a word or phrase in English that sounded like the Russian word.   For example, the Russian word for battleship is *linkór*.   American students were asked to use the word *Lincoln*, called the keyword, to help them remember this.   Atkinson and Raugh found that people who had used the keyword method learned substantially more English translations of Russian words than did the control group and that this advantage was maintained up to six weeks later.

Numerous subsequent studies have confirmed the effectiveness of the keyword method in FL and native language vocabulary learning (see Paivio & Desrochers, 1981; Pressley, Levin, & Delaney, 1982; Levin & Pressley, 1985; Cohen, 1987; Desrochers & Begg, 1987 for reviews).   It has been shown that keyword mnemonic techniques are more effective than are other direct methods such as rote rehearsal or placing vocabulary in the context of a meaningful sentence (Pressley et al., 1982; Nation, 1982). Sternberg (1987) states "for learning specific vocabulary, the keyword method of vocabulary teaching and learning is faster and more efficient than learning from context. . . . As far as I can tell, it may be the most effective of the currently available methods" (pp. 94–95).

The common explanation for the success of these systems is that the keyword enables people to combine in a single associative image the referent of one native word with that of a second native word that sounds like the foreign word, that is, the meanings of the native word and the keyword are integrated in one image. There are two stages in recall using keywords. The first stage of recalling the meaning of a foreign word involves remembering the native keyword that sounds like the foreign word. The second stage involves accessing an interactive image containing the referent of the keyword and "seeing" the object with which it is associated. By naming this object the learner accesses the native translation.

The involvement of keyword mediators introduces a number of additional potential psycholinguistic determinants of success:

1. *Reminding power of foreign word for keyword.* The first of Raugh and Atkinson's (1975) criteria for a good keyword is that it "sounds as much as possible like a part (not necessarily all) of the foreign word" (p. 2). Whereas it may be relatively easy to find English keywords that sound like some foreign words (e.g., for the German words *Blech, Böttcher, Decke, Flitter*), others are considerably more problematical (e.g., the German nouns *Abhilfe, Bleiarbeiter, Durchschlag*, and *Geschluchze*). (See Desrochers & Begg, 1987). Raugh and Atkinson demonstrate a correlation of .53 between the probability of a keyword being remembered given a Russian word and the probability of the English translation being remembered by different students using the same keyword as a mnemonic.

2. *Reminding power of keyword for foreign word.* Raugh and Atkinson's (1975) criterion applies here, too, but with even more importance because the keyword has to cue the pronunciation of the foreign word. So it has to sound as close as possible to the foreign word. Word recall is likely to be best if the keyword or part of it overlaps with the initial part or cluster of the foreign word to be recalled (Horowitz, Chilian, & Dunnigan, 1969; Loess & Brown, 1969; Desrochers & Begg, 1987). But it remains to be determined whether the best overlap is in terms of pronunciation or orthography or both.

3. *Imageability of keyword.* **Raugh and Atkinson's (1975)** second criterion is that "it is easy to form a memorable imagery link connecting the keyword and the English translation" (p. 2). Thus "concrete nouns may be good as keywords because they are generally easy to image; abstract nouns for which symbolic imagery comes readily to mind also may be effective keywords" (p. 2).

4. *Imageability of mediational sentence.* Atkinson and Raugh (1975) reported that the probability of remembering the image-based link between keyword and native word in one set of subjects correlated .49 with the relative recall of the native words (given the foreign word) by other students learning FL vocabulary under keyword instructions.

The range of these possible psycholinguistic factors is summarized in Figure 1 for learning both without (Fig. 1a) and with (Fig. 1b) keyword mediators. Although many of these variables

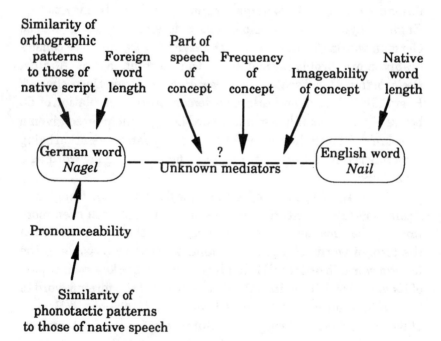

Figure 1a. Potential determinants of learnability of foreign language vocabulary without keyword mediation.

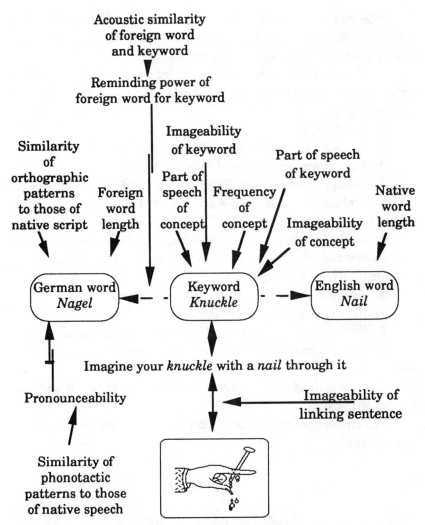

Figure 1b. Potential determinants of learnability of foreign language vocabulary with keyword mediation.

have been studied individually, their interrelationships remain to be determined. Furthermore, it is quite possible that each will make a different contribution depending on the learning strategy that students adopt—for example, repetition learners versus keyword learners.

The study reported below thus *concurrently* assessed the following effects and therefore *their interactions* on the "learnability" (Higa, 1965) of FL vocabulary:

1. Phonological content of the foreign word and the degree to which its phonotactic sequence accords with those found in the native language;
2. word class;
3. imageability of the concept;
4. foreign and native word lengths; and
5. orthographic content of the foreign word and the degree to which its phonotactic sequence accords with those found in the native language.

It further investigated whether, when students are instructed to use keyword mediation, the following factors play a determining role on FL learnability:

6. whether the keyword is a noun or a verb;
7. the imageability of the keyword;
8. the imageability of the whole mediational sentence;
9. the spoken overlap between the keyword and the foreign word;
10. the orthographic overlap between the keyword and the foreign word; and
11. the degree to which the keyword reminds people of the foreign word.

Methods

Vocabulary Learnability

Participants

Forty-seven L1 English-speaking undergraduates of psychology (13 males & 34 females) participated in this study. They were naïve as to the theoretical background to the research and spoke no German. The mean age was 24.2 (*SD* 6.2) years.

Apparatus and Procedure

All testing was done individually by means of a Macintosh computer programmed in Hypercard.

In German Vocabulary Learning Stage I, students were randomly allocated to one of four groups that had had the same exposure to German vocabulary but under different instructions. Two of the groups had to use the keyword method, two did not. Of the two groups using the keyword method, one was provided with a keyword that was a noun, the other was given the keyword as a verb, in a sentence devised by the experimenters. The groups were instructed as follows:

Own Strategy Group. "Please now do your best to learn the German translation of the following English words."

Repetition Group. "In order to learn the English-German pairs of words please repeat aloud each pair of words continuously until presentation of the subsequent pair of words. Please now do your best to learn the German translation of the following English words."

Noun Keyword and Verb Keyword Groups (The Imagery groups). "To help you learn the words, the computer will display for each German word an instruction to IMAGINE a specific scene that links the sound of the English and German words together in some way. You must try to produce in your mind's eye as vivid an image as possible of the scene. You may find it helpful to close your eyes while you think about it, but remember to study the German word properly first, and to open your eyes in good time for the next word-pair. The linking of the sounds may only be approximate, but you will find that the process of imagining a visual scene will help you to recall the words subsequently. Please now do your best to learn the German translations of the following English words."

The computer randomly assigned students to groups. This resulted in there being 10 students in the Own Strategy group, 10 in Repetition, and 8 and 19, respectively (a late-discovered bug in the "random" number seed) in the Noun and Verb Keyword Groups.

The German words used in this experiment are shown in Table 1, along with their English translations and the noun and verb keywords for these respective conditions.

In the vocabulary learning session, the students were intro-

Table 1
The Stimulus Material Used in This Experiment

GW	EW	Noun Keyword Sentence
Block A		
Sperre	barrier	Imagine a *sparrow* on a station *barrier*
Hose	trousers	Imagine *trousers* wrapped round a garden *hose*
Nehmen	to take	Imagine you *take* a *name in* your address book
Haben	to have	Imagine *harbours have* many ships
Ecke	corner	Imagine an *echo* in a *corner*
Dohle	jackdaw	Imagine a *jackdaw* with a *dollar* in its beak
Kaufen	to buy	Imagine you *buy* a *coffin*
Fliegen	to fly	Imagine *fleas fly* quickly
Leiter	ladder	Imagine a *lighter* at the foot of a *ladder*
Friseur	hairdresser	Imagine your *hairdresser* inside a *freezer*
Stellen	to put	Imagine you *put steel* girders in your house
Brauchen	to need	Imagine *brokers need* much experience
Block B		
Teller	plate	Imagine a fortune-*teller* with a pile of silver *plates*
Küche	kitchen	Imagine your *kitchen* and a *cook* in it
Mieten	to rent	Imagine you *rent meat* to friends in your room
Zahlen	to pay	Imagine *sailors pay* for hot rum
Klippe	cliff	Imagine nail-*clippers* on a *cliff*
Fahne	flag	Imagine a *flag* on a *fan*
Rufen	to call	Imagine you *call* a friend to put a new *roof* on a cottage
Graben	to dig	Imagine *crabs dig* holes in the sand
Schere	scissors	Imagine *shears* besides a pair of *scissors*
Rasen	lawn	Imagine your *lawn* covered in *raisins*
Stossen	to push	Imagine you *push stores* in a cupboard
Streichen	to paint	Imagine *strikers paint* slogans on walls

GW=German word; EW=English word; PoS=Part of speech of word to be learned; O=Order of words in mediation sentence

duced to the procedure with 12 practice words (not used in the experiment itself) whose order of presentation was randomized for each participant.

The procedure for each learning trial was: The English word

Verb Keyword Sentence	PoS	O
Imagine you *spare* a penny at a station *barrier*	N	GE
Imagine dirty *trousers* and *hose* them down	N	EG
Imagine you *take* and *name* a puppy	V	EG
Imagine you *harbour* criminals and *have* doubts about it	V	GE
Imagine you *echo* the sentiments of the person in the *corner*	N	GE
Imagine a *jackdaw* and *dole* out some bread to it	N	EG
Imagine you *buy* sweets and *cough*	V	EG
Imagine you *flee* quickly and *fly* away	V	GE
Imagine you *light* a fire at the foot of a *ladder*	N	GE
Imagine your *hairdresser* and *freeze her*	N	EG
Imagine you *put* one book down and *steal* another	V	EG
Imagine you *broke* a pen and *need* it	V	GE
Imagine you *tell a* story about silver *plates*	N	GE
Imagine your *kitchen* and *cook* a meal there	N	EG
Imagine you *rent* a room and *meet* friends in it	V	EG
Imagine you *sail* and *pay* for hot rum	V	GE
Imagine you *clip* a rope to a *cliff*	N	GE
Imagine *a flag* and *fan* yourself with it	N	EG
Imagine you *call* a friend and *roof* your cottage	V	EG
Imagine you *grab* a spade and *dig* with it	V	GE
Imagine you *shear* off some hair with a pair of *scissors*	N	GE
Imagine your *lawn* and *raise* its level	N	EG
Imagine you *push* and *store* things in a cupboard	V	EG
Imagine you *strike* out old graffiti and *paint* new slogans	V	GE

Table 1 (continued)
The Stimulus Material Used in This Experiment

GW	EW	Noun Keyword Sentence
Block C		
Schalter	counter	Imagine a seaside *shelter* with a candy-floss *counter*
Flasche	bottle	Imagine a *bottle* in a *flash* of lightning
Streiten	to quarrel	Imagine you *quarrel* about the Menai *straits*
Laufen	to run	Imagine bread *loaves run* down the street
Brücke	bridge	Imagine a small *brook* under a humpbacked *bridge*
Messer	knife	Imagine a *knife* in a *mess* of gravy
Treten	to step	Imagine you *step* on a stair *tread*
Tragen	to carry	Imagine *dragons carry* fire hoses
Nagel	nail	Imagine your *knuckle* with a *nail* through it
Birne	pear	Imagine a *pear* on a gas *burner*
Sagen	to tell	Imagine you *tell* someone *sago* is good for them
Reissen	to tear	Imagine *rice tears* a hole in a paper bag

GW=German word; EW=English word; PoS=Part of speech of word to be learned; O=Order of words in mediation sentence

was presented in a box at the left-hand top of the screen with the German translation accompanying at the right-hand top. As the stimuli were presented the German word was spoken. The speech in this experiment was recorded by a native female German speaker and digitized for later use using MacRecorder. If the students were in either of the two imagery conditions, the appropriate imagery mediation sentence was presented in a field underneath the two stimuli. After 7 seconds the German word was spoken again. The trial finished after 10 seconds when the screen cleared for one second before the next trial.

After a block of 12 learning trials, the student was tested on the material just presented. The first test block was German to English. The 12 German words were reordered randomly and for each test trial the German word appeared at the top left of the screen, it was spoken at the same time, and the student was

Verb Keyword Sentence	PoS	O
Imagine you *shelter* under a candy-floss *counter*	N	GE
Imagine a *bottle* and *flash* a light onto it	N	EG
Imagine you *quarrel* and *straighten* your tie	V	EG
Imagine you *loaf* about and then *run* off	V	GE
Imagine you *brook* no disagreement over the building of a humpbacks *bridge*	N	GE
Imagine a *knife* and *mess* it with gravy	N	EG
Imagine you *step* quietly as you *tread* on the stair	V	EG
Imagine you *drag* and *carry* fire-hoses	V	GE
Imagine you *knuckle* down to fixing a *nail*	N	GE
Imagine a *pear* and *burn* it	N	EG
Imagine you *tell* someone to *say go* when you are ready	V	EG
Imagine you *rise* up and *tear* a paper bag in half	V	GE

invited to type in the English translation. After the 12 German-to-English test trials the identical procedure was repeated in the reverse direction (i.e., from English to German) with the exception that the English word was not spoken.

On completion of the practice phase of the experiment (12 trials learning, 12 trials German-to-English test, 12 trials English-to-German test) the students entered the main vocabulary learning phase. Here they carried out this procedure three times for the 12 word-pairs of Block A; they then did the same for Blocks B and C in turn. (See Table 1.)

The students completed a second experimental session (German Vocabulary Learning Stage II) approximately one month (M=31.4 days, SD=4.5) after the first session. The students were tested for recall of the 12 practice pairs with the same testing procedure used in Stage I—first they gave the English translations for the 12 German words presented in random order, and then the German translations when presented with the English words.

Once the students had been tested for their long-term retention of the translations in both directions for the 12 practice pairs, they completed one set of trials relearning the practice words under the same instructions and condition as in German Vocabulary Learning Stage I. Subsequently a German-to-English test was carried out, followed by an English-to-German test as in Stage I.

This procedure was then repeated for Blocks A, B and C.

The recall scores for each word were pooled over all testing sessions and expressed as percentage correct for each condition. It is these scores that constitute the FL learning and recall data to be analyzed across words in the present study.

Psycholinguistic Determinants

The above procedures demonstrated that the receptive vocabulary most easy and most difficult to learn were, respectively, *Friseur-hairdresser* and *Zahlen-pay*. The easiest productive (native to foreign) pair was *trousers-Hose* and the hardest was *to rent-Mieten*. To determine the psycholinguistic factors that determined these relative difficulties, the following additional variables were measured:

Phonotactic Regularity of Foreign Word.

Accuracy in saying and learning a foreign word may be affected by the degree to which its pronunciation follows the sound patterns of the native language, that is, whether its component phonemes are common in the native language and whether they follow typical sequential orderings. There is a need for an exhaustive corpus of position-sensitive transitional frequencies of phonemes in spoken English. Given the lack of same we made do with the tables produced by Hultzén, Allen, and Miron (1964) from a small running text of 20,000 phonemes (roughly one page each from 11 different plays contained in a collection of drama for young people) delivered in "normal, modern, standard-colloquial American English" (Hultzén et al., 1964, p. 5). These tables give first- to fourth-order sequences and frequencies of phonemes. We had a phonetician transcribe the German words as spoken in these experiments and then calculated the summed biphoneme frequencies for each word (irrespective of position). Thus, for example, the word *Birne* (biːrnə) has the frequencies: #b=197+bi=33+ir=7+rn=14+ nə=25+ə#=325—>total=601. Because these totals are heavily influenced by word-length, the final measure of phonotactic regularity adopted was the average biphoneme frequency; thus for biːrnə the phonotactic regularity score was $^{601}/_6$=105.7. If a phoneme does not appear in American English, for example the /ç/ in *Küche*, the word was given a proportionately low regularity score with zero for both biphoneme combinations, /yç/ and /çə/. Of course these measures are mere approximations as they depend on the pronunciation of the speakers both in this experiment and in Hultzén et al. (1964), the ear and categorization pattern of the various transcribers, coarticulation effects, speech sampling, and so forth. However noisy a measure, in general the higher the resultant score, the more the pronunciation of the foreign word conforms to frequent sequential phoneme combinations in English.

Pronounceableness of the Foreign Word.

To check the pronounceableness of the German words, we had 7 English undergraduates (4 males and 3 females, age range 18–27 years), who had never learned any German, attempt to pronounce them after a single hearing. The German vocabulary, spoken as in the vocabulary learning experiments, was presented in a random order under Hypercard control. At the initiation of each trial, a word was spoken and the student repeated this 10 times as quickly as possible. A German speaker listened to each repetition and judged it correct or incorrect, entering 1 or 0 into the computer. The final input stopped a clock. Thus, for each student there was a score out of 10 for each word's correct repetition and a time (in 60ths of a second) for 10 repetitions.

The average accuracy score was 6.84 (*SD*=2.47) with high accuracy for *Leiter, Stossen, Streichen, Messer, Stellen,* and low accuracy for *Nehmen, Zahlen, Rufen,* and *Rasen.* The reliability was acceptable with a Cronbach's alpha across students of 0.71. The average time taken to say each word 10 times was 6.32 (*SD*=0.36) seconds. Pronunciation time varied as a function of written word length (*r*=0.46, *p*<.01). Cronbach's alpha across the 7 students was 0.83. There was the expected inverse relationship between pronunciation speed and accuracy (*r*=–0.37, *p*<.05).

Part of Speech of Concept

The part of speech of the word to-be-learned was classified as a binary variable with 0 for verbs and 1 for nouns.

Concept Imageability

The imageability of the concept was assessed using the procedure of Paivio, Yuille, and Madigan (1968) (whose norms themselves only address nouns and so fail to suffice for present purposes). Twenty-three first-year psychology students (5 males & 18 females, *M*=27.3 years, *SD*=9.6 years) rated the 36 English words for imageability on a 7-point scale. The full instructions are available from the authors. In summary these were: "Any word which, in your estimation, arouses a mental image (i.e., a mental picture or sound, or other sensory experience) very quickly and easily should be given a high imagery rating; any word that arouses a mental image with difficulty or not at all should be given a low imagery rating. Think of the nouns *apple* or *fact* and the verbs *to run* or *to know*. *Apple* or *to run* would probably arouse an image relatively easily and would be rated as high imagery; *fact* or *to know* would probably do so with difficulty and would be rated as low imagery. Your ratings will be made on a 7-point scale, on which 1 is the low imagery end of the scale and 7 is the high imagery end of the scale." The interrater reliability of this procedure was high (Cronbach's alpha across raters was 0.98). Unfortunately, only five of these words appeared in the Paivio et al. (1968) norms and, thus, it was impossible to triangulate to assess concurrent validity. The mean imageability ratings across students for each word were then used in later analyses. These ranged from 2.09 (*to need*) to 6.91 (*scissors*) (*M*=5.23, *SD*=1.52).

Concept Frequency

The best available index of concept frequency is word frequency in the native language. The Francis & Kucera (1982) norms that count the number of written occurrences in roughly the million words of the Brown Corpus were used to measure this factor. This has the advantage over other corpora in that it tags words for their syntactic class, thus distinguishing between different parts of speech or meanings of polysemous words or homonyms (cf. Thorndike & Lorge, 1944, analyses in which the count for *tear* includes its use as a verb and as nouns reflecting either sartorial or emotional raggedness). It should be noted, however, that the Brown Corpus reflects American rather than Northern-Welsh English usage, and thus this operationalization, although the best available, is only an approximation to our target of concept frequency. The frequency counts for our words ranged from 1 (*jackdaw*) to 12,458 (*to have*) and were heavily positively skewed. We therefore used log(10) of the Corpus frequencies in the analyses.

Orthography

Accuracy in writing the foreign word may be affected by the degree to which the orthography of the foreign word follows the spelling patterns of the native language.

The positional bigram counts of Solso and Juel (1980) were used to assess the English orthographic regularity of the German words. Positional bigram counts provide a more accurate esti-

mate of word orthography than do single letter positional counts
as they reflect multiple letter-connecting regularities—the true
frequencies of bigrams by position are preserved. For example,
the sum of bigram frequencies (SOBIF) of the regular word *mother*
is high (*mo*=1,721, *ot*=895, *th*=1,797, *he*=1,811, *er*=7,527;
SOBIF=13,751), that of the irregular word *avoid* is low (*av*=65,
vo=81, *oi*=81, *id*=345; SOBIF=1,248). Applying these procedures
to the German words we discover, for example, that, even ignoring
the dieresis, *Küche* has the lowest SOBIF at 99, whereas *Leiter*
has the highest at 14,013. The SOBIF score thus assesses the
conformity of the German words to regular English orthographic
sequential dependencies, but it is affected by word length
(Spearman's r=0.27 in our sample); the longer the word, the
higher the SOBIF. We therefore computed two other indices of
English sequential orthographic regularity. The first, AVBIF, is
the word's SOBIF divided by its length in letters. The other,
MINBIF, is the smallest bigram frequency of the bigrams consti-
tuting the word. MINBIF is thus particularly sensitive to words
with very uncommon spelling patterns that might cause the
learner considerable difficulty, for example, the *ck* in Positions 2
and 3 of *ecke* occurs in no English four-letter word counted in Solso
and Juel (1980); similarly the *hm* in *nehmen* is a very unusual
spelling by English standards; in contrast *rasen* is spelled thoroughly in accord with English spelling patterns with positional
BIFs all in excess of 500.

The measures AVBIF and MINBIF were both used as indices
of English sequential orthographic regularity in the statistical
analyses.

Word Length of Foreign and English Words.

These were simple letter counts.

Similarity of Foreign Word and Keyword

Orthographic. Three different measures of orthographic
similarity were computed and then summed as a total score. The

first was the number of letters that the German word and keyword have in common until the first mismatch, expressed as a proportion of the German word length (e.g., the keyword *sparrow* for *sperre* scores 2 for *sp*—a 0.33 overlap). The second was total letter overlap regardless of position (*sparrow* and *sperre* share *s,p,r,r*— a 0.66 overlap). The third was absolute positional letter overlap (again in this case *s, p, r, r*=0.66). The first measure heavily reflects the degree of overlap of the initial segments of the words, which Desrochers and Begg (1987) hold to be important. The others reflect any letter overlap that might serve as a reminding cue. The final orthographic similarity measure is the simple sum of these three aspects and ranges from 0.33 (Verb keyword *cough* for *Kaufen*) to 3.00 (keyword *hose* for *Hose*).

Acoustic. This was similarly assessed by having a linguist phonetically transcribe the German words as they were spoken in the experiment, and the associated Noun and Verb keywords. The same three overlap measures (initial, total, and absolute overlap) were computed for these phonemic transcriptions, expressed as a proportion of German word-length, and summed to give a total score. These ranged from 0.2 (the keyword *sago* [seigo] for *sagen* [zagǝn]) to 3.0 (the Verb keyword *clip a* [klipǝ] for *Klippe* [klipǝ]).

Reminding Power of Foreign Word for Keyword

The experimental procedure for determining reminding power was heavily influenced by that used by Atkinson and Raugh (1975, p. 132). We tested only the unidirectional association from foreign word to keyword.

A Macintosh computer was programmed in Hypercard to say each German word as it was spoken in the learning experiments and to show the associated keyword at the same time. Each trial consisted of the keyword being presented midscreen. The German word was spoken at keyword onset and repeated 3 and 6 seconds later. The screen went blank after 9 seconds and there was a 1-second intertrial interval. The training trial sequence comprised 6 practice items from Table 1, followed by the 36 test items in randomized order, finishing with 6 more filler items to remove recency effects. The test trials followed the same trial order. Each trial comprised the computer saying the German word at the same time as the trial number appeared on the screen; the word was repeated after 3 seconds, and the screen went blank after another 5 seconds. There was a 1-second intertrial interval. These experimental sequences were recorded onto video for use in the two experimental sessions proper. In the first of these, 30 first-year psychology students (9 males and 21 females, M=24.7 years, SD=9.1 years) learned the Noun keywords. In the second, 33 different first-year psychology students (5 males and 28 females, M=24.1 years, SD=7.5 years) learned the Verb keywords. The procedure was the same on both occasions. The students were instructed that they were to observe the video-monitors and that they were to try to learn the English (Key)word that went with each German word. They then attended to the training trials.

After a two-minute retention interval, filled with the havoc of the students talking to their neighbors, the test trials were presented and the students wrote down the (Key)word for each trial on a numbered answer sheet. These were later scored for correctness and the reminding power of each German word for its keyword calculated as the probability of the latter's correct recall over the group of students. The worst keyword in this respect was *sailors* for *Zahlen* (reminding probability=0.03), the best was *flash* for *Flasche* (1.0). The mean for the Noun keywords was 0.55 (0.27), that for the Verb keywords was 0.50 (0.27); this difference is not significant, $t(35)$=1.53, *n.s.*). The correlation between Verb and Noun keyword-reminding powers was significant (ρ=0.67, p<.001) demonstrating that, to a large degree, it is equally easy (or difficult) to find a useful keyword for a German word whether that keyword be a noun or a verb.

Keyword Imageability

The same procedure and instructions were used to assess the imageability of the keywords. The 36 Noun keywords from the

Noun Keyword Condition were combined with the 36 Verb keywords from the Verb Keyword Condition (in their infinitive form)
and these were then randomly ordered. Twenty different first-
year psychology students (3 males and 17 females, $M=25.8$ years,
$SD=8.6$ years) rated these keywords for imageability on a 7-point
scale. The interrater reliability was again high (Cronbach's alpha
across raters was 0.94). The mean imageability ratings across
students for each keyword were then used in later analyses. The
most imageable keyword was *coffin* (6.95) and the least was *to
broke* (1.6). The Noun keywords ($M=5.79$) were as a group more
imageable than were the Verb keywords ($M=4.55$), $F(1,70)=20.72$,
$p<.001$.

Mediating Sentence Imageability

High imageability of both keyword and English word does
not guarantee a highly imageable mediating sentence—these can
still be integrated to a lesser or greater degree (see, e.g., Bower,
1970; Bower & Winzenz, 1970; Winograd & Lynn, 1979). A similar
procedure to that described above was therefore used to separately assess the imageability of the mediating sentences. The 36
mediators from the Noun Keyword Condition were randomly
mixed with those from the Verb Keyword Condition and 20
different first-year psychology students (4 males and 16 females,
$M=19.7$ years, $SD=2.5$ years) rated these *sentences* for imageability
on a 7-point scale. The instructions emphasized that it was the
sentences as a whole that were to be assessed: "Any phrase which,
in your estimation, arouses a mental image (i.e., a mental picture
or sound, or other sensory experience) very quickly and easily
should be given a high imagery rating; any phrase that arouses a
mental image with difficulty or not at all should be given a low
imagery rating. Think of the phrases "The dog chased the cat" or
"The fact was known". "The dog chased the cat" would probably
arouse an image relatively easily and would be rated as high
imagery; "The fact was known" would probably do so with difficulty and would be rated as low imagery." The interrater reliability

was lower than when keywords in isolation were rated but was still acceptable (Cronbach's alpha across raters was 0.88). The mean imageability ratings across students for each mediating sentence were then used in later analyses. The most imageable mediating sentence was "Imagine HARBOURS HAVE many ships" (6.45), the least imageable was "Imagine BROKERS NEED much experience" (1.95). There was no significant difference between the imageability of the mediating sentences constructed from Noun or Verb keywords—the mean imageability was 4.6 in both cases, $F(1,70)<1$.

Results

Correlational Analyses

The Pearson correlations between the psycholinguistic variables are shown in Table 2.

There is a negative correlation between native word frequency and native word length ($r=-0.61$), confirming Zipf's law, and the longer items also tend to be nouns ($r=0.61$) and more imageable ($r=0.43$). The longer the foreign word, the longer it takes to pronounce ($r=0.52$) and the greater its chance of not conforming to the phonotactic ($r=-0.44$) and orthographic ($r=-0.30$) patterns of the native language. In this sample of words, the nouns that were learned better than the verbs tend to be less frequent ($r=-0.62$), and the more frequent items tend to be less imageable ($r=-0.59$); thus any positive effects of word class or imageability cannot be a confound of word frequency. The nouns are much more imageable than are the verbs ($r=0.80$). The two measures (bigram frequency) of orthographic sequential regularity intercorrelate ($r=0.54$) and orthographic sequential regularity is associated with phonotactic regularity ($r=0.63$ and $r=0.38$) and both pronunciation accuracy ($r=0.39$) and time ($r=-0.28$). Phonotactic regularity (controlled for word length) determines pronunciation time ($r=-0.55$).

The patterns of intercorrelation within the Noun and Verb

Table 2A
Pearson Correlations Between the Psycholinguistic Variables: Native and Foreign Word Factors

	EW Length	GW Length	EW Freq	PoS[a]	CI	AVBIF	MINBIF	Acc	Time	Phono Reg
								German Word		
								Pronunciation		
EW: Length	1.00									
GW: Length	0.03	1.00								
EW: Freq	−0.61**	0.02	1.00							
Part of Speech[a]	0.61**	−0.35*	−0.62**	1.00						
CI	0.43**	−0.19	−0.59**	0.80**	1.00					
GW: AVBIF	0.07	−0.09	−0.13	0.15	0.09	1.00				
GW: MINBIF	0.15	−0.30*	−0.20	0.18	0.19	0.54**	1.00			
GW: Pro Acc	0.02	0.14	−0.06	−0.11	−0.01	0.39**	0.14	1.00		
GW: Pro Time	0.30*	0.52**	−0.22	0.09	0.14	−0.28*	−0.01	−0.34*	1.00	
GW: Phono Reg	0.09	−0.44**	−0.01	0.33*	0.18	0.63**	0.38**	0.20	−0.55**	1.00

[a]Part of Speech, Noun=1, Verb=0.

*p<.05. **p<.01, one-tailed.

EW=English Word; GW=German Word; Freq=Frequency; CI=Concept Imageability; AVBIF=Average Bigram Frequency; MINBIF=Minimum Bigram Frequency; Pro Acc=Pronunciation Accuracy; Pro Time=Pronunciation Time; Phono Reg= Phonotactic Regularity

Table 2B

Pearson Correlations Between the Psycholinguistic Variables: Noun Keyword Factors

	NK Rem Power	NK Imageability	NLS Imageability	G&NK Overlap Orthographic	G&NK Overlap Spoken
NK: Reminding Power	1.00				
NK: Imageability	-0.04	1.00			
NLS: Imageability	0.00	0.39**	1.00		
G&NK: Orthographic Overlap	0.31*	-0.30*	0.05	1.00	
G&NK: Spoken Overlap	0.66**	-0.18	-0.08	0.24	1.00

Table 2C

Pearson Correlations Between the Psycholinguistic Variables: Verb Keyword Factors

	VK Rem Power	VK Imageability	VLS Imageability	G&VK Overlap Orthographic	G&VK Overlap Spoken
VK: Reminding Power	1.00				
VK: Imageability	-0.14	1.00			
VLS=Imageability	-0.03	0.36*	1.00		
G&VK: Orthographic Overlap	0.25	0.00	0.06	1.00	
G&VK: Spoken Overlap	0.62**	-0.23	-0.11	0.25	1.00

*$p<.05$. **$p<.01$, one-tailed.
NK=Noun Keyword; NLS=Noun Linking Sentence; G&NK=German and Noun Keyword; Rem Power=Reminding Power;
VK=Verb Keyword; VLS=Verb Linking Sentence; G&VK=German and Verb Keyword

keyword conditions are similar, with spoken overlap between the foreign word and keyword predicting reminding power ($r=0.66$ and $r=0.62$) much more than did orthographic overlap ($r=0.31$ and $r=0.25$). When the data for both Noun and Verb keywords are analyzed together, reminding power correlates 0.64 ($p<.001$) with spoken overlap and 0.29 ($p<.01$) with orthographic overlap. The standardized multiple regression equation predicting reminding power from these two variables results in a beta of 0.60 ($p<.001$) for spoken overlap and 0.14 ($n.s.$) for orthographic overlap, suggesting that the degree to which the keyword sounds like the foreign word is much more important than the degree to which they are spelled similarly.

Within each condition, the more imageable the keyword, the more imageable the mediating sentence that associates the foreign word and the keyword ($r=0.39$ for the nouns and 0.36 for the verbs) even though these ratings for keywords and sentences were performed by different groups of judges. In the experiment measuring imageability of the mediating sentence, the keyword and native word appeared equally often early or late in the mediational sentence. When we pooled the data for Noun and Verb keywords, a standardized multiple regression analysis predicting mediation sentence imageability from the imageability of the keyword and the native word resulted in betas of 0.28 ($p=0.02$) for the keyword and 0.21 ($p=0.07$) for the native word ($R^2=12\%$)— there is, unsurprisingly, little to choose between them. What *is* important is that, as far as is possible, *both* the native word and the keyword are imageable—if a compound imageability score is calculated as the multiple of the imageabilities of the keyword and native words, this compound predicts the imageability of the mediating sentence with a beta of 0.44 ($R^2=19\%$).

The Pearson correlations between the psycholinguistic variables and word recall in the two directions of translation and four conditions of the experiment are shown in Table 3.

Many of the correlations are significant. There is a strong negative correlation between recall and German word-length in all conditions of productive translation but less so in receptive

Table 3

Pearson Product Moment Correlations Between Psycholinguistic Factors and Recall of Vocabulary Under the Different Training Regimes

Condition Direction of Translation	Own Strategy		Repetition		Noun Keyword		Verb Keyword	
	E>G	G>E	E>G	G>E	E>G	G>E	E>G	G>E
English Word – Length	0.26	0.39**	0.21	0.35*	0.21	0.44**	0.42**	0.48**
German Word – Length	−0.70**	−0.34*	−0.63**	−0.29*	−0.63**	−0.11	−0.52**	−0.31*
English Word – Frequency	−0.11	−0.32*	−0.12	−0.24	−0.34*	−0.35*	−0.12	−0.24
Part of Speech (Noun=1, Verb=0)	0.56**	0.52**	0.51**	0.45**	0.64**	0.44**	0.56**	0.53**
Concept Imageability	0.37*	0.50**	0.42**	0.41**	0.53**	0.42**	0.39**	0.41**
German Word – AVBIF	0.16	−0.01	0.21	−0.06	0.39**	0.01	0.04	0.01
German Word – MINBIF	0.30*	0.17	0.31*	0.13	0.45**	−0.02	0.28*	0.16
German Word – Pronun Accuracy	−0.07	0.15	−0.08	0.10	0.03	0.21	0.00	−0.01
German Word – Pronun Time	−0.36*	−0.19	−0.35*	−0.19	−0.40**	−0.09	−0.19	−0.03
German Word – Phono Regularity	0.51**	0.26	0.47**	0.26	0.63**	0.08	0.40**	0.24

Condition Direction of Translation	Own Strategy		Repetition		Noun Keyword		Verb Keyword	
	E>G	G>E	E>G	G>E	E>G	G>E	E>G	G>E
NK — Reminding Power of GW					0.36*	0.61**		
NK — Imageability					0.11	0.21		
NLS — Imageability					0.17	0.25		
G & NK — Orthographic Overlap					0.56**	0.07		
G & NK — Spoken Overlap					0.25	0.30*		
VK — Reminding Power of GW							0.38**	0.41**
VK — Imageability							-0.06	0.00
VLS — Imageability							-0.06	0.01
G & VK — Orthographic Overlap							0.36*	0.12
G & VK — Spoken Overlap							0.31*	0.35*
Mean Recall[a]	0.56	0.66	0.66	0.71	0.52	0.73	0.48	0.63

* $p < .05$. ** $p < .01$. one tailed.

[a] from Ellis and Beaton (1993).

E=English; G=German; AVBIF=Average Bigram Frequency; MINBIF=Minimum Bigram Frequency; Pronun Accuracy=Pronunication Accuracy; Pronun Time=Pronunciation Time; Phono Regularity=Phonotactic Regularity; NK=Noun Keyword; VK=Verb Keyword; GW=German Word; VK=Verb Keyword; NLS=Noun Linking Sentence; VLS=Verb Linking Sentence.

translation. Nouns are easier to learn than are verbs in all conditions, as are highly imageable items, confirming Ellis and Beaton (1993). Further reassurance in the robustness of these effects is derived from the observation that the strongest correlation between concept imageability and recall (0.53) is found in the Noun Keyword condition in which participants were required to use imagery mediation and effective (imageable) keywords were provided.

The degree to which the foreign word conforms to the phonotactic patterns—and to a lesser degree the orthographic patterns—of the native language, strongly affects translating to the foreign language.

The degree to which the foreign word reminds students of the keyword in the present study predicts vocabulary recall in both Noun and Verb keyword conditions of our earlier study (Ellis & Beaton, 1993). This is somewhat stronger for receptive than for productive translation, but interpretation of this is qualified by the fact that the measure of reminding power was from the foreign word to the keyword and not the reverse. These associations with reminding power are paralleled by those of orthographic and spoken overlap between the foreign word and the keyword. There are no effects of degree of either keyword imageability or mediating sentence imageability within either the Noun keyword or Verb keyword conditions, but one should note the restricted range of imageability within each of these conditions. Remember, too, that *as a whole* Noun keywords are much more effective (Ellis & Beaton, 1993) and that the Noun keywords are significantly more imageable than are the Verb keywords (Methods section, above).

Causal Path Analyses

Some of these predictor variables are intercorrelated, and causal path analysis was therefore performed using LISREL (Jöreskog & Sörbom, 1984; Saris & Stronkhorst, 1984) to summarize the major effects while controlling for spurious relationships attributable to common causes. The data for the Noun and Verb keyword conditions were used making 72 observations in all. Two separate analyses were performed, one for FL learnability from native to foreign language and one for the reverse direction of translation. The paths permitted in the two models were the same, as shown in Figure 2. The exogenous variables were acoustic and orthographic similarities of foreign word and keyword, whether the keyword and native word was a Noun (1) or not (0), and two phonological variables: phonotactic regularity (reflecting the degree to which the foreign word conformed to the native pronunciation patterns) and pronunciation time. The intervening endogenous variables were (a) reminding power of foreign word for keyword and imageability of (b) keyword and (c) native word and (d) mediating sentence. The outcome endogenous variable was learnability. All shown paths were fitted in the models, but only the paths that were significant at least at the 5% level are drawn in solid lines with their accompanying path-weights.[1]

The path-weights in Figure 2 can be interpreted similarly to the betas that result from standardized regression analyses: Thus, for example, the 0.61 path-weight from Acoustic Similarity of Foreign Word and Keyword to Reminding Power of Foreign Word for Keyword implies that for each standard deviation unit increase in the former, one would expect a 0.61 standard deviation unit increase in the latter.

These analyses demonstrate:

1. In learning the foreign vocabulary for native words, the pronounceableness of the foreign word has a strong determining effect (0.37) depending on the degree to which it conforms to the phonotactic patterns of the native language. There is no such effect in the reverse direction.

2. Nouns are much more imageable than are verbs, very much so (0.80) for the native words but somewhat less for the keywords, when the designer was at pains to select keywords as nearly as possible the same, or similar, for noun and verb keyword conditions.

3. The imageability of both the keyword (0.28) and the native

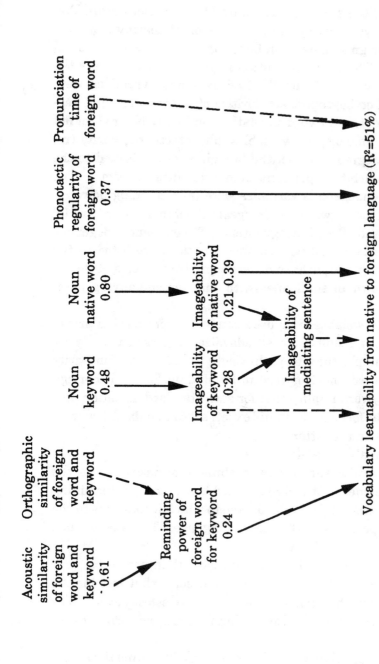

Figure 2a. LISREL causal path solutions predicting foreign language learnability (from native to foreign language). All permitted paths are shown, but the nonsignificant ones are shown as dashed lines.

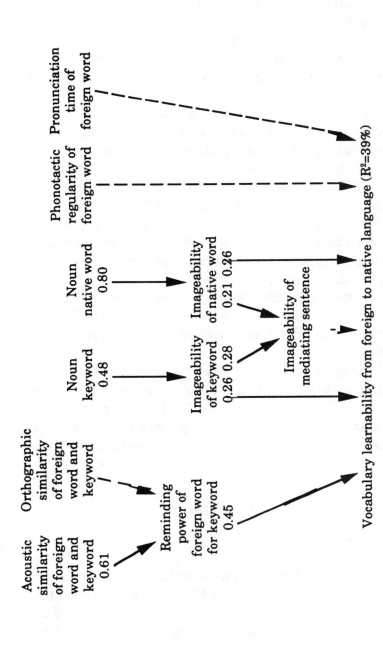

Figure 2b. LISREL causal path solutions predicting foreign language learnability (from foreign to native language). All permitted paths are shown, but the nonsignificant ones are shown as dashed lines.

word (0.21) affect the imageability of the mediating sentence that relates the two.

4. However, the imageability of these component words directly determines the learnability of the FL vocabulary. In neither analysis does mediating sentence imageability per se predict learnability.

5. The imageability of the native word is all-important in translating from native to foreign language; the imageability of the keyword only becomes a significant factor when translating from foreign to native language. This parallels the general finding that in PAL, imageability effects are much stronger for the stimulus word than for the response word (Paivio, 1971; Rubin, 1980); in translating from native to foreign language, it is the native word that is the stimulus, whereas the keyword is the stimulus member of the to-be-associated pair in translating from foreign to native language.

6. Acoustic similarity between foreign word and keyword much more importantly determines reminding power than does orthographic similarity (even though responses were typed in this experiment).

7. The reminding power of the foreign word for the keyword is a significant determinant of FL learnability in both directions of translation, but more so in going from foreign to native language (0.45) than from native to foreign language (0.24). Note, however, that reminding power was only assessed in the former direction.

Discussion

Phonological Factors

These "byword" analyses demonstrate significant correlations between the ease of pronunciation of FL words and their learnability. Gathercole and Baddeley (1989) demonstrated that young children's phonological short-term memory span (their ability to repeat novel nonwords in order) predicted their L1 vocabulary one year later, even when prior vocabulary levels were taken into account. In their reanalysis, Gathercole et al. (1991) showed that both nonword length and the degree to which nonwords were "word like" predicted ease of repetition of the nonwords. In the present study we have gone further; first, by directly measuring phonotactic regularity; second, by showing that this predicts long-term memorability; and third, by showing that this effect is independent of (a) mediational aspects between the novel word and its L1 translation equivalent by means of imagery and/or semantic association, and (b) the orthographic regularity of the novel word.

The results therefore lend further, more specific, support to theories positing a role of phonological short-term memory (Gathercole & Baddeley, 1989, 1990) and phonological long-term memory in vocabulary acquisition, whereby representation of the novel sound sequence of a new word in phonological short-term memory promotes its longer-term consolidation both for later articulation and as an entity with which meaning can be associated. The easier a novel word is in this respect, either because of its short length or because it conforms to the learner's expectations of phonotactic sequences of language, the easier it is to learn. Phonotactic regularity might allow the novel word to better match the learner's settings of excitatory and inhibitory links between sequential phonological elements (Estes, 1972) for input processes such as phonological segmentation or for output as articulatory assembly (Snowling, Chiat, & Hulme, 1991), either per se or as expectations of phonological sequences as influenced by regularities in the learner's lexica (Gathercole et al., 1991).

A number of studies, using different methodologies, converge on this conclusion. The first is a training study (Gathercole & Baddeley, 1990) in which children poor on nonword repetition were found to be slower than children who were good on nonword repetition at learning new vocabulary (phonologically unfamiliar names such as *Pimas* for toys). They were not slower to learn a new mapping for familiar vocabulary (familiar names like *Thomas* for the toys). Thus, it appears that temporary phonological encoding and storage skills are involved in learning new words. As Gathercole and Baddeley (1990) pointed out,

> Acquiring a new vocabulary item . . . must minimally involve achieving a stable long-term representation of a sequence of sounds which is linked with other representations specifying the particular instance or class of instances. The locus of the contribution of phonological memory skills seems most likely to be in the process of establishing a stable phonological representation as, in order to do this, a temporary representation has presumably to be achieved first. Immediate phonological memory seems an appropriate medium for this temporary representation and, presumably, constructing the stable long-term memory representation of the novel event will interact with the adequacy of this temporary representation. By this analysis, the better the short-term representation, the faster the long-term learning. (pp. 451–452)

A second source of evidence for a relationship between phonological memory and vocabulary acquisition comes from the study by Baddeley, Papagno and Vallar (1988) of an adult neuropsychological patient, PV, who appeared to have a highly specific acquired deficit of immediate phonological memory. PV was completely unable to make associations between spoken word and nonword pairs, despite showing normal phonological processing of nonword material. She had no difficulty, however, in learning new associations between pairs of words. In other words, temporary phonological memory is particularly involved in the long-term learning of *unfamiliar* phonological material.

This relationship holds for new words whether they are of native or foreign sources. Thus, Service (1992) demonstrated that the ability to represent unfamiliar phonological material in working memory (as indexed by Finnish children's ability to repeat aloud pseudowords that sounded like English) predicted FL (English) acquisition two and a half years later.

However, theories of FL vocabulary learning and the role of phonological memory systems typically fail to make the important distinction concerning direction of translation. The present study's findings suggest that phonological factors are more implicated in productive learning when the student has a greater cognitive burden in terms of sensory and motor learning. Ellis and Beaton (1993) demonstrate from individual differences analyses that although keyword techniques are efficient means for receptive vocabulary learning, for productive learning they are less effective than repetition (at least for learners naïve to the pronunciation patterns of the foreign language). The present byword analyses clarify this in that they demonstrate the strong effects of the foreign word's regularity of pronunciation (in terms of the phonotactic patterns of the native language) on the success of learning. Such an effect is absent in receptive learning.

These effects parallel those of Papagno, Valentine, and Baddeley (1991) who demonstrated, in a design comparable to ours in that it required productive vocabulary learning with written responses, that articulatory suppression (which presumably disrupts the articulatory loop component of STM) interfered with the learning of Russian vocabulary, but not of native language paired-associates, in Italian adults. English students, however, were not so disrupted in learning Russian, but were when learning Finnish words greatly dissimilar to English, a result that Papagno et al. attributed to the greater association value of Russian words for these students. Their results suggest that the articulatory loop is used in FL vocabulary acquisition when the material to be learned is phonologically unfamiliar and when semantic associations via native language cognates are not readily created, but it can be circumvented if the material readily allows semantic association. Taking together their results and ours, we would predict that (a) in such pairs of "different" languages, articulatory suppression will have a much greater effect on productive rather than receptive vocabulary learning; and (b) it will be much more detrimental for *ab initio* learners who are naïve to the pronunciation patterns of the foreign language. However, these experiments remain to be performed.

In conclusion, there is a considerable body of evidence that phonological factors are involved in (particularly productive) long-term vocabulary acquisition: (a) Individuals deficient in phonological STM have difficulty in acquiring the phonological representations of unfamiliar words; (b) phonological STM span predicts vocabulary acquisition in both L1 and L2; (c) interfering with phonological STM by means of articulatory suppression disrupts vocabulary learning when semantic associations between the native and foreign word are not readily available; (d) nonword length and word likeness predict repeatability; and (e) foreign language word regularity in terms of L1 phonotactics determines learnability.

How then should we conceptualize the development of vocabulary from the very beginnings of entry into a new language to full proficiency? What are the causal relationships between phonological STM and the phonological aspects of LTM for vocabulary? Gathercole and Baddeley (1989, 1990) demonstrated quite clearly that phonological STM predicts long-term vocabulary acquisition. Yet at the same time there are robust demonstrations of a LTM component of STM span that is independent of speech rate, that is, STM span is greater for FL lexical items that have been encountered more often (Hulme, Maugham, & Brown, 1991; Brown & Hulme, 1992). The direction of causation is neither STM to LTM, nor LTM to STM, but rather it is reciprocal. Both directions apply because new skills or knowledge invariably initially build upon whatever relevant abilities or knowledge are already present; then, as they are used, they legitimate and make more relevant (Istomina, 1975) those prior skills and knowledge, and so in turn cause their further development. This is the *normal* developmental pattern. The case of reading development is a clear example. Thus Ellis (1990; Ellis & Cataldo, 1990) demonstrated reciprocal interactions between reading, phonological awareness, spelling, and STM whereby, for example, initial levels of implicit phonological awareness determine the child's entry into reading, but reading itself causes development of phonological awareness. Similarly, Stanovich (1986) has persuasively argued the case for reciprocal relationships and bootstrapping effects in reading more generally: "In short, many things that facilitate further growth in reading comprehension ability—general knowledge, vocabulary, syntactic knowledge—are developed by reading itself" (p. 364). He refers to these as "Matthew effects"—"unto those who have shall be given"—the more you know, the easier it is to learn more—such is growth and development.

Vocabulary acquisition is no exception to this rule:

> A further possibility is that nonword repetition ability and vocabulary knowledge develop in a highly interactive manner. Intrinsic phonological memory skills may influence the learning of new words by constraining the retention of unfamiliar phonological sequences, but in addition, extent of vocabulary will affect the ease of generating appropriate phonological frames to support the phonological representations. (Gathercole et al., 1991, pp. 364–365)

The novice FL learner comes to the task with a capacity for repetition of L1 words. This capacity is determined by (a) constitutional factors, (b) metacognitive factors (e.g., knowing that repetitive rehearsal is a useful strategy in STM tasks), and (c) cognitive factors (phonological segmentation, blending, articulatory assembly). Such cognitive language processing skills occur at an implicit level in input and output modules that are cognitively impenetrable (Fodor, 1983) *but whose functions are very much affected by experience*—hence, for example, frequency and regularity effects in reading (Morton, 1969; Baron & Strawson, 1976; Seidenberg, Waters, Barnes, & Tanenhaus, 1984; Brown, 1987; Paap, McDonald, Schvaneveldt, & Noel, 1987), spelling (Barron, 1980; Barry & Seymour, 1988), and spoken word recognition (Morton, 1969; Marslen-Wilson, 1987).

The degree to which such relevant skills and knowledge (pattern recognition systems for speech sounds, motor systems for speech production) are transferable and efficient for L2 word repetition is dependent on the degree to which the phonotactic patterns in the L2 approximate to those of the L1, hence the phonotactic regularity effects at both language and individual word levels. Here then we have long-term knowledge affecting phonological STM, that is, Gathercole et al.'s linguistic hypothesis.

The "good language learner" (Naiman, Fröhlich, Stern, & Todesco, 1978) knows that repetition and practice of new vocabulary are useful strategies (O'Malley, Chamot, Stewner-Manzanares, Kupper, & Russo, 1985). In so doing, the good learner acquires long-term L2 vocabulary. Here we have phonological STM determining long-term vocabulary acquisition (Gathercole & Baddeley, 1989, 1990).

As their L2 vocabulary extends, as they practice hearing and producing L2 words, so good language learners automatically and implicitly acquire knowledge of the statistical frequencies and sequential probabilities of the phonotactics of the L2. Their input and output modules for L2 processing begin to abstract knowledge of L2 regularities, thus they become more proficient at short-term repetition of novel L2 words. And so L2 learning lifts itself up by its bootstraps.

Mediations and Associations—Imageability and Meaningfulness

Nouns are far easier to learn as FL vocabulary than are verbs. This is of little surprise in the conditions in which students were encouraged to use keyword imagery mediation. Here the byword analyses in large part parallel the individual differences analyses of Ellis and Beaton (1993) in that they demonstrate that the imageability of both the keyword and the native word determines the effectiveness of keyword methods of FL vocabulary learning. Greater effectiveness depends upon greater imageability, which in turn is best promoted by choosing nouns as keywords.

To our knowledge, ours is the first demonstration of the effects of keyword imageability and the directional interaction whereby keyword imageability is more important in translating from foreign to native language than from native to foreign language. However novel in the keyword literature, a comparable effect is standard in research concerning imagery effects in PAL, in which the imageability of the stimulus member of the pair has much more effect than does that of the response (Paivio, 1971; Rubin, 1980). These findings, taken together with the interactions between keyword effectiveness and individual differences in Gordon Imagery Control (Ellis & Beaton, 1993), strongly confirm interpretation of the keyword technique in terms of theories of imagery.

However, nouns are also far easier to learn as FL vocabulary than are verbs even when students are *not* instructed to use imagery mediation. Within the literature on organization and memory, mediation is discussed predominantly in terms of semantic links. A relationship might be made between the stimulus and response words because it taps into preexisting semantic links; thus, at the extreme, highly associated pairs are easy to learn (Jenkins, Mink, & Russell, 1958). Otherwise students may choose from a wide variety of strategies: for example, to attempt to link the two items in a meaningful sentence (as in the sentence generation condition of Bower and Winzenz, 1970). The possibilities are endless—even with research on nonsense syllables, Baddeley (1976) wrote:

> Anyone who has worked with nonsense syllables will know that, despite the effort put into scaling their association value, familiarity, pronounceableness, and so forth, the correlation between these measures and the learning of individual syllables is low.... The probable reason for this lack of consistency is that subjects will use any strategy they can devise to give meaning to an item or pair. .... Given a flexible and ingenious subject, it is hardly surprising that no measure based on a single coding dimension has proved to be an accurate or reliable predictor of learning. Indeed, the best way of predicting the difficulty of a nonsense syllable pair is still to ask subjects (Prytulak, 1971), presumably because subjects can base their judgements on the whole range of possible coding strategies, whereas most measures are based on a single coding dimension. (p. 273)

With meaningful material we give the fertile mind even more scope, and with imageable material yet more again.

There are diverse psychological theories of meaning, but many posit that the element representing a word in semantic memory is associated with a number of features or, more fully, predicates. This assumption has been used to analyze work in sentence verification (e.g., Anderson, 1976), category prototypes (e.g., Rosch, 1975), concepts (e.g., Schank & Abelson, 1977), basic categories (e.g., Rosch, 1976), similarity (e.g., Tversky, 1977), metaphor (e.g., Ortony, 1979), episodic memory (e.g., Tulving, 1983), semantic priming (e.g., Meyer & Schvaneveldt, 1971), and deep dyslexia (Jones, 1985). All of these models are concerned to represent meanings, and propositional representations are well suited to this end—knowledge is represented as a set of discrete symbols that are linked by associational relationships to form propositions; concepts of the world are thus represented by formal statements, with the meaning of a concept given by the pattern of relationships among which it participates. (See Rumelhart & Norman, 1985, for a review.) Meaningful concepts have many relationships; less meaningful ones have few. When Rubin (1980) factor-analyzed 51 psycholinguistic variables measured for 125 words and Paivio, Yuille, & Madigan (1968) imageability, (a) meaningfulness (m, associative frequency, and categorizability), and (b) concreteness loaded on the *same* factor, suggesting that these measures have much in common. Another way of operationalizing this definition of meaning is to measure the "ease of predication" of the word, that is, the ease with which what the word refers to "can be described by simple factual statements" (Jones, 1985, p. 6; e.g., a *dog* is a type of animal, a *dog* barks when angry, a *dog* has four legs, a *dog* wags its tail when pleased, a *dog* often lives in a kennel, etc., vs. an idea . . .). When Jones (1985) had participants rate 125 nouns for ease of predication, there was a very high correlation ($r=.88$) between this measure and Paivio et al. imageability. When he chose a measure of predication time (the mean number of seconds taken to produce two predicates for each word) there was a correlation of $r=-0.72$ with Paivio et al. imageability (Jones, 1988). These are high correlations; it seems that imageability and predictability go hand in hand.

Schwanenflugel, Harnishfeger & Stowe (1988) and Schwanenflugel (1991) argued that the greater meaningfulness of imageable words arises from their greater "context availability" (Schwanenflugel, 1991, p. 242), a concept very similar to predictability. In this view imageable concepts, as a result of their experientially based cores, more easily allow access of relevant world knowledge, or "inner provided contexts" (Harnishfeger & Stowe, 1988, p. 501) that add meaning relationships to the word. The common feature of all of these theories is that things experienced and analyzed visually are imageable things are meaningful things about which we have coordinate and subordinate semantic information.

Gentner (1982) emphasized the parallelism of vision that allows for ready associations: Good concrete objects are cohesive collections of precepts because objecthood is created by spatial relationships among perceptual elements. Perceptual elements packaged into noun referents are highly cohesive (i.e., have many internal relationships to one another), whereas perceptual elements packaged into verb referents are distributed more sparsely through the perceptual field and have fewer internal relationships with one another. Thus, noun concepts are richer and nouns are more easily mapped onto discrete perceptual experiences. Hence, they are more meaningful and more easily acquired in either first or second languages. Similarly Ellis (1993a) proposed that imageability effects in verbal learning reflect the fact that visual imageability confers meaning, or, as Lakoff & Johnson (1980) and Barsalou (1991) suggested, symbols are grounded in our perceptual experience, that is, imageable items are meaningful items are memorable items.

Keyword Mediation

Finally, the present results confirm the two-stage view of keyword mediation proposed by Raugh and Atkinson (1975) that a useful keyword must be (a) highly imageable *and* (b) an effective reminder of the foreign word; that is, imageability is needed for the link between native word and keyword, but the keyword and the foreign word must also be similar enough to effect their mutual reminding. The beta of 0.44 between the compound of native and keyword imageabilities and FL vocabulary learnability confirms the imagery mediation stage of the process. That the reminding power of the foreign word for keyword (as measured above) is a separate stage is demonstrated by its separate and significant effects in the causal path analyses (Fig. 2). These analyses also demonstrate that effective reminding is achieved by having the keyword as acoustically similar to the foreign word as possible; orthographic similarity is of less concern.

Individual Differences and Instructional Techniques

These analyses have concentrated on the factors that make *words* easier or harder to acquire. Allied questions concern (a) which *people* are better at learning FL vocabulary, that is *individual differences*, and (b) *effective methods* of learning, that is, *instructional techniques*. Our companion paper (Ellis & Beaton, 1993) addresses these issues. It demonstrates that keyword techniques are more effective for receptive learning, but that repetition is superior for production. (This is the individual differences replication of the word pronounceableness effects discussed here.) Performance is optimal when learners combine both strategies. The nature of the keyword is crucial; whereas imageable noun keywords promote learning, verb keywords may actually impede it. Students left to their own devices report using imagery mediation 33% of the time, and in turn, noting similarity between the foreign and native words 19%, sentence mediation between a keyword and the native word 4%, sound similarity 4%, and rote repetition 2% of the time. Students high in Imagery Control naturally adopt imagery mediation strategies and perform better as a result. However, people can be encouraged to use this technique effectively; and when this is done, Imagery Control no longer predicts performance.

Provisos

Before reaching our general conclusions we must emphasize the limitations of this research. The study focused on the very beginning stages of vocabulary learning, and one cannot assume that learning occurs in similar ways at different stages of proficiency (Meara, 1984). Our operationalization of vocabulary learning treats it simply as the learning of word pairs, and we have in no sense addressed the implicit learning of vocabulary (Ellis, 1993b, 1994a). The testing procedures involved typed responses, and furthermore they revealed nothing about the extent to which students can manipulate the foreign language words that they have "learned"; for example, we have not assessed whether students can use these lexical items in a sentence demonstrating that they understand their meaning, nor have we ascertained whether the students know in which contexts these lexical items can be used. Further research is needed to answer these and related questions.

Practical Corollaries

The second-language learner must acquire the pronunciation elements and their compounds in the foreign tongue as well as the graphemes and their patterns of orthographic combination in the foreign script—all this on top of the mappings of word meanings between the two languages. Keyword techniques can be very effective in promoting the semantic mappings, but they can do little for the phonological and orthographic aspects unless the learner is fortunate enough to be studying an FL that is sufficiently related to the mother tongue that there exists therein a host of cognates that will serve as effective keywords in that they closely share acoustic and orthographic similarity to the FL lexicon. Here, particularly, it is not as important that the keyword sound like the foreign word, but rather that the foreign word sound just like the keyword—a subtle but important distinction. If this is not the case, and it is often very difficult to find suitable keywords in this respect (see Nation, 1987; Hall, 1988), then the learner must also be encouraged to practice the pronunciations and writings of the FL to develop phonological and graphemic pattern-recognition and motor programs by some other means, such as repetition.

Note

[1]We could have tested other theoretically motivated models. For example, there are good reasons to expect that there are independent effects of part of speech on learnability that are not mediated by imageability (Gentner, 1982; Schwanenflugel et al. 1988; Schwanenflugel, 1991). Indeed, this is certainly the case from the data: In Table 3 in each of the eight cases, part of speech is a numerically better predictor of learnability than is concept imageability. Furthermore, in each of these cases, hierarchical regression analyses in which imageability is forced in at the first stage invariably demonstrate that word class makes a further significant contribution to the explained variance. Notwithstanding this, we chose to limit the analysis to the current model in which effects of word class are mediated by imagery for both theoretical and practical reasons: (a) much of the advantage of nouns over verbs is due to the fact that words are grounded in our imagery memories of perceptual experiences (thus Gentner, 1982, arguing that object concepts are given to us by the world whereas predicate concepts form a system that the child must discover, demonstrates that even as far as nouns are concerned, those that appear in the child's first words are all either concrete or proper nouns; they center on concrete precepts not abstract vagaries); (b) we are investigating the effects of imagery keyword mediation in which it is clear that there is an advantage of imagery over semantic association (Bower & Winzenz, 1970) and it is precisely the nature of these imagery effects that we wish to explore; (c) in our experiment, imagery and word class are so confounded ($r=0.80$) that if both native and keyword word class were entered as direct effects of learnability, extending the models in Figure 2, then there would be little variance left for imagery to explain. A factorial experiment in which part of speech is crossed with imagery in its full range for both nouns and verbs is needed to properly disentangle effects of word class and imageability.

References

Anderson, J. P., & Jordan, A. M. (1928). Learning and retention of Latin words and phrases. *Journal of Educational Psychology*, 19, 485–496.

Anderson, J. R. (1976). *Language, memory, and thought*. Hillsdale, NJ: Erlbaum.

Atkinson, R. C., & Raugh, M. R. (1975). An application of the mnemonic keyword method to the acquisition of a Russian vocabulary. *Journal of Experimental Psychology: Human Learning and Memory, 104,* 126–133.

Baddeley, A. D. (1976). *The psychology of memory.* New York: Basic Books.

Baddeley, A. D., Papagno, C., & Vallar, G. (1988). When long-term learning depends on short-term storage. *Journal of Memory & Language, 27,* 586–595.

Baron, J., & Strawson, C. (1976). Use of orthographic and word specific knowledge in reading words aloud. *Journal of Experimental Psychology: Human Perception & Performance, 2,* 386–393.

Barron, R. W. (1980). Visual and phonological strategies in reading and spelling. In U. Frith (Ed.), *Cognitive processes in spelling* (pp. 195–214). London: Academic Press.

Barry, C., & Seymour, P. H. K. (1988). Lexical priming and sound-to-spelling contingency effects in nonword spelling. *Quarterly Journal of Experimental Psychology: Human Experimental Psychology, 40*(A), 5–40.

Barsalou, L. W. (1991, July). *Structure and flexibility in concepts.* Keynote address at the International Conference on Memory, University of Lancaster, Bailrigg.

Beaton, A., Gruneberg, M/. & Ellis, N. C. (in press). Retention of foreign vocabulary learned using the keyword method: A ten-year follow-up. *Second Language Research.*

Berndt, R. S., Reggia, J. A., & Mitchum, C. C. (1987). Empirically derived probabilities for grapheme-to-phoneme correspondences in English. *Behavior Research Methods, Instruments & Computers, 19,* 1–9.

Bower, G. H. (1970). Imagery as a relational organizer in associative learning. *Journal of Verbal Learning and Verbal Behavior, 9,* 529–533.

Bower, G. H., & Winzenz, D. (1970). Comparison of associative learning strategies. *Psychonomic Science, 20,* 119–120.

Brown, G. D. A. (1987). Resolving inconsistency: A computational model of word naming. *Journal of Memory & Language, 26,* 1–23.

Brown, G. D. A., & Hulme, C. (1992). Cognitive psychology and second-language processing: The role of short-term memory. In R. J. Harris (Ed.), *Cognitive processing in bilinguals* (pp. 105–122). Amsterdam: North Holland.

Carroll, J. B. (Ed.). (1956). *Language, thought and reality: Selected writings of Benjamin Lee Whorf.* Cambridge, MA: MIT Press.

Carroll, J. B., & Sapon, S. M. (1955). *Modern language aptitude test.* New York: The Psychological Corporation/Harcourt Brace Jovanovich.

Carter, R. (1987). *Vocabulary: Applied linguistic perspectives.* London: Allen & Unwin.

Carter, R., & McCarthy, M. (1988). *Vocabulary and language teaching.* London: Longman.

Christian, J., Bickley, W., Tarka, M., & Clayton, K. (1978). Measures of free recall of 900 English nouns: Correlations with imagery, concreteness, meaningfulness, and frequency. *Memory & Cognition, 6*, 379–390.

Cohen, A. D. (1987). The use of verbal and imagery mnemonics in second-language vocabulary learning. *Studies in Second Language Acquisition, 9*, 43–62.

Cohen, A. D., & Aphek, E. (1980). Retention of second language vocabulary over time: Investigating the role of mnemonic association. *System, 8*, 221–236.

Davelaar, E., & Besner, D. (1988). Word identification: Imageability, semantics, and the content-functor distinction. *Quarterly Journal of Experimental Psychology:* Human Experimental Psychology, *40A*, 789–799.

Desrochers, A., & Begg, I. (1987). A theoretical account of encoding and retrieval processes in the use of imagery-based mnemonic techniques: The special case of the keyword method. In M. A. McDaniel & M. Pressley (Eds.), *Imagery and related mnemonic processes: Theories, individual differences, and applications* (pp. 56–77). New York: Springer-Verlag.

Dukes, W. F., & Bastian, J. (1966). Recall of abstract and concrete words equated for meaningfulness. *Journal of Verbal Learning and Verbal Behavior, 5*, 455–458.

Ehri, L. C. (1977). Do adjectives and functors interfere as much as nouns in naming pictures? *Child Development, 48*, 697–701.

Ellis, A. W., & Young, A. W. (1988). *Human cognitive neuropsychology.* Hillsdale, NJ: Lawrence Erlbaum.

Ellis, N. C. (1990). Reading, phonological skills and short-term memory: Interactive tributaries of development. *Journal of Research in Reading, 13*, 107–122.

Ellis, N. C. (1991). In verbal memory the eyes see vividly, but ears only faintly hear, fingers barely feel and the nose doesn't know: Meaning and the links between the verbal system and modalities of perception and imagery. In C. Cornoldi & M. A. McDaniel (Eds.), *Imagery and cognition* (pp. 313–330). New York: Springer-Verlag.

Ellis, N. C. (1993a). *Imagery, meaning and memory.* Manuscript submitted for publication.

Ellis, N. C. (1993b) Rules and instances in foreign language learning: Interactions of explicit and implicit knowledge. *European Journal of Cognitive Psychology, 5*, 289–318.

Ellis, N. C. (1994a). Consciousness in second language learning: Psychological perspectives on the role of conscious processes in vocabulary acquisition. *AILA Review, 11*, 37–56.

Ellis, N. C. (1994b). Vocabulary acquisition: The implicit ins and outs of explicit cognitive mediation. In N. C. Ellis (Ed.), *Implicit and explicit learning of languages* (pp. 211–282). London: Academic Press.

Ellis, N. C. (in press). The psychology of foreign language acquisition: Implications for CALL. *International Journal of Computer Assisted Language Learning.*

Ellis, N. C., & Beaton, A. (1993). Factors affecting the learning of foreign language vocabulary: Imagery keyword mediators and phonological short-term memory. *Quarterly Journal of Experimental Psychology: Human Experimental Psychology, 46A,* 533–558.

Ellis, N. C., & Cataldo, S. (1990). The role of spelling in learning to read. *Language and Education, 4,* 1–28.

Estes, W. K. (1972). An associative basis for coding and organisation in memory. In A. W. Melton & E. Martin (Eds.), *Coding processes in human memory* (pp. 161–190). Washington, DC: V. H. Winston.

Faust, G. W., & Anderson, R. C. (1967). Effects of incidental material in a programmed Russian vocabulary lesson. *Journal of Educational Psychology, 58,* 3–10.

Fodor, J. A. (1983). *The modularity of mind: An essay on faculty psychology.* Cambridge, MA: MIT Press.

Francis, W. N., & Kucera, H. (1982). *Frequency analysis of English usage: Lexicon and grammar.* Boston: Houghton Mifflin.

Frincke, G. (1968). Word characteristics, associative-relatedness and the free-recall of nouns. *Journal of Verbal Learning and Verbal Behavior, 7,* 366–372.

Gathercole, S. E., & Baddeley, A. D. (1989). Evaluation of the role of phonological STM in the development of vocabulary in children: A longitudinal study. *Journal of Memory & Language, 28,* 200–213.

Gathercole, S. E., & Baddeley, A. D. (1990). The role of phonological memory in vocabulary acquisition: A study of young children learning new names. *British Journal of Psychology, 81,* 439–454.

Gathercole, S. E., Willis, C., Emslie, H., & Baddeley, A. D. (1991). The influences of number of syllables and wordlikeness on children's repetition of nonwords. *Applied Psycholinguistics, 12,* 349–367.

Gentner, D. (1982). Why nouns are learned before verbs: Linguistic relativity versus natural partitioning. In S. A. Kuczaj II (Ed.), *Language development: Vol. 2. Language, thought, and culture* (pp. 301–334). Hillsdale, NJ: Erlbaum.

Gilhooly, K. J., & Gilhooly, M. L. (1979). Age-of-acquisition effects in lexical and episodic memory tasks. *Memory & Cognition, 7,* 214–223.

Hall, J. W. (1988). On the utility of the keyword mnemonic for vocabulary learning. *Journal of Educational Psychology, 80,* 554–562.

Henning, G. H. (1973). Remembering foreign language vocabulary: Acoustic and semantic parameters. *Language Learning, 23,* 185–196.

Higa, M. (1965). The psycholinguistic concept of "difficulty" and the teaching of foreign language vocabulary. *Language Learning, 15,* 167–179.

Horowitz, I. M., Chilian, P. C., & Dunnigan, K. P. (1969). Word fragments and their redintegrative powers. *Journal of Experimental Psychology, 80,* 392–394.

Hulme, C., Maughan, S., & Brown, G. D. A. (1991). Memory for familiar and unfamiliar words: Evidence for a long-term memory contribution to short-term memory tasks. *Journal of Memory & Language, 30,* 685–701.

Hultzén, L. S., Allen, J. H. D. Jr., & Miron, M. S. (1964). *Tables of transitional frequencies of English phonemes.* Urbana: University of Illinois Press.

Ijaz, I. H. (1986). Linguistic and cognitive determinants of lexical acquisition in a second language. *Language Learning, 36,* 401–451.

Istomina, Z. M. (1975). The development of involuntary memory in preschool age children. *Soviet Psychology, 13,* 5–64.

Jenkins, J. J., Mink, W. D., & Russell, W. A. (1958). Associative clustering as a function of verbal association strength. *Psychological Reports, 4,* 127–136.

Jones, G. V. (1985). Deep dyslexia, imageability, and ease of predication. *Brain & Language, 24,* 1–19.

Jones, G. V. (1988). Images, predicates, and retrieval cues. In M. Denis, J. Engelkamp, & J. T. E. Richardson (Eds.), *Cognitive and neuropsychological approaches to mental imagery* (pp. 89–98). Dordrecht, Holland: Nijhoff.

Jöreskog, K. G., & Sörbom, D. (1984). *Lisrel VI user's guide.* Uppsala, Sweden: University of Uppsala, Department of Statistics.

Kellog, G. S., & Howe, M. J. A. (1971). Using words and pictures in foreign language learning. *Alberta Journal of Educational Research, 17,* 87–94.

Lakoff, G. (1987). *Women, fire, and dangerous things: What categories reveal about the mind.* Chicago: University of Chicago Press.

Lakoff, G., & Johnson, M. (1980). *Metaphors we live by.* Chicago: University of Chicago Press.

Levin, J. R., & Pressley, M. (1985). Mnemonic vocabulary acquisition: What's fact, what's fiction? In R. F. Dillon & R. R. Schmeck (Ed.), *Individual differences in cognition* (Vol. 2, pp. 145–172). New York: Academic Press.

Loess, H., & Brown, A. (1969). Word fragments as aids to recall a whole word. *Journal of Experimental Psychology, 80,* 384–386.

Marslen-Wilson, W. D. (1987). Functional parallelism in spoken word-recognition. *Cognition, 25,* 71–102.

Meara, P. (1984). The study of lexis in interlanguage. In A. Davies, C. Criper, & A. Howatt (Eds.), *Interlanguage* (pp. 225–235). Edinburgh: Edinburgh University Press.

Meyer, D. E., & Schvaneveldt, R. W. (1971). Facilitation in recognizing pairs of words: Evidence of a dependence between retrieval operations. *Journal of Experimental Psychology, 90,* 227–234.

Morton, J. (1969). Interaction of information in word recognition. *Psychological Review, 76,* 165–178.

Morton, J., & Patterson, K. (1980). "Little words—No!". In M. Coltheart, K. Patterson, & J. C. Marshall (Eds.), *Deep dyslexia* (pp. 270–285). London: Routledge & Kegan Paul.

Naiman, N., Fröhlich, M., Stern, H. H., & Todesco, A. (1978). *The good language learner: A report.* Toronto: Ontario Institute for Studies in Education.

Nation, I. S. P. (1982). Beginning to learn a foreign language vocabulary: A review of the research. *RELC Journal, 13,* 15–36.

Nation, I. S. P. (1987). *Teaching and learning vocabulary* (Occasional Publication No. 7). Wellington, New Zealand: Victoria University of Wellington, English Language Institute,

O'Malley, J. M., Chamot, A. U., Stewner-Manzanares, G., Kupper, L, & Russo, R. P. (1985). Learning strategies used by beginning and intermediate ESL students. *Language Learning, 35,* 21–46.

Ortony, A. (1979). *Metaphor and thought.* Cambridge: Cambridge University Press.

Paap, K. R., McDonald, J. E., Schvaneveldt, R. W., & Noel, R. W. (1987). Frequency and pronunciability in visually presented naming and lexical decision tasks. In M. Coltheart (Ed.), *Attention and performance XII: The psychology of reading* (pp. 221–244). Hillsdale, NJ: Erlbaum.

Paivio, A. (1968). A factor-analytic study of word attributes and verbal learning. *Journal of Verbal Learning and Verbal Behavior, 7,* 41–49.

Paivio, A. (1971). *Imagery and verbal processes.* New York: Holt, Rinehart and Winston.

Paivio, A., & Desrochers, A. (1981). Mnemonic techniques in second language learning. *Journal of Educational Psychology, 73,* 780–795.

Paivio, A., Yuille, J. C., & Madigan, S. A. (1968). Concreteness, imagery and meaningfulness values for 925 nouns. *Journal of Experimental Psychology Monographs, 76*(1, Pt. 2), 1–25.

Paivio, A., Yuille, J. C., & Smythe, P. C. (1966). Stimulus and response abstractness, imagery and meaningfulness, and reported mediators in paired-associate learning. *Canadian Journal of Psychology, 20,* 362–377.

Papagno, C., Valentine, T., & Baddeley, A. (1991). Phonological short-term memory and foreign-language vocabulary learning. *Journal of Memory & Language, 30,* 331–347. `

Patterson, K. E. (1981). Neuropsychological approaches to the study of reading. *British Journal of Psychology, 72,* 151–174.

Postman, L. (1962). The effects of language habits on the acquisition and retention of verbal associations. *Journal of Experimental Psychology, 64,* 7–19.

Pressley, M., Levin, J. R., & Delaney, H. D. (1982). The mnemonic keyword method. *Review of Educational Research, 52,* 61–91

Pressley, M., Levin, J. R., & Miller, G. E. (1981). The keyword method and children's learning of foreign vocabulary with abstract meanings. *Canadian Journal of Psychology, 35,* 283–287.

Raugh, M. R., & Atkinson, R. C. (1975). A mnemonic method for learning a second-language vocabulary. *Journal of Educational Psychology, 67,* 1–16.

Rodgers, T. S. (1969). On measuring vocabulary difficulty: An analysis of item variables in learning Russian-English vocabulary pairs. *International Review of Applied Linguistics, 7,* 327–343.

Rosch, E. (1975). Cognitive representations of semantic categories. *Journal of Experimental Psychology: General, 104,* 192–233.

Rosch, E. (1976). Basic objects in natural categories. *Cognitive Psychology, 8,* 382–439.

Rubin, D. C. (1980). 51 properties of 125 words: A unit analysis of verbal behaviour. *Journal of Verbal Learning and Verbal Behavior, 19,* 736–755.

Rubin, D. C. (1983). Associative asymmetry, availability and retrieval. *Memory and Cognition, 11,* 83–92.

Rumelhart, D. E., & Norman, D. A. (1985). Representation of knowledge. In A. M. Aitkenhead & J. M. Slack (Eds.), *Issues in cognitive modeling: A reader* (pp. 15–62). Hillsdale, NJ: Lawrence Erlbaum.

Saris, W. E., & Stronkhorst, L. H. (1984). *Causal modelling in nonexperimental research: An introduction to the LISREL approach.* Amsterdam: Sociometric Research Foundation.

Schank, R. C., & Abelson, R. (1977). *Scripts, plans, goals, and understanding: An inquiry into human knowledge structures.* Hillsdale, NJ: Erlbaum.

Schwanenflugel, P. (1991). Why are abstract concepts hard to understand? In P. Schwanenflugel (Ed.), *The psychology of word meanings* (pp. 223–250). Hillsdale, NJ: Erlbaum.

Schwanenflugel, P. J., Harnishfeger, K., & Stowe, R. W. (1988). Context availability and lexical decisions for abstract and concrete words. *Journal of Memory & Language, 27,* 499–520.

Seibert, L. C. (1927). An experiment in learning French vocabulary. *Journal of Educational Psychology, 18,* 294–309.

Seidenberg, M. S., Waters, G. S., Barnes, M. A., & Tanenhaus, M. K. (1984). When does irregular spelling or pronunciation influence word recognition? *Journal of Verbal Learning and Verbal Behavior, 23,* 383–404.

Service, E. (1992). Phonology, working memory, and foreign-language learning. *Quarterly Journal of Experimental Psychology: Human Experimental Psychology, 45A,* 21–50.

Shapiro, S. I. (1969). Response word frequency in paired-associate learning. *Psychonomic Science, 16,* 308–309.

Snowling, M., Chiat, S., & Hulme, C. (1991). Words, nonwords, and phonological processes: Some comments on Gathercole, Willis, Emslie, and Baddeley. *Applied Psycholinguistics, 12,* 369–373.

Solso, R. L., & Juel, C. L. (1980). Positional frequency and versatility of bigrams for two- through nine-letter English words. *Behavior Research Methods & Instrumentation, 12,* 297–343.

Stanovich, K. E. (1986). Matthew effects in reading: Some consequences of individual differences in the acquisition of literacy. *Reading Research Quarterly, 21,* 360-407.

Sternberg, R. J. (1987). Most vocabulary is learned from context. In M. G. McKeown & M. E. Curtis (Eds.), *The nature of vocabulary acquisition.* Hillsdale, NJ: Lawrence Erlbaum.

Thorndike, E. L., & Lorge, I. (1944). *The teacher's word book of 30,000 words.* New York: Teachers College, Columbia University.

Tulving, E. (1983). *Elements of episodic memory.* Oxford: Clarendon Press.

Tversky, A. (1977). Features of similarity. *Psychological Review, 84,* 327–352.

Underwood, B. J., & Schulz, R. W. (1960). *Meaningfulness and verbal learning.* Chicago: Lippencott.

Venezky, R. L. (1970). *The structure of English orthography.* The Hague, Holland: Mouton.

Wang, W. S.-Y. (1971). The basis of speech. In C. E. Reed (Ed.), *The learning of language* (pp. 89–105). New York: Appleton-Century-Crofts.

Wimer, C., & Lambert, W. E. (1959). The differential effects of word and object stimuli on the learning of paired-associates. *Journal of Experimental Psychology, 57,* 31–36.

Winograd, E., & Lynn, D. S. (1979). Role of contextual imagery in associative recall. *Memory and Cognition, 7,* 29–34.

Zipf, G. K. (1935). *The psycho-biology of language: An introduction to dynamic philology.* Boston: Houghton Mifflin.

The Effect of Imagery-Based Mnemonics on the Long-Term Retention of Chinese Characters

Alvin Y. Wang and *Margaret H. Thomas*
University of Central Florida

Authors' Statement: *The research reported here suggests that imagery-based memories can be especially prone to long-term forgetting. Frankly, we were not wholly prepared for this finding because it ran counter to many prevailing models of memory. Since then, our laboratory has replicated many times this dramatic decline in long-term memories associated with imagery-based mnemonics. For example, we have documented this effect when the keyword mnemonic is applied to the learning of a second language (e.g., French and Tagalog) and to learning obscure English words. Despite the immediate superiority of using keywords, we find that this imagery-based mnemonic produces consistently greater long-term forgetting compared to a nonmnemonic strategy such as rote rehearsal. We typically obtain results that are similar to those shown in Figure 2 of our reprinted paper.*

What lessons have we been able to draw from this program of research? First, we have stood steadfastly by our original conclusion that language teachers should not assume that learning strategies that boost immediate performance will confer advantages in the long

---

Study 1 was presented at the annual meeting of the Southeastern Psychological Association in Atlanta, Georgia during April 1990.

This research was partially supported by a research grant awarded to the first author by the Division of Sponsored Research at the University of Central Florida. Matthew Lau and Millie Fernandez assisted in stimuli preparation and data collection. The insightful comments of two anonymous reviewers made this a better paper.

term. That is, techniques that foster rapid learning in the classroom may not well serve the student later. Second, whereas rote rehearsal is not a "glitzy" learning strategy, it does seem to promote long-term retention. Perhaps this is a reiteration of what language teachers have known all along—"practice makes perfect". Third, our original finding has prompted us (and others) to investigate the theoretical basis for learning strategies that promote effective long-term performance. Perhaps imaginal codes produce distinctiveness cues that are available only in the short-term; however, relational (i.e., semantic) cues are needed to support long-term retention. And finally, all of these lessons underscore a basic tenet of language acquisition—that successful learning should lead to relatively permanent changes in performance.

Alvin Y. Wang and Margaret H. Thomas
University of Central Florida, 1994

It is well documented that mnemonic devices will enhance acquisition performance and immediate recall compared to either rote learning or unstructured learning (see Bellezza, 1981, for a review). Imagery-based mnemonic devices such as the keyword technique, the method of loci, and the one-is-a-bun pegword system all display strong positive effects when acquisition and immediate recall are assessed. In terms of language learning, the keyword technique in particular has received a great deal of attention with respect to its influence upon second-language learning. The beneficial application of keyword mnemonics has been demonstrated for several second languages, including French, German, Latin, Spanish, Russian, and Tagalog (Atkinson, 1975; Atkinson & Raugh, 1975; Pressley, Levin, Nakamura, Hope, Bispo, & Toye, 1980; Derochers, Pressley, Levin, & Delaney, 1982; Gelinas, & Wieland, 1989; Thomas, Wang, Ouellette, & Porcelli, 1990; Wang, Thomas, & Ouellette, 1992).

Interestingly, whereas imagery-based mnemonic devices produce substantial benefits for learning and immediate recall, there exists no direct evidence indicating that they confer long-term advantages when forgetting is evaluated. For instance, the few studies that have examined this issue have not provided a definitive interpretation of their results in that the same participants were used for both immediate and delayed tests of recall (e.g., Groninger, 1971; Ott, Butler, Blake, & Ball, 1973; Pressley & Levin, 1985; Rosenheck, Levin, & Levin, 1989). Because a participant's learning speed and recall performance tend to be correlated (Underwood, 1954; Wang, 1991), and because tests of immediate recall provide an additional opportunity to learn (Slamecka & Katsaidi, 1988), measures of long-term retention that have not controlled for differences in degree of original learning will be confounded. The presence of this confounder in the aforementioned studies has rendered conclusions regarding the long-term effect of mnemonic devices problematic. To control for the confound established by repeated measures testing, the two present studies examined immediate and delayed recall using a between-students design.

Interestingly, with the exception of these earlier studies, it seems that the long-term influence of mnemonic devices has been assumed rather than empirically tested.[1] Theoretically, several memory models have predicted reduced forgetting under conditions in which material is acquired mnemonically. For instance, the "levels of processing" approach (Craik & Lockhart, 1972), the dual coding view (Paivio, 1971), and the attribute models of memory (Bregman, 1968) all expect less forgetting when mnemonic devices are used rather than rote learning. In these memory models, elaborative strategies such as mnemonic devices are presumed to increase the durability or retrievability of memories relative to simple repetition. Stated differently, elaborative rehearsal should produce less forgetting compared to maintenance (rote) rehearsal. Thus, Paivio (1971) has asserted that "the use of mnemonic pegs can reduce forgetting over long retention intervals" (p. 338).

Recently, we conducted a series of studies that examined the issue of long-term retention of second-language vocabulary (Thomas et al., 1990; Wang et al., 1992). Specifically, we compared the retention rates for second-language vocabulary words that were learned using either the keyword technique or by rote learning.

The critical first step of this technique is for the experimenter to supply participants with keywords that are phonetically similar to an aspect of a second-language vocabulary item. For example, *eye* is an appropriate keyword because it corresponds to the pronunciation of the second syllable in the Spanish word for horseman *caballero*. Next, the learner is asked to form an interactive image that incorporates both the keyword and *caballero*'s English translation. A suitable image might the eye of a horse. Later, on tests of cued recall, *caballero* will elicit the keyword *eye*, which, in turn, allows the learner to retrieve the image incorporating the English translation, horseman.

To avoid the confound between acquisition and retention performance, all of our earlier studies used a between-students 2×2 factorial design. The two factors were Learning Condition (mnemonic vs. rote) and Time (immediate vs. delay). In Study 1, French words were learned and recalled either immediately or after a one-week delay. In Studies 2 and 3, the same basic procedure was followed except that Tagalog (the national language of the Philippines) words were used as second-language stimuli. These studies differed in terms of the number of study trials given to participants in the rote learning condition. Despite differences in language stimuli and variations in procedure, a remarkably consistent pattern emerged across all three studies. First, when the number of study trials was equal, the keyword technique produced significantly higher levels of immediate recall compared to rote learning. This result replicates earlier research demonstrating the effectiveness of mnemonic devices for acquisition performance and immediate recall. Second, we also determined that keyword mnemonics do not confer any long-term advantages beyond the immediate test of recall. Indeed, in all of these experiments, greater forgetting was obtained for items acquired using the keyword technique compared with items acquired using rote learning.

Although unanticipated by the memory models discussed above, these results are understandable when the notion of *encoding variability* is taken into account (Martin, 1972; Hasher

& Johnson, 1975). In this view, experimenter-imposed encodings may be readily retrieved when testing is immediate because temporal and contextual cues associated with keyword encodings are still available. However, after a delay, spontaneous participant-generated encodings will regain their prominence and thereby interfere with keyword retrieval. For example, the encoding evoked by the keyword *eye* may be only one of several possible encodings for the word *caballero*. However, if *ball* (or *cab*) was a learner's spontaneous encoding, then it will more likely be reinstated after a delay compared to *eye*. In contrast, given the cognitive demands of rote learning, fewer opportunities for producing spontaneous encodings may be expected. Yet, the few participant-generated encodings that are produced will likely be reinstated after an extended period of time. Consequently, less long-term forgetting will be obtained under conditions of rote learning compared to experimenter-imposed mnemono-technics.

The rationale for the current studies was to extend these findings (Thomas et al., 1990; Wang et al., 1992) by assessing the effect of an experimenter-supplied, imagery-based mnemonotechnic other than the keyword system. We began with the notion that "image-hospitable" language material would provide the ideal test for studying the long-term effect of an imagery-based learning strategy. Consequently, selected Chinese characters (ideographs) were chosen as language stimuli because their etymological heritage is based upon ideographic rather than phonetic representation. The elaborative strategy that we developed takes advantage of the imagery and symbolism that is suggested visually by many Chinese characters. Thus, participants in the mnemonic learning condition were given a brief description of each ideograph's etymological origin with respect to its visual components. Because our intention was to have participants simply recall each character's meaning, there was no attempt to have learners pronounce any of the Chinese language stimuli. The highly visual nature of this mnemonic system was emphasized during both acquisition and recall by prompting participants to integrate the appearance of each ideograph with an experimenter-supplied image that would assist in the recall of its English equivalent. In contrast, rote learning participants traced over the ideograph and wrote its English equivalent as many as six times each. Although a few participant-generated encodings are inevitable, the requirement to trace and write reduced this spontaneous activity in a manner analogous to verbalized rote learning used in our previously cited research.

Study 1 tested the delayed recall of 30 ideographs after a two-day retention period, whereas in Study 2, delayed recall of 24 ideographs followed a one-week interval. In the first experiment, total study time for the two learning conditions was identical. In Study 2, learning time was increased for the rote learning group so that their immediate recall levels would be comparable to the mnemonic group. For both studies the critical question was the same: would any long-term advantage accrue to the mnemonic group?

Study 1

Method

Participants. A total of 64 undergraduate students served as participants in partial fulfillment of class requirements in an Introductory Psychology course. Because they were contacted at the start of the fall semester, none had participated in any prior psychological study. All were native English speakers and none had any familiarity with the Chinese language. Participants were randomly assigned to one of the four treatment conditions.

Design and Materials. A 2×2 between-students design was used in partial replication of our earlier research. The two factors were Time (immediate vs. delay test) and Learning Condition (rote vs. imagery). Because there are two retention periods, it is possible to plot the lines relating retention (y axis) and time (x axis) for each learning condition. In this analysis, the steeper the slope of the line, the greater the forgetting over time. Accordingly, a Condition × Time interaction, as revealed by a 2×2 Analysis of

Variance (ANOVA) would suggest different rates of forgetting for material learned under different study conditions (Slamecka & McElree, 1983).

The stimuli consisted of 30 Chinese ideographs along with their English translations. These characters were selected because their visual qualities were based directly upon a picture from their etymological past. Therefore, with proper instruction, recall of their meanings may be derived from the visual image that is evoked upon the presentation of any of these characters. For instance, consider the ideographs for *prisoner* and *nest* shown in Figure 1. The ideograph for *prisoner* is actually a combination of the symbol for *man* (the inverted Y-shape) surrounded by the four walls of a room. Similarly, the more complex ideograph for *nest* is derived from the juxtaposition of three simpler symbols: a tree (the lower portion of the ideograph), a bird's feathers (the three strokes at the top), and the actual nest denoted by the box shape occupying the middle of the ideograph. Consequently, the ability to form the appropriate image to each ideograph would permit learners access the meanings (English equivalents) of these Chinese characters. As many as three different colors were used for slides in the mnemonic condition so that the various elements of an ideograph were easily discernable to participants. The following are the English equivalents for the 30 Chinese ideographs used in Study 1: angry, ask, black, boundary, bright, calculate, clasp, crowd, dawn, east, faithfulness, good, hear, I, leak, loyal, mother, nest, old, pen, prisoner, rich, safe, see, sit, straight, urine, wife, wisdom, woods.[2]

Prisoner

Nest

Figure 1. Examples of two Chinese ideographs and their English equivalents

To reduce item sequence effects, groups of up to 4 participants studied the material using different random orderings of
stimuli from other groups during acquisition. In addition, two
different versions of the cued (written) test for recall were also
devised.

Procedure. Total study time for each of the Chinese characters and their English translations was held constant at 30
seconds in both learning conditions. For participants in the rote
learning condition, ideographs and their English equivalents
were presented on booklets using black and white characters
across three study trials. Each page in the booklet contained an
English word and its corresponding Chinese ideograph followed
by a blank space. Participants turned the pages in the booklets at
a 10-second rate and traced over each Chinese character twice and
wrote its English translation twice during this interval. Thus, by
the end of acquisition, each ideograph and its English equivalent
was written a total of six times in the rote condition: twice for each
of the three study trials.

In contrast, participants receiving experimenter-supplied
images were instructed to recognize the ideographic qualities of
Chinese characters and to relate the unique visual aspects of each
character to its English equivalent. All 30 ideographs in this
learning condition were shown using color slides. There was only
one acquisition trial in this condition; however, each slide was
viewed in conjunction with its mnemonic description for a total of
30 seconds. All imagery-based descriptions were presented via
prerecorded cassette tapes. For instance, the Chinese character
for *prisoner* was described as visually symbolizing the concept of
four walls depicted in black ink, surrounding a man symbolized by
red ink. Similarly, the ideograph for *nest* was described as the
combination of a tree (green ink), bird's feathers (blue ink), and
the nest drawn in brown ink.

Immediately after acquisition, a three-minute "general knowledge" questionnaire was given to all participants to eliminate
recency effects and to minimize the chance of spontaneous rehearsal. This 24-item, paper-and-pencil test included topics that

were unrelated to any of the study material (e.g., "Was Frank Sinatra born in New Jersey or Sicily?").

Half of the participants in each learning condition were tested either immediately or after a two-day retention period. Retention was assessed using tests of cued recall in which the Chinese ideographs were presented in black ink on a test sheet. Participants were allowed an unlimited amount of time to write down the English equivalents to each ideograph in the appropriate blank spaces. To discourage spontaneous rehearsal of the study material during the delay interval participants were led to believe that the experiment was only concerned with their preferences for various types of learning strategies. This cover story was first introduced at the beginning of each experimental session and then reiterated at the end of acquisition for delay participants. A debriefing questionnaire administered to all participants after completion of their recall tests indicated that the cover story was successful—only about 10% of the participants in any of the treatment conditions indicated that they thought about the study materials during the retention period.

Results

To evaluate errors of omission and commission, recall was scored both stringently and leniently. The stringent recall analysis scored an item as correct only if an English word was written next to its appropriate Chinese ideograph. The lenient recall method scored any English equivalent as correct regardless of its placement on the test sheet. Because there were virtually no errors of commission, only the analysis of stringent recall will be discussed. Figure 2 depicts mean stringent recall as a function of learning condition and retention interval. A 2×2 completely randomized Analysis of Variance indicated that there was no main effect of Condition, $F(1, 60)=2.32$. However, there was a main effect for Time, $F(1, 60)=35.23$, $p<.001$, indicating that forgetting had occurred in both learning conditions. More critical was the presence of a significant Condition×Time interaction, $F(1,$

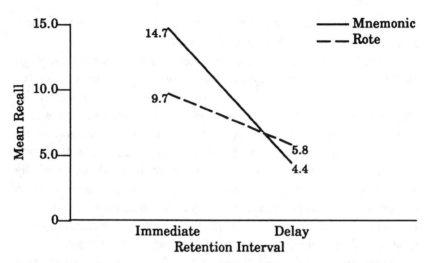

Figure 2. Mean stringent recall in Study 1 as a function of Learning Condition (mnemonic vs. rote learning) and Time (immediate vs. two-day delay)

60)=7.18, $p<.01$. Fisher's Least Significant Difference (LSD) Test indicated that whereas mnemonic instruction was superior to rote learning on the immediate test for recall, retention levels for both learning conditions were highly comparable after a two-day delay, $LSD=3.37$, $p<.05$. In fact, more than twice as many ideographs were forgotten in mnemonic compared to rote learning condition (10.3 vs. 3.9 items, respectively). The steeply sloped line representing the mnemonic learning condition in Figure 2 reflects this finding. Therefore, it appears that greater forgetting occurs under conditions of experimenter-supplied images compared to rote learning. This finding corroborates other evidence indicating that the keyword technique produces greater forgetting than does rote learning (Thomas et al., 1990; Wang et al., 1992).

Study 2 was designed to replicate this finding across a longer retention interval (one week rather than two days). Another rationale for Study 2 was prompted by the argument that the relatively low immediate recall of the rote learning group in Study 1 (about 30% of the items) constituted a floor effect that minimized the chance for substantial long-term forgetting to occur. Therefore, Study 2 was also devised to determine whether experimenter-provided images would confer a long-term advantage when the immediate recall performance of both learning conditions was equated. Pilot studies had indicated that an additional (seventh) study trial in conjunction with a reduction in the total number ideographs (from 30 to 24) would boost the immediate recall performance of the rote learning condition to sufficient levels.

Study 2

Method

Participants. Students enrolled in an introductory psychology class participated in partial fulfillment of course requirements. Participants that had participated in any other psychological study on learning and memory were not included in the analysis. Also, no participants had any familiarity with the Chinese language. Therefore, the data are based upon a final N=80 native English speakers. Participants were tested in groups of up to four individuals, and assignment to one of the four treatment conditions (n=20) was random.

Design and Materials. As in Study 1, a 2×2 factorial design was used with Time (immediate vs. delay) and Learning Condition (rote vs. imagery) as the between-participants factors. However, in contrast to the earlier study, the delay recall interval was lengthened from two days to one week. Also, 24 ideographs were selected from the total pool of 30 items used in Study 1. The criterion for selection was that each written character should contain the fewest number of written strokes, thereby simplifying the writing task of participants in the rote learning condition. The English equivalents of the 24 chosen ideographs were: angry, ask, black, boundary, bright, calculate, clasp, dawn, east, faithfulness, good, hear, I, loyal, mother, nest, old, prisoner, rich, see, sit, straight, wife, and woods.

Procedure. The total exposure times to each stimulus were

30 seconds and 42 seconds for the mnemonic and rote learning conditions, respectively. Study items (an ideograph and its English equivalent) in the rote learning condition were presented on individual pages in booklets. Acquisition for participants in this condition occurred across seven trials during which a page was turned every 6 seconds. Participants were instructed to trace each ideograph and to write its English translation during this 6-second interval. The Study 1 controls for reducing item sequence effects were also used in the present investigation.

Participants receiving imagery-based instructions were treated in the same manner as Study 1. Similarly, the immediate and delayed tests of cued recall were administered in the manner described earlier. In addition, the same cover story was used at the beginning and end of acquisition to reduce the likelihood that participants would rehearse the items during the delay interval. The cover story proved successful because only about 15% participants in either delay condition indicated that they had thought about the material during the retention period.

Results

Figure 3 shows mean cued recall as a function of Time and Learning Condition. Because the analyses for stringent and lenient recall were virtually identical, discussion will be confined to stringent recall. A 2×2 completely randomized ANOVA revealed that the main effect of Time, $F(1, 76)=112.16, p<.001$, and Learning Condition were significant, $F(1, 76)=4.30, p<.04$. The two-way interaction was not obtained, $F<1$. That Fisher's Least Significant Difference Test indicated that the two learning conditions did not differ from one another on either the immediate or delayed test of recall, $LSD=2.56, p<.05$ is probably due to the conservative nature of this statistic. Two critical observations become apparent when this pattern of results is considered. First, our attempt to boost the immediate recall levels of the rote learning group proved successful. Second, despite equating the immediate recall performance of the two learning conditions, no

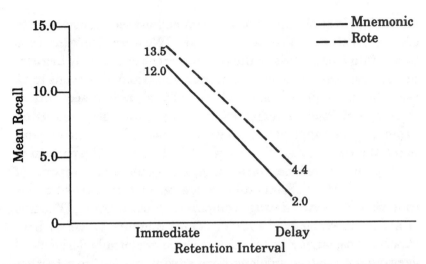

Figure 3. Mean stringent recall in Study 2 as a function of Learning Condition (mnemonic vs. rote learning) and Time (immediate vs. one-week delay)

support was garnered for the notion that imagery-based mnemonics produce long-term benefits when recall is assessed against rote learning. This later finding corroborates the pattern of results reported in Study 1.

General Discussion

We reported two studies that assessed both immediate and delayed recall of English equivalents of Chinese ideographs learned either under conditions of rote learning or imagery-based instruction. In Study 1, when total exposure time was held constant (30 seconds) across learning conditions (i.e., mnemonic vs. rote learning), there was a distinct advantage for imagery-based instruction on the immediate test of cued recall. Nevertheless, when cued recall was assessed two days later, retention levels for the mnemonic and rote learning conditions were highly comparable. The rationale for Study 2 was to replicate this finding with a one-week retention interval. In addition, we asked whether this pattern of results would be obtained when the immediate recall performance of both learning conditions was equated. We were able to increase immediate recall levels in the rote learning condition by increasing the total exposure time for study items (from 30 seconds to 42 seconds) and by providing an additional study trial of acquisition. Once again, Study 2 indicated that ideographs acquired using experimenter-supplied images were no more likely to be remembered than were items that were rote rehearsed. The pattern of findings presented here are congruent with earlier reports of greater forgetting of second-language vocabulary learned under conditions of keyword usage compared to rote learning (Thomas et al., 1990; Wang et al., 1992). Thus, contrary to widely held expectations, supplying learners with mnemonically derived images did not produce any long-term advantages for the retention of second-language vocabulary items.

Indeed, the present studies suggest that Chinese ideographs acquired via experiment-supplied, imagery-based mnemonics were especially prone to forgetting. As suggested earlier, one possible explanation for the greater forgetting associated with these mnemonic devices concerns the notion of encoding variability (Martin, 1972; Hasher & Johnson, 1975). In this view, the mnemonic description accompanying each ideograph may differ from the spontaneous, preexperimental encodings of individual participants. The presence of contextual and temporal cues associated with these experimenter-imposed images would be expected to enhance immediate recall performance. However, it will be the spontaneous participant-generated encodings that are more likely to be reinstated after an extended retention interval. Thus, suggesting that an ideograph represents a nest does not mean that learners will consistently arrive at this interpretation, especially after an extended delay. Consequently, the immediate advantage that may accrue to material studied with experimenter-imposed images will be largely evanescent in nature.

The concept of encoding variability also applies to the recall performance of the rote learning groups in the present studies. Whereas the requirements of repetitively tracing a Chinese ideograph and writing an English word may be operationally defined as rote learning, the possibility exists that automatic and spontaneous encodings will still occur (Pressley & Levin, 1985). In effect, instructions to rote rehearse will not eliminate the activation of implicit knowledge. To the extent that these encodings integrate the semantic properties of the studied items, long-term forgetting will be somewhat diminished for rote learning groups. Thus, the durability of some of their memories is due to the occasional, yet inevitable activation of self-generated encodings that may function mnemonically.

This analysis draws support from other research that has directly examined the efficacy of experimenter-supplied versus participant-generated encodings (Hasher & Johnson, 1975; Pelton, 1969; Schwartz, 1971; Wall & Routowicz, 1987; Wang, 1983). All of these studies employ variations of a yoked-experimental design in which the elicited encodings of one group of learners are collected and "carried-over" to another group of participants studying the same material. Typically, the collected encodings are obtained from participants who had received some form of mnemonic instruction, such as the use of interactive imagery. The findings reported by all of these studies is that experimenter-supplied encodings are not as effective as are participant-generated encodings, even when the specific encodings involved are identical. Stated more concretely, successful long-term retention of a Chinese ideograph such as *nest* may be expected if students had thought of the mnemonic image themselves. In contrast, long-term retention may not be as successful if the mnemonic image for *nest* was teacher-supplied rather than student-generated.

The present findings suggest that instruction in the use of mnemonic strategies should emphasize the ability of learners to discover and apply their own mnemonic cues. Pedagogically, teachers should not assume that providing mnemonic devices to their students will "automatically" strengthen memories for the study material; a strict reliance on teacher-supplied mnemonics can produce immediate benefits in the classroom, but long-term advantages may prove more elusive.

Notes

[1]A rich history of debate concerning the use of mnemonotechnics antecedes the present discussion by several centuries. For many medieval thinkers and writers, "the art of memory" was considered vital for the development of cultured eloquence and effective rhetoric (Yates, 1966). However, not all early scholars were convinced. As the historian J. D. Spence (1984) notes in *The Memory Palace of Matteo Ricci*, Cornelius Agrippa stated that "monstrous images" dulled one's natural memory and often "caused madness and frenzy instead of profound and sure memory". In a similar manner, Francis Bacon concluded that mnemonic devices were fundamentally barren and of "ostentation prodigious".

[2]A list of stimulus materials (both Chinese and English), as well as their imagery-based descriptions may be requested from the first author.

References

Atkinson, R. C. (1975). Mnemonotechnics in second -language learning. *American Psychologist, 30,* 821–828.

Atkinson, R. C., & Raugh, M. R. (1975). An application of the mnemonic keyword method to the acquisition of Russian vocabulary. *Journal of Experimental Psychology: Human Learning and Memory, 104,* 126–133.

Bellezza, F. S. (1981). Mnemonic devices: Classification, characteristics, and criteria. *Review of Educational Research, 52,* 247–275.

Bregman, A. S. (1968). Forgetting curves with semantic, phonetic, graphic, and contiguity cues. *Journal of Experimental Psychology, 78,* 539–546.

Craik, F. I. M., & Lockhart, R. S. (1972). Levels of processing: A framework for memory research. *Journal of Verbal Learning and Verbal Behavior, 11,* 671–684.

Derochers, A., Gelinas, C., & Wieland, L. D. (1989). An application of the mnemonic keyword technique to the acquisition of German nouns and their grammatical order. *Journal of Educational Psychology, 81,* 25–32.

Groninger, L. D. (1971). Mnemonic imagery and forgetting. *Psychonomic Science, 23,* 161–163.

Hasher, L., & Johnson, M. K. (1975). Interpretive factors in forgetting. *Journal of Experimental Psychology, 1,* 567–575.

Martin, E. (1972). Stimulus encoding in learning and transfer. In A. W. Melton & E. Martin (Eds.), *Coding processes in human memory* (pp. 59–84). Washington, DC: V. H. Winston & Sons.

Ott, E. C., Butler, D. C., Blake, R. S., & Ball, J. P. (1973). The effect of interactive-image elaboration on the acquisition of foreign language vocabulary. *Language Learning, 23,* 197–206.

Paivio, A. (1971). *Imagery and verbal processes*. New York: Holt, Rinehart and Winston.

Pelton, L. H. (1969). Mediational construction vs. mediational perception in paired associate learning. *Psychonomic Science, 17*, 220–221.

Pressley, M., & Levin, J. R. (1985). Keywords and vocabulary acquisition: Some words of caution about Johnson, Adams, and Bruning (1985). *Education Communication and Technology, 33*, 277–284.

Pressley, M., Levin, J. R., & Delaney, H. D. (1982). The mnemonic keyword method. *Review of Educational Research, 52*, 61–91.

Pressley, M., Levin, J. R., Nakamura, G. V., Hope, D. J., Bispo, J. G., & Toye, A. R. (1980). The keyword method of foreign vocabulary learning: An investigation of its generalizability. *Journal of Applied Psychology, 65*, 635–642.

Rosenheck, M. B., Levin, M. E., & Levin, J. R. (1989). Learning botany concepts mnemonically: Seeing the forest and the trees. *Journal of Educational Psychology, 81*, 196–203.

Schwartz, M. (1971). Subject-generated versus experimenter-supplied mediators in paired-associate learning. *Journal of Experimental Psychology, 87*, 389–395.

Slamecka, N. J., & Katsaidi, L. T. (1988). Normal forgetting of verbal lists as a function of prior testing. *Journal of Experimental Psychology: Learning, Memory, & Cognition, 14*, 716–727.

Slamecka, N. J., & McElree, B. (1983). Normal forgetting of verbal lists as a function of their degree of learning. *Journal of Experimental Psychology: Learning, Memory, & Cognition, 9*, 384–397.

Spence, J. D. (1984). *The Memory Palace of Matteo Ricci*. New York: Viking.

Thomas, M. H., Wang, A. Y., Ouellette, J., & Porcelli, L. (1990, April). *The keyword mnemonic and remembering a foreign language*. Paper presented at the annual meeting of the Southeastern Psychological Association, Atlanta, GA.

Underwood, B. J. (1954). Speed of learning and amount retained: A consideration of methodology. *Psychological Bulletin, 51*, 276–282.

Wall, H. M., & Routowicz, A. (1987). Use of self-generated and others' cues in immediate and delayed recall. *Perceptual and Motor Skills, 64*, 1019–1022.

Wang, A. Y. (1983). Individual differences in learning speed. *Journal of Experimental Psychology: Learning, Memory, and Cognition, 9*, 300–312.

Wang, A. Y. (1991). Assessing developmental differences in retention. *Journal of Experimental Child Psychology, 51*, 348-363.

Wang A. Y., Thomas, M. H., & Ouellette, J. A. (1992). Keyword mnemonic and retention of second-language words. *Journal of Educational Psychology, 84*, 520–528.

Yates, F. A. (1966). *The art of memory*. Chicago: University of Chicago Press.

SECTION III

LEXICAL ACQUISITION AND USE IN COMMUNICATION TASKS

Classroom Interaction, Comprehension, and the Acquisition of L2 Word Meanings

Rod Ellis, Yoshihiro Tanaka, and Asako Yamazaki
Temple University Japan

Author's Statement: *This paper reports on an attempt to examine the role of premodified and interactionally modified input in the acquisition of word meanings in a classroom context. Although a number of previous studies have demonstrated that giving learner opportunities to negotiate meaning when they fail to understand promotes comprehension, no previous study has been able to support the claim that interactionally modified input facilitates language acquisition. This paper, then, is to be seen primarily as a contribution to the study of input and interaction in L2 acquisition. The decision to focus on the acquisition of word meaning (rather than the acquisition of grammatical structures) was taken for two reasons. First, descriptive studies have shown that meaning negotiation is frequently triggered by learners' failure to understand specific lexical items. Second, in an experimental study involving relatively little exposure to the L2, it is much easier to measure gains in knowledge of word meaning than it is gains in grammatical knowledge.*

The study provides evidence to support claims that interactionally modified input is especially beneficial in facilitating the acquisition of word meanings. Further research is needed to demonstrate whether it also facilitates the acquisition of other aspects of language (e.g., grammatical structures) and also to explore which specific properties of this type of input aid acquisition.

Rod Ellis, Temple University, Philadelphia, 1995

The authors acknowledge the help they have received from Tere Pica and from a number of anonymous reviewers.

When second language (L2) learners experience communication problems and have the opportunity to negotiate solutions to them, they are able to acquire new language. This claim, which originated in the work of Long (1981), has been referred to as the *interaction hypothesis* (Ellis, 1990). The hypothesis advances two major claims about L2 acquisition:

1. Comprehensible input is necessary for acquisition;
2. Modifications to the interactional structure of conversations in the process of negotiating solutions to communication problems help make input comprehensible to the learner.

The first claim originates in Krashen's (1980) *input hypothesis*. However, whereas Krashen emphasized the role of simplified input and contextual support in making input comprehensible, Long argued that negotiated interaction is especially important. This is based on Long's (1981) finding that whereas few "input" differences were found in speech addressed to L2 learners as compared to speech addressed to native speakers, several "interaction" differences were noted. For example, although there was no difference in type-token ratio or number of S-nodes/T-units,[1] there were significant differences in the frequency of conversational modifications.

Long (1983a) has provided a detailed account of the conversational modifications involved in negotiating meaning. They include comprehension checks (speaker checks whether interlocutor has understood something), confirmation checks (speaker attempts to ascertain whether s/he has heard or understood something interlocutor said) and clarification requests (speaker requests help in understanding something interlocutor said). These devices provide learners with opportunities to resolve their comprehension difficulties and therefore make negotiation of meaning possible.

According to the interaction hypothesis, therefore, L2 acquisition is promoted if learners have opportunities to solve communication problems by means of conversational modifications. Long (1981) demonstrated that communication tasks involving a two-way exchange of information (e.g., where learners have to find the difference between two nearly identical pictures) lead to more conversational adjustments than do tasks involving only a one-way exchange of information (e.g., giving instructions). Long (1983b) argued, therefore, that two-way exchanges of information ought to provide more comprehensible input and thus promote acquisition more effectively than one-way exchanges of information. He has also argued, on the basis of a study of interaction in ESL lessons at the elementary level in the United States, that "the SL classroom offers very little opportunity to the learner to communicate in the target language or to hear it used for communicative purposes by others" (Long 1983b; 348). In other words, comprehensible input obtained through meaning negotiation is in poor supply in many classrooms. Because comprehensible input is seen as necessary for acquisition to take place, this lack of opportunity to negotiate meaning is considered an impediment to acquisition.

The interaction hypothesis (Fig. 1) (Long, 1983b, p. 214) can be tested by examining (a) whether negotiated modification of conversation leads to comprehensible input and (b) whether comprehensible input leads to language acquisition.

Pica, Young, and Doughty (1987) specifically addressed the claim that negotiated modification promotes comprehension. As

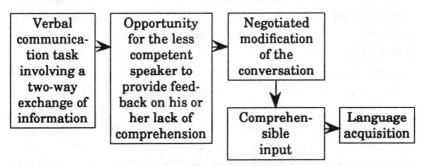

Figure 1. Model of the interactive hypothesis.
Note. From *On TESOL '82: Pacific Perspectives on Language Learning and Teaching* (p. 214) by M. Clarke and J. Handscombe (Eds.), 1983, Washington, DC: TESOL. Copyright 1983 by TESOL. Reprinted with permission.

their study provided a basis for the studies we undertook, we will report it in some detail. They divided 16 low-intermediate female learners into two groups. One group received directions requiring them to choose and place items on a small board illustrated with an outdoor scene. These directions were derived from "baseline" directions (i.e., directions produced in interaction between native speakers of English). These were systematically modified in order to increase redundancy and decrease complexity. The other group received the baseline directions, but were given opportunities individually to seek verbal assistance from a researcher if they did not understand. Thus, although the learners in this group all received the same baseline directions, they participated in nego-tiation to different extents and, as a result, received differing amounts of interactionally modified input. In this way, the researchers aimed to compare the effects of (a) *premodified input* and (b) *interactionally adjusted input* on comprehension (mea-sured as the number of correct learner responses to the directions). The results indicated that interactionally adjusted input did result in higher levels of comprehension (88% vs. 69%). The input from the restructured interactions was quantitatively greater, more elaborate, and more redundant than both premodified and baseline input. Also, an analysis of individual directions showed that "modifications of interaction were most effective in achieving comprehension when the learners had difficulty in understanding the input but were superfluous when the input was easily under-stood" (Pica et al., 1987, p. 747). The study, then, supports that part of the interaction hypothesis that claims modifying conversa-tion through negotiation results in better comprehension.

Pica et al.'s (1987) study did not address whether learners need to participate actively in the negotiation of meaning or whether it suffices for them simply to have access to input interactionally adjusted through the efforts of others. Pica (1992) reports a study that examined this question. This study had three groups: (a) negotiators, who had opportunities to actively negoti-ate the meaning of the directions, (b) observers, who observed the negotiators but did not themselves negotiate, and (c) listeners, who performed the task later, listening to the teacher read directions based on the interactionally modified input with no opportunity for interaction. The comprehension scores of the three groups were negotiators 88%, observers 78%, and listeners 81%, but the differences were not statistically significant. However, when Pica examined the results for individual learners in the three groups, she found some evidence that, whereas learners who have achieved a high level of comprehension ability do not need to rely on negotiation to comprehend input, those with low levels of comprehension ability do. She noted this result's compatibility with Long's (1983b) assertion that negotiation is of special value in the early stages of L2 acquisition.

The postulated relationship between negotiated interaction and comprehension has not gone unchallenged, however. First, two studies suggested that the kind of elaborate input that can result from negotiation does not always aid comprehension. Derwing (1989) found that native speakers (NSs) who included more information (in describing a film they had seen) when addressing learners than when addressing other NS interlocutors were less successful in communicating with the learners than were those NSs who did not elaborate as much. Ehrlich, Avery, and Yorio (1989) also found that NSs differed in the amount of information they gave to learners in a problem-solving task. Whereas some adopted a "skeletonizing" strategy (i.e., provided only the basic information needed), others adopted an "embroidering" strategy (i.e., provided information that expanded and embellished beyond what was required). Ehrlich et al. reported that the embroiderers created problems for the learners by making it difficult for them to identify essential information and the source of communication problems. On the basis of this study, the authors concluded that "the role of negotiations within the second language acquisition process is still an open question" (Ehrlich et al., p. 411). These two studies suggest that the greater quantity of input that results from negotiation may not in itself aid comprehension. Of course, perhaps not so much the quantity as the quality of negotiated input is important.

There is another reason why negotiation may be less beneficial for comprehension than Long (1983b) has surmised. Both Hawkins (1985) and Aston (1986) have pointed out that learners may sometimes feign comprehension after negotiation rather than continue to demonstrate incomprehension to their interlocutors. Aston argues for a social perspective on what he calls "trouble-shooting procedures" to complement Long's psycholinguistic perspective. He points out that excessive troubleshooting procedures may jeopardize communication from a social point of view.

To sum up, the first part of the interaction hypothesis (negotiation of meaning aids comprehension) has largely been established, although some doubts persist, mainly because we know little about how negotiation contributes to comprehension. In contrast, the second part (comprehension leads to acquisition) is much less secure. First, there is no direct empirical support for it. Second, there are strong theoretical arguments against it.

Comprehension and Acquisition

Long (1981, 1983b) gives only indirect empirical evidence to support a close relationship between comprehension and acquisition. He places considerable store on the fact that evidence from studies of hearing children with deaf caretakers shows that "acquisition is either severely delayed or does not occur at all if comprehensible input is unavailable" (1983b, p. 209). However, the one study that has attempted to establish a direct relationship between negotiated interaction and acquisition failed to find supporting evidence. Loschky (1989) investigated three groups of L2 learners of Japanese exposed to sentences containing locative expressions under three conditions: (a) baseline input (i.e., unsimplified input), (b) premodified input, and (c) interactionally modified input. Like Pica et al., (1987), Loschky found that those learners receiving interactionally modified input achieved higher comprehension scores than the others. However, when he tested for retention of the locative constructions, he found no advantage for the group receiving interactionally modified input.

A number of theoretical attacks on the claim that comprehension leads to acquisition (Ellis, 1991; Færch & Kasper, 1986; Greg., 1984; Sharwood Smith, 1986; White, 1987) hinge on the point that the processes responsible for comprehension and for acquisition are not the same. Rost (1990) defines listening comprehension as "essentially an inferential process based on the perception of cues rather than straightforward matching of sound to meaning" (p. 33). In other words, comprehension involves top-down processing, which obviates the need for learners to attend to the actual forms present in the input. In line with current theorizing that acquisition can only take place if learners notice new material in the input (Schmidt, 1990), we can hypothesize that when comprehension takes place by means of inferencing based on an existing schema the learners do not notice new material and therefore do not acquire it. As Færch and Kasper (1986) argued, only when there is a "gap" between the input and the learner's interlanguage and—crucially—when the learner perceives this gap as a gap in linguistic knowledge, can acquisition take place.

However, to abandon the general claim that comprehension is important for acquisition runs counter to intuition. Clearly, if learners receive input they do not understand, they will not learn much from it, if only because they are likely to "switch off" their attention very rapidly. Ellis (1991) has suggested that a weaker form of the interaction hypothesis can be maintained if it is accepted that (a) comprehension does not necessarily lead to acquisition and (b) that only some interactional modifications (those that cause learners to notice new material in the input) promote the kind of comprehension that fosters acquisition. Assumption A is, of course, compatible with Krashen's (1980) and Long's (1983b) view that comprehensible input will only work if learners are developmentally ready to attend to the structures in the input.

Finally, we should note that the claims advanced regarding the importance of comprehensible input in L2 acquisition do not preclude a role for learner production. Swain (1985) has argued

convincingly that learners may need access to what she calls
"pushed output" in order to advance to higher levels of grammatical proficiency. She suggested that pressure to produce language
that is concise and appropriate may help learners test hypotheses
about the L2 and encourage them to engage in syntactic as
opposed to semantic processing. Swain's arguments in favor of
"comprehensible output" are not intended to displace those in
favor of comprehensible input, but rather to complement them.

Given the lack of any direct empirical support for the interaction hypothesis, we obviously need a study that investigates
whether negotiated interaction does set up the conditions for
acquisition. However, the success of such studies could depend on
how well they operationalize the concept of acquisition—so far, a
cloudy area in interaction studies.

Lexical Acquisition

Discussions of the interaction hypothesis typically refer to
acquisition, without specifying what is to be acquired. Probably
Krashen (1980) and Long (1981, 1983a, 1983b), along with most
other SLA researchers of the 1970s and early 1980s, saw *acquisition* primarily in terms of the mastery of the L2's grammatical
system. Other language levels—phonology, vocabulary, and discourse—were paid scant attention. Meara (1980) considered
vocabulary a "neglected aspect of language learning" (p. 221).

There are, however, good reasons for considering the interaction hypothesis in relation to vocabulary acquisition. Sato (1986)
has pointed out that meaning negotiation may sometimes work
against, rather than for, the acquisition of morphological features, as comprehension of problematic utterances can be achieved
without learners having to attend to such features in the input.
This is less likely in the case of troublesome lexical items. Whereas
learners may not be aware of a grammatical source of their
incomprehension, they are much more likely to recognize a lexical
source and therefore to seek clarification of its meaning. In fact,
an examination of the examples of meaning negotiation provided

in the published studies indicates that the problem source is often lexical.

The main foci of vocabulary acquisition research have been the effectiveness of various strategies for memorizing new items (e.g., Cohen, 1990) and the extent learners are successful in inferring the meaning of new items from written texts (e.g., Li, 1989). In addition, some work has investigated the effects of listening to stories on vocabulary acquisition (e.g., Elley, 1989). Brown (1993) has also examined the effects of the frequency and saliency of words in oral input from a videodisk program. However, the role of oral input in L2 vocabulary acquisition has received very little attention—in a 1993 collection of papers only Brown's (1993) dealt with oral input—and, to the best of our knowledge, the role of interaction has not been considered at all.

The acquisition of a new lexical item is a complex process. It involves discovering the frequency with which the item is used in speech and writing, its situational and functional uses, its syntactic behavior, its underlying form and the forms that can be derived from it, the network of associations between it and other items, its semantic features and, of course, the various meanings associated with the item (Richards, 1976). Furthermore, as Carter (1987) emphasized, learning to recognize an item is different, and presumably, less difficult, than learning how to produce it. Unfortunately, we as yet know little about how L2 learners gradually acquire all this information. One could reasonably suppose that learners begin by ascertaining one meaning of an L2 item—by establishing its referent, by identifying an L1 equivalent or by some other means—and then gradually fill out their knowledge of the item as they subsequently encounter it.

In the studies reported below, we will be concerned with the recognition of L2 word meanings as a possible test of the interaction hypothesis. That is, we will examine to what extent learners acquire an understanding of the basic reference of a number of items which have concrete referents by testing their ability to supply L1 translations of the items or label pictures. We are interested in the extent to which an interactional context, where learners can negotiate problems in understanding sentences containing these items, enables them to obtain a foothold in the process of acquiring them. We thus ask the following research questions:

1. Does interactionally modified input result in better comprehension of L2 word meanings than either unmodified or premodified input?

2. Does interactionally modified input result in better retention of L2 word meanings than either unmodified or premodified input?

These general question can be broken down into a set of more specific hypotheses to be tested:

1. Input gathered through interaction (direct or observed) will differ in quantity, redundancy, and complexity from input gathered either by unmodified instruction (baseline input) or by listening to input derived from previously recorded interactions (premodified input).

2. Learners who receive input through direct or observed interaction will achieve higher levels of L2 comprehension than those exposed to unmodified instruction or to premodified input.

3. Learners in interactive situations will learn and retain more L2 words that those receiving the other two types of input.

4. Learners in interactive situations who actively participate in negotiating meaning will achieve higher levels of L2 comprehension that those who do not.

5. Learners in interactive situations who actively participate in negotiating meaning will learn and retain more L2 words than those who do not.

These hypotheses address the relative advantages of nonmodified, premodified, and interactionally modified input on both comprehension and vocabulary learning. They also address the important issue of whether direct participation in interaction leads to better comprehension and vocabulary learning than does indirect participation.

Method

Two separate studies, which we will call the Saitama Study and the Tokyo Study, were undertaken in different teaching contexts. However, the design of both was the same. This afforded a number of advantages, in particular, enabling us to establish how much the results were influenced by situational factors.

Participants

In the Saitama Study, the participants were 79 third-year students at a public high school in Saitama, Japan. They had studied English for five years previously. The students had been divided into three classes (28 in Group 1, 27 in Group 2, and 24 in Group 3) according to their previous English grades at the school, the aim being to create groups of equal ability. They were studying an elective course, English IIA, the goal of which was to develop listening and speaking ability.

In the Tokyo Study, the participants were 127 first-year high-school students in a Tokyo metropolitan high school, Japan. They had studied English for three years previously. They were in three intact classes (43 in Group 1 and 42 each in Groups 2 and 3). The classes were of equal overall academic ability, as measured by a school entrance examination, which included a test of English.[2] They all received six English classes each week, one of which was taught by a native speaker of English.

One important difference between the students in the two studies was that the students in the Tokyo Study generally had high expectations of entering a prestigious Japanese university on completion of high school whereas those in the Saitama Study did not. English is a required subject in the entrance examinations of universities in Japan.

Design

Both studies utilized the same multifactorial design with two dependent variables (listening comprehension and vocabulary acquisition) and two independent variables (premodified input and negotiated input). The three groups in both studies were designated Baseline Group (B), which functioned as a control group, the Premodified Group (PM) and the Interactionally Modified Group (IM). Each group experienced the following:

1. *The pretest*: This was administered to all the groups one month prior to the commencement of the treatment.

2. *The treatment*: This took the form of a listening task performed by a different native speaker in each study and completed within one class period (about 45 minutes). The native speakers were both Assistant English Teachers in the schools in question. In the Saitama Study, the teacher was male and American with one year's experience of teaching English. In the Tokyo Study, the teacher was female and British with several years' teaching experience. The nature of the treatment differed from group to group, as described below.

3. *The posttests*: The participants in the two experimental groups (PM and IM) in both studies completed two posttests, one 2 days after the treatment and the other about a month later. The participants in the control group (B) of the Tokyo Study also completed these posttests. However, the students in the control group (B) of the Saitama Study did not, because they were inadvertently taught the target items by another teacher unaware that they were part of the study.

4. *The follow-up test*: This was administered one month after the second posttest when the students returned from summer vacation, about $2\frac{1}{2}$ months after the treatment.

Instruments

The purpose of the pretest was to establish a set of lexical items unknown to the students. It consisted of 65 English words that they were asked to translate into Japanese. These words included a set of words labeling a kitchen, which were designated as potential target items, distracter items such as *fireplace* and *closet*, and a number of basic words likely to have been already acquired by the students. On the basis of the results, we selected 18 items, all unknown by the students, as target items in the Saitama Study. We chose 19 items, which were unknown by at least 88% of the students, for the Tokyo Study. The items chosen for the two studies overlapped but were not identical, as the students' previous lexical knowledge differed slightly.

The first posttest required the students to translate the target items into Japanese. In case they did not know the Japanese equivalent of an item, they were allowed to write down a circumlocution or paraphrase. In the Saitama Study, the 18 items were: *sink, scouring pad, shelf, lid, garbage can, canister, broom, pot holder, stove, saucepan, faucet, dishwashing liquid, counter, eggplant, dustpan, plate, dish drainer,* and *ladle.* In the Tokyo Study, the 19 items were: *sink, dish drainer, cabinet, shelf, eggplant, lid, faucet, scouring pad, outlet, broom, dustpan, saucepan, stove, pot holder, garbage can, counter, blender, plate canister.* Participants were awarded one mark for each correctly translated item.

The second posttest was the same as the first in both studies, except that the order of the target items was changed to mitigate against any possible test-taking effect.

In the follow-up test all the students in each study were given a picture of a kitchen and a list of their target items in English. We asked them to use all the items in the list to label the picture. They were awarded one mark for each object in the picture they labeled correctly.

Treatment

The treatment took the form of a listening task in which we asked the students to listen to a set of directions. Each direction included the name of a kitchen utensil and reference to a specific position in a picture of a kitchen. We provided the students with individual pictures of the different kitchen utensils and a matrix picture of the kitchen. (The materials for this task can be found in Appendix A.) The students demonstrated their comprehension by choosing from the individual pictures of kitchen utensils and then writing the number of the chosen picture in the correct position in the matrix picture in accordance with the teacher's directions. Each student's matrix picture was collected at the end of the treatment. Their performance on this task provided a measure of comprehension; their responses to a direction were awarded one mark if (a) they chose the correct utensil and (b) also located this object in the correct position in the matrix picture. The students were familiar with the locational expressions used in the directions (e.g., *in, on top of, the right side, on*) as a result of previous instruction; failure to comprehend a direction occurred when they were unable to identify the correct object or the part of the kitchen (e.g., *sink, floor, stove*) in which to place it.

Although the task that each group was asked to perform was the same, the directions that they listened to differed. Two versions of these directions were prepared.

The baseline directions. These were derived from an audio-recording of two native speakers performing a version of the same task. They each in turn chose one of the kitchen utensils and gave instructions to the other about where to position it in the matrix picture. We prepared a transcript of their interactions and used it to write a set of baseline directions. For example:

> We have an apple. And I'd like you to put the apple in the sink.
> Can you find the scouring pad? Take the scouring pad and put it on top of the counter by the sink—the right side of the sink.

There were 15 such directions in the Saitama Study and 16 in the Tokyo Study.

The premodified directions. To prepare these, the task was performed by three students drawn from the same population as those in the two studies. These students interacted with a native speaker giving the baseline directions. The students were allowed to request clarification if they did not understand. The interactions were audio-taped and transcribed. We derived modified versions of the baseline directions from the transcriptions of these interactions, incorporating the increased redundancy that had resulted from the native speaker's repetitions and paraphrases of problematic items. We adjusted the transcribed directions in only one respect: If they became overly long, the object's name and location were repeated at the end. Examples are:

> I have an apple. And I'd like you to put the apple in the sink. A sink is a hole and you wash dishes inside it and you fill it with water. It's a hole in a counter to put water and dishes.
>
> Can you find the scouring pad? A scouring pad—*scour* means to clean a dish. A scouring pad is a small thing you hold in your hand and you clean a dish with it. Take the scouring pad and put it on top of the counter by the sink— on the right side of the sink.

The premodified input contained many more repetitions of the items than did the baseline input. We decided to ensure that the premodified directions were spoken more slowly than the baseline directions, as in the preliminary task the students frequently asked the native speaker to speak more slowly.

The task was performed in three different ways:

Baseline Group (B). The control group in each study listened to the teachers read the baseline version of the directions at about 180 words per minute (wpm). A short pause between each direction allowed the students to write down their answers on the matrix picture and the native-speaking teachers to check they had done so. No interaction between students and teachers was allowed.

The Premodified Group (PM). The students in this group listened to the premodified version of the directions. The native-speaking teachers read each direction slower (about 90 wpm), pausing to check that the students had written down their answers after each direction. No interaction between students and teachers was allowed.

The Interactionally Modified Group (IM). The students in this group listened to the baseline version of the directions read at the same speed as for the control group (180 wpm). However, whereas the students in the other two groups were not permitted to interact with the teacher, those in Group 3 were. Because Japanese high-school students are often reluctant to interact, the teacher wrote a number of formulas for requesting clarification on the board, for example:

Will you please speak more slowly?
What is a ———?
Will you say it again?
Where do I put the ———?
Could you say it again?

The native speakers modified the initial directions in accordance with students' requests,[3] thereby repeating many items. We placed no limit on the length of the interaction resulting from a single direction. However, to ensure that comprehension of the task would be based only on spoken input, we instructed the teachers not to use any gestures. The interactions were audio-taped and transcriptions prepared.

Results

The results reported below provide data about our five hypotheses for both studies: (a) the redundancy and complexity of the input made available to the three groups, (b) the comprehension scores achieved by the three groups, (c) the relationship between interactional modifications and comprehension, (d) the vocabulary acquisition scores of the three groups and, for the Tokyo Study only, (e) the relationship between individual students' active participation in meaning negotiation and their comprehension and vocabulary acquisition scores.

The results, therefore, will examine the following:

1. *Redundancy* in the input: the number of times a target item is repeated in a direction.

2. *Complexity*: the number of S-nodes over T-units per direction (see Note 1)

3. *Comprehension*: whether the participants were able to identify the right objects and place them in the correct locations in the matrix picture of the kitchen

4. *Vocabulary acquisition*: the scores obtained on the translation posttests and the picture-identification follow-up test

5. *Interactional modifications*: the number of requests for clarification, requests for confirmation, and comprehension checks made by either a student or the teacher in accomplishing each direction

An Input Analysis

As might be expected, the length of the treatment given to each group varied considerably. In the case of the Saitama Study, the control group (B) received about 6 minutes of instruction, the premodified group (PM) about 10 minutes, and the interactive group (IM) about 45 minutes. The times in the Tokyo Study were approximately 10 minutes, 20 minutes, and 45 minutes, respec-

Table 1
An Analysis of the Three Kinds of Input

Type of Input	Quantity	Redundancy	Complexity
Saitama Study			
1. Baseline	20.07	1.27	1.00
2. Premodified	48.53	4.40	1.07
3. Interactionally Modified	98.73	14.73	1.05
Difference Between 2 & 3	$t=3.55$	$t=3.79$	$t=0.62$
	$df=28$	$df=28$	$df=28$
	$p<.001$	$p<.001$	$p=.54$ns
Tokyo Study			
1. Baseline	19.19	1.13	1.02
2. Premodified	49.31	4.94	1.09
3. Interactionally Modified	77.50	13.25	1.21
Difference Between 2 & 3	$t=2.526$	$t=4.104$	$t=2.090$
	$df=30$	$df=30$	$df=30$
	$p<.05$	$p<.001$	$p<.05$

Quantity=Number of words per direction; Redundancy=Number of repetitions of target items per direction; Complexity=S-nodes/T-units per direction

tively, for the three groups. Clearly, then, the IM group was exposed to more input than the other two groups. The analysis shown in Table 1 confirms this difference. In both studies, the number of words per direction was substantially greater in the IM input than in the PM input, which was more than double than that of the baseline input.

The input available to the three groups also differed with regard to redundancy. We computed a redundancy score by counting the number of repetitions of the target item (e.g., *pot holder*) and the location for the item (e.g., *over the stove*) in each direction and then calculating the mean number of repetitions in the input available to each group. As Table 1 shows, the difference between the interactionally modified input and the baseline/ premodified input is considerable. In the Saitama Study, the interactionally modified input contained a mean of 14.73 repetitions per direction and in the Tokyo Study a mean of 13.25.

Complexity of input (measured by calculating S-nodes/T-units per direction—see Note 1) differed much less. In the Saitama Study, the differences were negligible. In the Tokyo Study, however, the interactionally modified input was significantly more complex than the premodified input ($p<.05$).

In summary, in both studies the IM group received more input (longer directions) and also more redundant input (more repetitions of the key items) as a result of the interaction that took place. However, the IM group experienced more complex input only in the Tokyo Study.

Comprehension of the Directions

We calculated the comprehension scores for correctly carrying out the directions for all the learners in each group (see Appendix B) and tested the differences between the three groups by a one-way analysis of variance (ANOVA). The results are shown in Table 2. In the case of the Saitama Study, the ANOVA revealed a significant difference in the three groups. A post-hoc Scheffé test (Table 3) indicated that the students in the IM group

Table 2
Comparison of Comprehension Scores Across Three Groups

Source of Variance	SS	df	MS	F
Saitama Study				
Between Groups	802.44	2	401.22	48.64*
Within Groups	626.90	76	8.25	
Tokyo Study				
Between Groups	1680.39	2	840.20	113.37*
Within Groups	919.02	124	7.41	

*p< .05

Table 3
Scheffé Test of Differences in Comprehension Across the Three Groups

Group	Baseline Group	Premodified Group	Interactionally Modified Group
Saitama Study			
Mean	2.32	4.04	9.91
Baseline Group		2.13	10.28 *
Premodified Group			2.13 *
Tokyo Study			
Mean	1.20	6.79	10.69
Baseline Group		8.14 *	14.74 *
Premodified Group			6.58 *

*p< .05

achieved significantly higher comprehension scores than both the B group and the PM group. The IM group outscored the PM group on every single direction. However, the difference between the comprehension scores of the B group and the PM group was not significant. In the Tokyo Study, similar results were obtained. Again, the IM group obtained the highest comprehension score, with PM next and B group last. In this case, however, the difference between the PM group and the B group was sufficient to reach statistical significance ($p<.05$). In fact, on three directions the PM group outscored the IM group, indicating a much higher level of comprehension in this group than in the equivalent group in the Saitama Study.

Taken together, the studies demonstrate that the group receiving interactionally modified input comprehended the directions more fully than did either the group receiving baseline input or the group receiving premodified input. Premodified input was also found to facilitate comprehension in the Tokyo Study.

The Relationship Between Interactional
Modifications and Comprehension

The comprehension scores for each direction (see Appendix C) indicated that whereas the opportunities for interaction enabled the IM group to comprehend some directions much more successfully than the PM group, there were other directions where interaction proved less effective. Given that Long (1983b) argued that it is not interaction per se but rather modified interaction that is important for acquisition, we examined whether the number of modifications (defined as requests for clarification, requests for confirmation, and comprehension checks) could account for this difference. We counted individual utterances performing each of these functions, identifying instances where the discourse context made it clear the communicative purpose was that of negotiating meaning.

We reasoned that if interactional modifications facilitated acquisition, they would occur with higher frequency in those directions where the difference between the PM group's and the IM group's comprehension scores was considerable than in those directions where the difference in comprehension scores was less marked. We identified the four directions where the difference was greatest and the four where it was smallest in each study and then counted the number of modifications occurring in the interactional sequences triggered by these directions. The results are shown in Table 4.

Table 4
Interactional Modifications in Relation to Comprehension Score
Differences Between Premodified and Interactionally Modified Groups

Directive	Comprehension Difference (IM–PM scores)	Interactional Modifications
Saitama Study		
1	79.3%	3
6	75.4%	7
8	65.7%	4
14	60.0%	4
Total		18
Mean		4.5
7	6.2%	9
15	12.9%	4
2	14.3%	12
12	12.9%	4
Total		29
Mean		7.25

U' (Mann Whitney Test–Small Sample Case)= 2; p=ns

Tokyo Study		
16	50.0%	4
7	47.7%	10
4	42.8%	2
2	35.7%	7
Total		23
Mean		5.75
10	–9.5%	2
14	–9.5%	6
13	–4.7%	2
8	4.8%	3
Total		13
Mean		3.25

U' (Mann Whitney Test–Small Sample Case)=6; p=n.s.

In the Saitama Study, more modifications occurred on those directions where the difference between the PM and IM group's comprehension scores was least. In the Tokyo Study, the opposite result was obtained; more modifications occurred in those directions where the IM group performed much better than the PM group. However, when we tested the differences between the number of modifications in the two sets of directions by means of the Mann Whitney test, we found they were nonsignificant in both studies. In other words, the frequency of modifications was not significantly related to comprehension scores.

Vocabulary Acquisition

In the case of the Tokyo Study, the extent to which the three groups acquired the target lexical items was measured by means of two posttests (one administered two days after the treatment and the other approximately two weeks later) and a follow-up test (administered approximately six weeks after the treatment). In the case of the Saitama Study, no posttest or follow-up scores are available for the B (control) group for reasons already explained. (The scores for individual learners in the two studies can be found in Appendix B.)

In the case of the Tokyo Study, we compared the differences in the three groups' vocabulary acquisition scores in Posttest 1, Posttest 2 and the follow-up test of the three groups by means of separate ANOVAs. The results are reported in Table 5. These show significant group differences in all three tests. Post-hoc Scheffé tests were carried out to identify specific differences between the means of the three groups. The results are shown in Table 6. In the case of the Saitama Study, we could only compare the vocabulary acquisition scores of the PM and IM groups. The results of the *t*-tests used to make this comparison are shown in Table 7.

In the Saitama Study, the IM group demonstrated the ability to accurately supply translation equivalents of the target items to a greater extent than the PM group shortly after the treatment (Posttest 1) and they also maintained this advantage over a two-week period (Posttest 2). Furthermore, this group was better able to match the target items with pictures than the PM group six

Table 5
Vocabulary Acquisition Scores Across Three Groups in the Tokyo Study

Source of Variance	SS	df	MS	F
Posttest 1				
Between Groups	262.16	2	131.08	19.32*
Within Groups	841.29	124	6.78	
Posttest 2				
Between Groups	145.92	2	72.96	11.32*
Within Groups	798.89	124	6.44	
Follow-up Test				
Between Groups	118.09	2	59.05	9.54*
Within Groups	767.67	124	6.19	

*p<.05

Table 6
Scheffé Test of Differences Across Three Groups in the Tokyo Study

Group	Baseline Group	Premodified Group	Interactionally Modified Group
Posttest 1			
Mean	2.02	4.02	5.55
Baseline Group		3.38*	4.90*
Premodified Group			2.93*
Posttest 2			
Mean	2.53	4.29	5.10
Baseline Group		3.12*	3.93*
Premodified Group			2.18
Follow-up Test			
Mean	4.05	5.60	6.36
Baseline Group		2.89*	3.65*
Premodified Group			2.11

*p<.05

Table 7
Vocabulary Acquisition Scores in Two Groups in the Saitama Study

	n	M	SD	t value	df	p
Posttest 1						
PM Group	27	2.52	2.38			
IM Group	24	6.00	2.72	4.88	49	<.001
Posttest 2						
PM Gpoup	27	2.59	2.02			
IM Group	24	4.75	2.66	3.28	49	<.002
Follow-up Test						
PM Group	27	4.70	2.30			
IM Group	24	7.08	3.34	2.99	49	<.004

PM=Premodified; IM=Interactionally Modified

weeks after the instruction (follow-up test). However, it is not possible to say whether either the IM or PM group had performed better than the B group.

In this respect, the Tokyo Study is crucial. The PM and IM groups outperformed the B group on all three vocabulary tests, the results reaching statistical significance in each test ($p<.05$). Thus both short- and longer-term advantages in vocabulary acquisition were evident when learners had access to modified input. The comparisons between the PM and IM groups were less clear-cut, however. Whereas the IM group outscored the PM group on vocabulary learning in Posttest 1, this advantage was lost in Posttest 2 and in the follow-up test. In other words, the group receiving interactionally modified input outscored that receiving premodified input in vocabulary acquisition, but only in the short term.

A detailed examination of the results for the two posttests is revealing. In both the Saitama Study and the Tokyo Study, the vocabulary acquisition scores for the IM group reduced slightly from Posttest 1 to Posttest 2. In the Saitama Study, the vocabulary acquisition scores for the PM group stayed almost the same. However, in the Tokyo Study, the scores for the PM group increased slightly. This, together with the fact that the difference in the Posttest 1 vocabulary scores between the IM and PM groups was initially greater in the case of the Saitama Study than the Tokyo Study, accounts for the difference in results between the two studies.

Meaning Negotiation, Comprehension,
and Vocabulary Acquisition

The relationship between learners' active participation in the classroom interaction experienced by the IM group and their comprehension of the directions and acquisition of the target items was investigated in the Tokyo Study only. Of the 42 learners in the IM group, only 7 engaged actively in meaning negotiation. The others simply listened. Table 8 gives the comprehension scores and the vocabulary acquisition scores in the three tests for these 7 learners. From this it can be seen that 3 of the 7 learners achieved comprehension scores above the mean, 3 achieved vocabulary acquisition scores above the mean for Posttest 1, 4 achieved above the mean for Posttest 2, and 5 achieved above the mean for the follow-up test. It appears, then, that those learners who engaged in active meaning negotiation

Table 8
Comprehension and Vocabulary Acquisition Scores of Learners
Participating Actively in Meaning Negotiation in the Tokyo Study

	Comprehension Score	Posttest 1	Posttest 2	Follow-up Test
Group Mean	10.7	5.5	5.1	6.4
Participant 1	3	7	6	7
Participant 2	5	4	4	7
Participant 3	5	11	9	10
Participant 4	9	3	4	5
Participant 5	0	5	4	2
Participant 6	4	8	8	7
Participant 7	5	4	6	9

did not enjoy a clear advantage in either comprehension or vocabulary acquisition over those who just listened.

Discussion

The studies were designed to investigate five hypotheses, all based on the interaction hypothesis. We will now consider each of these hypotheses in the light of the results reported above.

Research Hypothesis 1

The first hypothesis was that the interactionally modified input experienced by the IM group would differ in quantity, redundancy, and complexity from the baseline input or the premodified input experienced by the PM groups. It was important to find support for this hypothesis, for unless we could show that the opportunity to negotiate communication problems affected the nature of the input the learners received there was no basis for examining the relationship between negotiated input and comprehension/vocabulary acquisition. In fact, the input analysis reported in Table 1 demonstrates clearly that negotiation leads to more input and more redundant input than baseline input. Furthermore, this difference is also evident when special efforts have been made to premodify the baseline input to make it more comprehensible to learners. Contradictory results regarding complexity of input were obtained. A difference was found in the input experienced by the PM and IM groups in the Tokyo Study only, where, contrary to Hypothesis 1, the IM group received more complex input than the PM group.

It might be argued that the difference between the negotiated and premodified input reflects our failure to make the necessary adjustments to the baseline input to ensure that the premodified input was properly matched to the learners' level. However, considerable care was taken to ensure that the premodified directions were delivered at a slow speed and that the teacher provided wait time for the learners to process each one. It is simply difficult to predict precisely what adjustments are needed in vacuo. The whole point of interactionally adjusted input is that it occurs in context when learners signal their comprehension difficulty.[4] It responds to problems rather than predicting them.

Research Hypothesis 2

The second hypothesis is also supported by the results of both studies. The learners in the IM group, who were given the opportunity to negotiate their comprehension problems, were more successful in carrying out the directions correctly. The opportunity to hear key target items repeated and to receive definitions of these items on demand helped them to understand the directions and thus gain higher comprehension scores.

However, maybe the advantage experienced by the interactionally modified group derived not so much from the fact that they could negotiate nonunderstanding as from the fact that they had more time to process the directions and were exposed to more input. Time does seem to have been a factor. The learners in the IM group enjoyed a considerable time advantage over the learners in the B and PM groups and outperformed both in comprehension. Also, the PM learners in the Tokyo Study were given considerably more time to process the directions than were the PM learners in the Saitama Study (20 minutes as opposed to 10), which may have been one reason why they outscored them. More input may also help because it increases redundancy, although, as we noted above, it is not so much the overall quantity of input as the opportunity to receive more input at times when comprehension problems arise that is important. Clearly, from this study we cannot determine whether interaction aids comprehension simply because of the additional time and input it provides or because of qualitative features of the input that it creates. The important point is that it seems natural for the quantity of input to increase when interaction takes place. Trying to examine qualitative features independently of attendant quantitative features may be like trying to investigate how fish swim out of water.

Although interactionally modified input appears to facilitate comprehension, there seems to be no direct relationship between the frequency of interactional modifications (requests for clarification, confirmation checks, and comprehension checks) and comprehension. Directions that stimulated large numbers of modifications were not necessarily the ones where the IM group learners outscored the PM learners. It is, of course, not the interactional modifications themselves that facilitate acquisition but rather the modified input they give rise to. Probably the key lies in discovering the relationship between interactional modification and input modification (see Pica, 1992).

The transcripts of the negotiated directions show that comprehension is something that learners have to work at. They need to identify and address specific problems in the input and to build up comprehension of a linguistically difficult utterance in steps. This is what the opportunity to negotiate gives them, as this example from the Saitama Study illustrates:

T: We have an apple. And I'd like you to put the apple in the sink.
S: What is the sink?
T: Sink is a place to wash dishes. It's a hole where you wash dishes.
S: One more time please.
T: We have an apple. And I'd like you to put the apple in the sink.
S: What is sink?
T: Sink is a hole and you wash dishes in the hole.

The mean comprehension score for this item was 90% in the IM group but only 10.7% in the PM group. The opportunity to negotiate, therefore, clearly helped. In fact, though, there were relatively few interactional modifications in this sequence. How then did the negotiation aid comprehension? The answer seems to lie in the students' ability to identify the source of their comprehension difficulty (*sink*), to make this clear to the teacher and to persist until they had elicited a definition they understood. Gass (1988) has pointed out that there is an important difference between *comprehensible* and *comprehended* input; "comprehensible input is controlled by the person providing input... comprehended input is learner-controlled" (p. 204). As our example sequence illustrates, the opportunity to negotiate gives learners some control over the input. How they make use of this control is important.

However, premodified input can also aid comprehension. In both studies, the learners receiving premodified input achieved higher levels of comprehension than those receiving baseline input, although only in the Tokyo Study did the difference reach statistical significance. The important point is that even when premodified input can be shown to work, it does not work as well as negotiated input. Thus, both studies found that, in general, the learners receiving negotiated input understood the directions better than those receiving premodified input.

Research Hypothesis 3

Comprehending input does not guarantee the acquisition of new word meanings, as the processes of comprehension and acquisition are not identical. However, negotiated comprehension may facilitate acquisition because it induces learners to notice unknown items in the input. If this were the case, we might expect that those learners who experienced negotiated input would acquire more new items than those who did not.

The results lend some support to this argument. In the Saitama Study, the learners who experienced interactionally adjusted input achieved higher vocabulary acquisition scores in the immediate posttest than did those who received premodified input and, importantly, maintained this advantage over time. In the Tokyo Study we were able to show that modified input in general led to more word meanings being acquired than unmodified input. Also, in this study, the learners in the IM group outperformed those in the PM group on the immediate posttest.

We cannot know for certain what in the interactions helped learners to acquire the new items, but we can speculate that the following may have been important:

1. Learners were able to pinpoint precisely the source of their comprehension difficulty. Because of the way the task was described, this was almost invariably the target items.

2. The learners were given multiple opportunities to hear the new items, which may have helped them develop auditory images of the new items.

3. The learners had ample time to process the new items.

4. The learners were able to identify the meanings of the new items by relating the spoken forms to their pictorial referents (Krashen, 1985).

5. The long-term storage of these items may have been facilitated by having the learners carry out an action involving the items (Asher, 1977). That is, the act of responding nonverbally to a directive may help to "fix" new items associated with the action in memory.

We can further speculate that the interactionally modified input was potentially facilitative in all five ways. Premodified input is also helpful—as shown by the Tokyo Study—but less so, perhaps because it is less effective where Factors 1, 2, and 3 above are concerned.

In the Tokyo Study, we found a long-term advantage for interactionally modified input over baseline input but no such advantage over premodified input; the PM group almost caught up with the IM group by Posttest 2 and was not significantly different from the IM group in the follow-up test. Besides, the difference between the PM and IM groups in Posttest 1 was not as great in the Tokyo Study as in the Saitama Study. One possible explanation lies in the overall proficiency of the learners in the two studies. The learners in the Tokyo Study came from a prestigious Tokyo high school and were expected to do well academically, whereas those in the Saitama Study came from a less prestigious and less academically successful public high school. Therefore the learners in the Tokyo Study were probably more proficient overall in English than those in the Saitama Study.

There is, however, another reason why no long-term effect for negotiation was evident in the Tokyo Study. Informal contact with a number of the PM group learners following Posttest 2 revealed that several of them had made efforts to study the new vocabulary privately. This reflected their general high level of motivation to learn English and to do well in tests. If this is the reason, it merely demonstrates what is well-known: New words can be effectively acquired through study and memorization (Nation, 1990). Effective as negotiation may be in promoting vocabulary acquisition, it is certainly not the only way in which new words can be learned. Learners who do not have opportunities to interact in the L2 may be able to compensate by utilizing alternative learning strategies.

Finally, we make no claim that the learners in these studies had fully acquired the new items. Exposure to unknown concrete nouns in premodified or interactionally adjusted input was clearly sufficient to give the learners a knowledge of their word meaning, as was demonstrated by the post- and follow-up tests. We cannot, however, say whether it also gave them a knowledge of how to use these items productively in English sentences.[5] Nor can we say whether similar exposure would enable learners to acquire a knowledge of the meaning of other parts of speech (e.g., adjectives and verbs) or of abstract nouns.

Research Hypothesis 4

In the introduction, we noted that the interaction hypothesis is unclear as to whether active participation in negotiation is required in order for learners to benefit from interactionally adjusted input or whether learners can benefit simply by listening to others negotiate. Hypothesis 4 stated that learners who engaged in active negotiation would achieve higher levels of comprehension than those who merely listened. However, this hypothesis was not supported by the results obtained for the Tokyo Study. Apparently, other factors are responsible for the interlearner variation in comprehension evident in this study.

Research Hypothesis 5

The Tokyo Study also failed to demonstrate that active participation in negotiating meaning was advantageous for vocabulary acquisition. Those learners who listened to others negotiate achieved similar scores to those who engaged actively. Again, other factors must have been responsible for the interlearner variation. Our study, then, lends some support to the claim that active participation may be less important for acquisition than is sometimes claimed. (See Ellis, 1988, for a discussion of the role of participation in L2 acquisition.)

However, neither did our study show that active participation had any detrimental effect on either comprehension or acquisition. Those learners who participated actively did not do any worse than those who just listened.

The finding that active participation is neither necessary nor detrimental to comprehension/ acquisition is important. First, it suggests that listening tasks of the kind used in our study can be beneficially employed in lock-step instruction, with the whole class attending to input supplied by the teacher. This has the advantage of ensuring that learners have access to well-formed input.[6] (See Prabhu, 1987, for arguments in favor of teacher-led task-based instruction.) Second, it suggests that teachers do not have to make efforts to ensure that opportunities for negotiating meaning are evenly distributed across all the learners in the class. It may be sufficient to allow learners to volunteer responses. The work required to comprehend difficult input may be performed publicly through interaction or covertly through mental activity. Those learners who prefer the quieter route can be left to benefit from the interactional activity of their more public comrades.

Implications

Whereas a number of earlier studies have demonstrated that negotiation facilitates comprehension (e.g., Loschky, 1989; Pica et al., 1987), no studies have shown that interactionally adjusted input promotes acquisition. The interaction hypothesis, therefore, has received only partial empirical support. Crucial evidence supporting a direct link between meaning negotiation and language acquisition has been missing. Our studies were designed to address this lack.

Our results confirm the results of earlier studies regarding the role of interaction in comprehension. We have suggested that interaction helps learners work toward comprehension because it gives them control over the input they receive and enables them to systematically identify and solve comprehension problems. In this respect, it is superior to premodified input. Along with Gass (1988), we would argue that it is not comprehensible input but comprehended input that is important and that interaction provides the means by which learners can successfully strive to comprehend.

Our studies' main contribution, however, lies in the support they give for the claim that interactionally modified input facilitates acquisition. One study provides the first clear evidence that access to modified input promotes acquisition.[7] Both show that interactionally modified input leads to the acquisition of more word order meanings than does premodified input. The cornerstone of the interaction hypothesis, therefore, is alive and well. It should be noted, however, that the studies also indicate that premodified input can be effective in promoting acquisition.

These studies have not shown (or tried to show) how interactionally modified input aids acquisition. We have suggested it may help learners notice the items that cause their comprehension problems, construct clear auditory images of these items, and obtain information that helps them to solve comprehension problems. We have argued that learners achieve comprehension because interaction gives them a degree of control over the input they receive and because it buys them time to focus their attention on key or problematic items. Without the opportunity to stop the flow on input, learners may become swamped.

In passing, we note that the positive effects on comprehension and acquisition were achieved by means of a one-way communication task. In the listening task we used, only the teacher had access to the information to be exchanged. Earlier research has suggested that two-way tasks result in more interactional modifications than one-way tasks. Although this may be true, the one-way task used in this study led to interaction that benefited both comprehension and lexical acquisition. It is not clear how sharing the information between teacher and students in a two-way task could have enhanced comprehension or acquisition. Also, along with other researchers (e.g., Ehrlich et al., 1989), we are not convinced that the sheer number of modifications is what is important for either comprehension or acquisition, a caveat bolstered by our results (the absence of any relationship between frequency of interactional modifications and comprehension).

Although our studies support a causative relationship between negotiated interaction and acquisition, we acknowledge the complexity of the acquisition process and the fact that different aspects of language (phonology, vocabulary, morphology, and syntax) may not be acquired in the same way. Our studies examined only vocabulary acquisition, and only the acquisition of the meaning of concrete nouns. It does not follow that negotiated interaction will promote the acquisition of other aspects of the L2 or even that it is important in other aspects of vocabulary acquisition. These issues await investigation.

Finally, we would like to point to a methodological feature. We made use of a single design in two separate studies that drew on different but related populations of learners. This enabled us to compare results across studies and identify where there were similarities, thus allowing us to report our findings with some confidence. It also enabled us to identify where there were differences, suggesting where variables other than those we had tried to control came into play. This dual-study method, thus, helps to establish which findings are robust and generalizable and which are subject to situational variation.

Notes

[1]A T-unit is an independent clause together with any associated dependent clauses. S-nodes are indicated by tensed and untensed verbs. For example, the following T-unit has two S-nodes: "When you make a milk shake, you mix it in a blender".

[2]We did not obtain standardized measures of the participants' proficiency in order to ensure the comparability of the three groups. To have done so would have been to interfere unduly with their instructional program. Also, we felt that comparability of the groups was best assured by demonstrating that there were no group differences with regard to knowledge of the target lexical items. This was achieved by means of the pretest. We would also like to emphasize that it was the policy of both schools to construct classes of equal ability and that in the opinion of the two researchers who carried out the empirical investigations this had been achieved.

[3]There were a total of 59 requests for clarification made by the learners in the Saitama Study, a mean of 3.9 per direction. In the Tokyo Study there were 43 requests for clarification, a mean of 2.7 per direction. Thus, the studies were reasonably successful in prompting the students to request clarification.

[4]In support of this claim, it should be noted that not all the premodified and negotiated directions differed with regard to length and redundancy. For example, in Study 1 there was little difference in the premodified and interactionally modified version of Direction 1.

[5]We consider it likely that productive use of new target items is also fostered by interaction. However, it is possible that this aspect of vocabulary acquisition requires opportunities for learners to *use* items they have begun to acquire and to receive feedback from other speakers. Swain's (1985) notion of *pushed output* may prove to be important where productive use of new items is concerned.

[6]It is, in fact, difficult to envisage how this task could have been performed successfully other than with the teacher taking charge of the input. Given that the directions contained items that were unknown to most of the learners, it would have been very difficult for learners to supply each other with input that led to comprehension. Such tasks do not lend themselves to small groupwork.

[7]It is not clear why these studies found that negotiation aided acquisition, whereas Loschky's (1989) study did not. One possibility lies in the target item. Whereas the target items of our studies were lexical, those in Loschky's study were prepositional particles. Clearly, much work remains to be done to investigate which items or structures are acquirable through interaction and which are not.

References

Asher, J. (1977). *Learning another language through actions: The complete teachers' guidebook.* Los Gatos, CA: Sky Oaks Publications.

Aston, G. (1986). Trouble-shooting in interaction with learners: The more the merrier? *Applied Linguistics, 7,* 128–143.

Brown, C. (1993). Factors affecting the acquisition of vocabulary: Frequency and saliency of words. In T. Huckin, M. Hughes, & J. Coady (Eds.), *Second language reading and vocabulary learning* (pp. 263–286). Norwood, NJ: Ablex.

Carter, R. (1987). *Vocabulary: Applied linguistic perspectives.* London: Allen and Unwin.

Cohen, A. (1990). *Language learning: Insights for learners, teachers, and researchers.* New York: Newbury House/Harper Row.

Derwing, T. M. (1989). Information type and its relation to nonnative speaker comprehension. *Language Learning, 39,* 157–172.

Ehrlich, S., Avery, P., & Yorio, C. (1989). Discourse structure and the negotiation of comprehensible input. *Studies in Second Language Acquisition, 11,* 397–414.

Elley, W. B. (1989). Vocabulary acquisition from listening to stories. *Reading Research Quarterly, 24,* 174–187.

Ellis, R. (1988). The role of practice in classroom language learning. *AILA Review, 5,* 20–39.

Ellis, R. (1990). *Instructed second language acquisition.* Oxford: Blackwell.

Ellis, R. (1991). The interaction hypothesis: A critical evaluation. In E. Sadtono (Ed.), *Language acquisition and the second/foreign language classroom* (pp. 179–211). Singapore: Regional English Language Centre.

Færch, C., & Kasper, G. (1986). The role of comprehension in second language acquisition. *Applied Linguistics, 7,* 257–274.

Gass, S. M. (1988). Integrating research areas: A framework for second language studies. *Applied Linguistics, 9,* 198–217.

Gregg, K. (1984). Krashen's monitor and Occam's Razor. *Applied Linguistics, 5,* 79–100.

Hawkins, B. (1985). Is the appropriate response always so appropriate. In S. M. Gass & C. G. Madden (Eds.), *Input in second language acquisition* (pp. 162–178). Rowley, MA: Newbury House.

Krashen, S. D. (1980). The theoretical and practical relevance of simple codes in second language acquisition. In R. C. Scarcella & S. D. Krashen (Eds.) *Research in second language acquisition* (pp. 7–18). Rowley, MA: Newbury.

Li, X. (1989). Effects of contextual cues on inferring and remembering meanings of new words. *Applied Linguistics, 10,* 402–413.

Long, M. H. (1981a). Input, interaction and second language acquisition. In H. Winitz (Ed.), *Native language and foreign language acquisition* (pp. 259–78). Annals of the New York Academy of Sciences 379.

Long, M. H. (1983a.) Native speaker/non-native speaker conversation and the negotiation of comprehensible input. *Applied Linguistics, 4*, 126–41.

Long, M. H. (1983b). Native speaker/non-native speaker conversation in the second language classroom. In M. Clarke & J. Handscombe (Eds.), *On TESOL '82: Pacific perspectives on language learning and teaching* (pp. 207–225). Washington, DC: TESOL.

Loschky, L. (1989). *The effects of negotiated interaction and premodified input on second language comprehension and retention.* Unpublished master's thesis, University of Hawaii, Honolulu.

Meara, P. (1980). Vocabulary acquisition: A neglected aspect of language learning. *Language Teaching and Linguistics: Abstracts, 15*, 221–246.

Nation, P. (1990). *Teaching and learning vocabulary.* New York: Newbury House/Harper Row.

Pica, T. (1992). The textual outcomes of native speaker-non-native speaker negotiation: What do they reveal about second language learning? In C. Kramsch & S. McConnell-Ginet (Eds.), *Text and context: Cross-disciplinary perspectives on language study* (pp. 198–237). Lexington, MA: D. C. Heath and Company.

Pica, T., Young, R., & Doughty, C. (1987). The impact of interaction on comprehension. *TESOL Quarterly, 21*, 737–758.

Prabhu, N. S. (1987). *Second language pedagogy.* Oxford: Oxford University Press.

Richards, J. (1976). The role of vocabulary teaching. *TESOL Quarterly, 10*, 77–89.

Rost, M. (1990). *Listening in language learning.* London: Longman.

Sato, C. (1986). Conversation and interlanguage development: Rethinking the connection. In R. R. Day (Ed.), *Talking to learn: Conversation in second language acquisition* (pp. 23–45). Rowley, MA: Newbury House.

Schmidt, R. (1990). The role of consciousness in second language learning. *Applied Linguistics, 11*, 129–158.

Sharwood Smith M. (1986). Comprehension vs. acquisition: Two ways of processing input. *Applied Linguistics, 7*, 239–256.

Swain, M. (1985). Communicative competence: Some roles of comprehensible input and comprehensible output in its development. In S. M. Gass and C. G. Madden (Eds.), *Input in second language acquisition* (pp. 235–252). Rowley, MA: Newbury House.

White, L. (1987). Against comprehensible input: The input hypothesis and the development of second language competence. *Applied Linguistics, 8*, 95–110.

Appendix A: Materials Used in the Listening Task

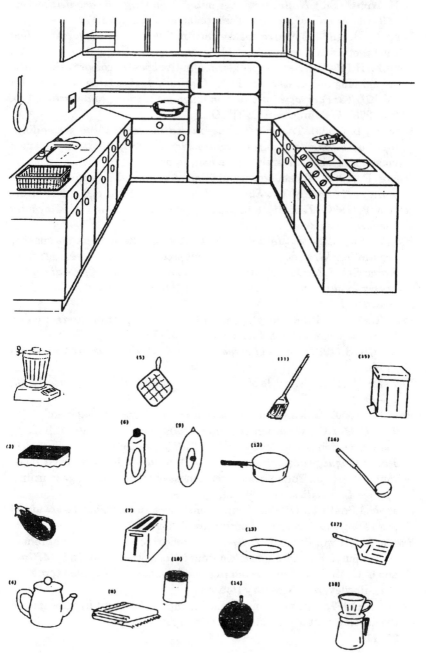

Table B–1
Comprehension and Vocabulary Acquisition Scores for Individual Learners

Learner	B Group				PM Group				IM Group			
	1	2	3	4	1	2	3	4	1	2	3	4
Saitama Study												
1	1				2	1	2	5	4	0	0	5
2	0				7	4	3	3	3	2	1	2
3	2				3	1	2	5	3	3	1	3
4	0				4	1	2	1	13	8	6	9
5	6				0	0	0	2	13	11	6	7
6	2				4	3	3	6	10	6	5	7
7	3				2	2	0	7	9	7	5	10
8	5				3	5	5	6	7	6	7	7
9	1				1	1	3	7	12	4	5	5
10	8				6	0	1	2	13	8	10	9
11	0				6	2	2	5	15	12	7	14
12	1				3	2	2	5	10	7	6	9
13	1				2	0	1	1	8	3	3	3
14	5				1	1	1	2	9	6	5	7
15	4				8	8	7	8	12	7	7	4
16	2				3	2	3	4	12	7	7	12
17	2				3	1	3	3	9	8	7	11
18	1				5	1	0	5	12	6	3	5
19	1				8	2	0	4	12	5	1	2
20	4				4	6	6	7	12	6	2	5
21	2				1	1	2	3	9	7	7	12
22	4				3	6	3	4	3	4	3	7
23	4				0	1	2	6	14	8	8	10
24	1				11	9	8	10	14	3	2	5
25	0				7	3	2	2				
26	2				9	3	4	7				
27	2				3	2	3	7				
28	1											

Table B–1 (continued)
Comprehension and Vocabulary Acquisition Scores for Individual Learners

Learner	B Group				PM Group				IM Group			
	1	2	3	4	1	2	3	4	1	2	3	4
Tokyo Study												
1	2	2	1	3	7	3	2	4	15	14	11	10
2	0	0	0	1	6	4	4	6	4	4	5	7
3	1	3	4	6	2	2	1	4	16	4	6	5
4	2	4	2	6	2	2	3	3	13	7	5	7
5	1	2	0	3	9	5	4	5	10	6	8	7
6	2	1	2	2	3	4	6	5	13	5	5	7
7	1	1	2	5	8	3	5	5	6	6	3	7
8	3	3	7	6	7	3	3	4	11	10	9	9
9	0	3	3	3	10	11	12	10	9	7	6	6
10	3	5	5	5	7	2	3	3	7	2	2	3
11	1	2	3	5	10	7	6	8	15	12	9	10
12	3	3	4	5	2	3	3	5	13	12	12	11
13	1	3	3	9	15	6	5	9	6	3	2	3
14	5	2	4	3	14	11	10	12	5	1	1	3
15	2	4	6	6	9	5	5	8	16	9	5	8
16	0	0	5	7	6	1	2	5	6	5	3	5
17	4	5	4	5	5	5	7	7	13	10	8	8
18	3	5	5	7	13	9	9	7	14	10	9	11
19	0	1	2	2	7	6	3	5	13	4	4	7
20	1	0	2	2	4	1	0	1	8	2	2	3
21	1	1	2	4	7	1	1	1	13	2	2	5
22	1	1	1	4	9	1	4	7	9	3	4	5
23	1	1	1	4	4	0	0	1	10	1	0	1
24	2	2	3	5	8	5	5	4	9	3	3	6
25	3	1	2	4	6	2	2	5	11	5	4	2
26	2	2	1	3	4	3	2	3	10	4	4	10
27	1	0	1	0	9	4	5	8	11	8	7	11
28	4	0	1	5	4	4	2	6	9	2	2	8
29	1	0	0	4	7	5	6	5	14	8	9	10
30	2	4	6	3	7	4	7	7	14	1	3	4
31	5	1	0	3	4	2	3	5	14	8	6	5
32	2	2	2	3	3	1	1	7	16	8	7	6
33	1	0	0	0	12	7	7	11	11	8	7	8
34	5	4	6	5	7	6	7	6	7	3	3	2

Table B–1 (concluded)
Comprehension and Vocabulary Acquisition Scores for Individual Learners

Learner	B Group				PM Group				IM Group			
	1	2	3	4	1	2	3	4	1	2	3	4
Tokyo Study												
35	2	1	1	5	2	4	2	5	13	4	5	6
36	3	1	5	3	7	5	8	10	14	2	5	7
37	0	5	2	4	9	4	5	8	9	4	4	4
38	3	0	1	3	4	4	2	3	5	4	6	9
39	2	4	3	3	11	6	5	8	10	11	10	11
40	2	2	2	4	8	3	7	4	9	3	1	0
41	3	4	4	6	4	1	1	3	9	5	4	5
42	4	0	0	5	3	4	5	2	9	3	3	5
43	0	2	2	3								

1=Comprehension; 2=Posttest 1; 3=Posttest 2; 4=Follow-up Test

Table C–1
Mean Comprehension Scores on Each Direction for Groups 2 and 3

Direction	Group 2 %	Group 3 %	Difference (Group 3–Group 2)
Saitama Study			
1. sink	10.7	90.0	79.3
2. scouring pad/counter	35.7	50.0	14.3
3. ladle	39.3	76.7	37.4
4. shelf	28.6	60.0	31.4
5. lid	17.9	66.7	48.8
6. garbage can/stove	17.9	93.3	75.4
7. canister	7.1	13.3	6.2
8. broom	14.3	80.0	65.7
9. pot holder	25.0	66.7	41.7
10. saucepan	46.4	76.7	30.3
11. faucet	0.0	26.7	26.7
12. dishwashing liquid	53.6	73.3	19.7
13. eggplant	35.7	76.7	41.0
14. dustpan	3.6	63.6	60.0
15. plate/dish drainer	57.1	70.0	12.9
Tokyo Study			
1. sink	59.5	92.9	33.4
2. scouring pad/counter	40.5	76.2	35.7
3. cabinet	45.2	78.6	33.4
4. shelf	38.1	80.9	42.5
5. lid	42.9	73.8	30.9
6. garbage can/stove	33.3	57.1	23.8
7. canister	30.9	78.6	47.7
8. broom	59.5	64.3	4.8
9. pot holder	21.4	33.3	11.9
10. saucepan	59.5	50.0	–9.5
11. faucet	16.7	45.2	28.5
12. eggplant	66.7	76.2	9.5
13. dustpan	21.4	16.7	–4.7
14. plate/dishdrainer	61.9	52.4	–9.5
15. outlet	52.4	69.0	16.6
16. blender	33.3	83.3	50.0

Reading, Dictionaries,
and Vocabulary Learning

Stuart Luppescu
University of Chicago

Richard R. Day
University of Hawaii

Author's Statement: *Our original research interests lay along the lines of vocabulary acquisition, and inferring meaning from context, while reading. Could dictionary use have an effect on this? When we began to investigate this topic, we were struck by the lack of previous research. Surely something as ubiquitous and essential as the dictionary would have been the subject of much study. Not so. We found there had been almost no work done on the value of dictionaries, their use, selection, or effect on vocabulary learning.*

The results we came up with were also surprising. For one thing, we expected that dictionaries would not have a significant effect on the amount of vocabulary learned. As foreign language learners and as ESL teachers we have observed the ephemeral nature of the memory of words we and our students have looked up in the dictionary. Moreover, some theories of language acquisition predict that vocabulary that is learned in context may have greater permanence than words that are looked up in the dictionary. Thus, we were quite surprised when the group that used dictionaries during reading did significantly better than the group that did not. The other unexpected finding was that in some cases, using the dictionary can inhibit vocabulary learning. This was attributed to the effect of a large number of entries in the dictionary presumably confusing the stu-

The authors appreciate the help given by all the teachers who cooperated with us in this study. In addition, we are indebted to Naoko Matsushima for her help in data entry. Our appreciation is also extended to Benjamin D. Wright and Terry Santos for their comments on previous versions of this report.

229

dents. We take this as a strong argument for explicit instruction and practice in dictionary use in the foreign language classroom.

One of the unanswered questions in the original study was whether the enabling effect of dictionary use on vocabulary learning would decline over time. This was tested by Ha (1992), who found that even when the test was given as much as three weeks after the students had read the passage, the group that used dictionaries did significantly better on the vocabulary test than the group that did not. The most important question raised by this study is whether the results can be generalized beyond a single vocabulary test given after reading a single passage: In general, over the long term, will the student who uses a dictionary acquire more vocabulary than a student who does not? Ha's work seems to indicate that the vocabulary learning that we detected may not be fleeting, but can be permanent.

Stuart Luppescu, University of Chicago, 1994

The importance of vocabulary knowledge in reading comprehension is well-established. For example, Wittrock, Marks and Doctorow (1975) found that, in certain contexts, a sentence, or even an entire text, could be made incomprehensible by the occurrence of a single unknown vocabulary item. Anderson and Freebody (1981) in a review of research on vocabulary learning stated that many researchers have discovered that vocabulary knowledge is an excellent predictor of general language ability (p. 77). Moreover, some measures of word difficulty have proved to be important factors in estimating readability (p. 80). Perfetti (1985) claimed that word recognition skill is an independent predictor of reading comprehension. The importance of vocabulary has also been demonstrated in studies of reading in context. Stanovich (1980), for example, showed that skilled readers are less dependent on context than are less skilled readers. Finally, eye movement research has established that readers sample three or four content words and half the function words on a page because so little information is obtained outside the foveal vision because the perceptual span is limited to a few letters (Rayner & Pollatset, 1985; Just & Carpenter, 1987).

Of interest for the present study is the source of vocabulary knowledge. We are particularly interested in the role that dictionaries play in the learning of second language vocabulary. To our knowledge, despite certain investigations of dictionary use (e.g., Bensoussan, Sim, & Weiss, 1984; Laufer, 1990), no studies have investigated the relationship between vocabulary learning and the use of dictionaries while reading in a second or foreign language. The purpose of the present study is to examine the role that bilingual dictionaries play in the learning of vocabulary while reading.

Research has determined that first language learners can learn vocabulary through reading. In a well-known study, Saragi, Nation, and Meister (1978) had native speakers of English read *A Clockwork Orange* by Anthony Burgess, which includes a large number of words of Russian origin. Most of the Russian-origin words (called nadsat) occur in the book in sufficient context and frequency for readers to understand their meaning. And, in fact, participants who had read the book performed far more effectively than would have been expected by chance on a vocabulary test of nadsat words.

Pitts, White, and Krashen (1989), in a replication of the Saragi study, found that second language learners of English, when given sections of *A Clockwork Orange* to read, were able to infer the meanings of nadsat words. Day, Omura, and Hiramatsu (to appear) gave Japanese high-school and university students of English a vocabulary test after they had read a passage that contained the tested words. The students scored significantly higher on the test than did students who took the test without having read the passage.

Second language researchers have also investigated the use of glosses while reading as a source of vocabulary learning. Jacobs and Dufon (1990) studied the effectiveness of glosses in vocabulary learning while reading. They found a significant effect for the use of glosses in the target language, English. On a delayed vocabulary test, however, this significance was not apparent.

The present study focuses on the contribution that the use of bilingual dictionaries might make in the learning of vocabulary.

This focus is of particular importance given the role that dictionaries play in second language learning. At the least, the purchase of a dictionary is considered a necessity for many foreign language students; however, the merits of this purchase to vocabulary learning have not yet been empirically demonstrated. Baxter (1980, p. 330) is of the opinion that continued use of a bilingual dictionary is harmful to the development of proficiency in the second language. He argues strongly for the use of a monolingual English learner's dictionary, claiming that it "not only demonstrates that definition is an alternative to the use of lexical items, but it also provides the means to actually employ definition" (1980, p. 334). Bensoussan et al. (1984) found that the use of bilingual dictionaries while reading had no effect on scores on a comprehension test.

The present study, however, deals only with the role of dictionaries in vocabulary learning and does not address the role that bilingual dictionaries play in reading comprehension. This study compares the amount of vocabulary learning that takes place when students use a dictionary while reading, and when they read without using a dictionary.

Our hypothesis is that there will be no significant difference in the measure of vocabulary learned by participants using bilingual dictionaries and those not using dictionaries. This hypothesis is based on two considerations. First, Krashen (1982, pp. 80–81) implied that vocabulary that is naturally acquired is more persistent and more likely to be remembered than is vocabulary that is explicitly learned through memorization or dictionary use. Second, most foreign language learners probably have had experiences similar to that of the authors, in which words looked up in the dictionary are quickly forgotten. This may seem like anecdotal evidence, but for lack of substantial empirical evidence, we feel it is better than none at all. We believe that these factors would offset any advantage gained from looking up words in the dictionary.

In addition, we were interested in discovering if the use of dictionaries caused an increase in the time needed to read a text.

Many people believe (e.g., Nuttall, 1982, p. 69), and indeed it seems to be common sense, that interrupting to consult a dictionary slows the reading process. However, empirical validation of this belief is lacking. Our hypothesis was that the students using dictionaries would take a significantly longer time to read the text than would those not using dictionaries.

Method

Participants

Participants in this study were 293 first- and second-year students studying English as a foreign language at two universities in Japan. They were typical of most Japanese college students in that they had completed 6 years of English instruction in high school. Japanese students at this level have studied English grammar extensively, but seldom have much practical or communicative ability in the language.

Design

Participants were randomly assigned by class to either a control or a treatment group; 148 in the former group, and 145 in the latter. Although it was not possible to assign people individually to treatment or control groups, the students had all completed 6 years of junior high-school and high-school English study, and were in required first-year university English classes. The students were assigned to classes according to their names. Because we cannot conceive of any correlation between name and ability, we consider the design of the experiment to be equivalent to assigning individual students randomly to either the treatment or the control group.

At least one control group and one treatment group were at each university. Students in the treatment group read a short story and were allowed to use their bilingual dictionaries. The control group also read the same short story but were not allowed to use their dictionaries. A comparison of the amount of vocabulary learned by the two groups was based on a comparison of the scores on a vocabulary test of the control group and the treatment group. The data were analyzed with BIGSCALE (Wright, Linacre, & Schulz, 1989), which produced person measures and item calibrations used in the study.[1] These measures and calibrations were analyzed with SYSTAT statistical software.

Materials

We selected a short story previously used by Day et al. (to appear) because it had been demonstrated to be of interest to a similar population (college-level Japanese EFL students) and because it contained vocabulary items and grammatical structures that these students could mainly understand. This short story contained 17 target words that Day et al. had identified as words that participants in their study did not know or found difficult. They had edited the original text to provide opportunities for the words to occur with ample frequency and in sufficient contexts to allow students to make reasonable guesses about their meanings. The study reported here focused on these 17 words. The text of the short story appears in the appendix; words featured in the test are printed in italics.

The vocabulary test was a multiple-choice type with five choices per item: one key, three distractors, and one *I don't know* choice. The test is the same as the one used by Day, Omura, and Hiramatsu (1991). The test initially consisted of 27 items. After a pilot administration, some items were eliminated as already known by at least half the students, and some were eliminated on the basis of fit, as determined by Rasch analysis provided by BIGSCALE (Wright et al., 1989). A comparison of the amount of vocabulary learned by the two groups was based on a comparison of the scores of each of the treatment groups. Each correct answer was scored 2 points, *I don't know* was scored 1 point, and each incorrect answer was scored 0 points. The rationale for our scoring was that students who knew that they did not know the meaning of certain words demonstrated greater vocabulary awareness than did those mistakenly thinking that they knew the meaning. Because the number of *I don't know* responses was so small, this partial credit scoring system had a negligible effect on the measures obtained and yielded no additional illuminating information compared to a dichotomous 1/0 *correct/incorrect* scoring system (i.e., both *incorrect* and *I don't know* were scored 0). For this reason, the simpler *correct/incorrect* scoring was ultimately adopted.

Procedure

Participants were given the short story and asked to read it. They were not told in advance that there would be any kind of a test on the reading. The students were told to take as much time as they needed to read the passage. As a part of the reading rate study, the students in both groups were asked to note the time when they started to read and the time they finished the passage. Each of the students in the dictionary group had a bilingual English-Japanese dictionary, although the choice of dictionary was left to the individual student. These students were told that they were free to use the dictionary to look up any words they were unsure of, and which they wanted to look up. The students in the other group were not permitted to use dictionaries while reading. Immediately after reading the passage, the students took the vocabulary test. They were instructed not to guess, but to choose the option *I don't know* when they did not know the meaning of a word. The students were not permitted to refer to their dictionaries during the test.

It is important to stress that this study investigated the effect of the use of bilingual dictionaries on vocabulary learning while reading. The present investigation was not able to consider how, or even *if*, dictionaries were actually used by the students. Because the two groups took the test under otherwise identical conditions, we must infer that any difference between the performance of the two groups is due to the use of dictionaries. Further, given the work by Day et al. (1991), which established that a comparable pilot group of participants in general had difficulty recognizing or did not know the target words, we also must infer that when the students in the dictionary condition used their bilingual dictionaries, they were most likely looking up the meanings of the target words.

Results

Two of the test items (4 & 10) fit the model poorly (had high infit statistics) and were eliminated from the analysis (see note 1).[2] Items 4 and 10 were deleted, and then the analysis was done on each of the groups separately with the calibrations for the items anchored on scores for all respondents to make the scores for both groups comparable. Table 1 is a summary of the scores for the dictionary and the nondictionary groups. Notice that the mean score of the dictionary group was considerably higher than that of the group that did not use dictionaries. The reliability of the measures, reported in the second to last line of Table 1, is low. This tendency is almost certainly the result of using a very short test, producing lower than ideal sample variation and higher than ideal error.

Table 2 gives the two-sample *t*-test results. The difference of the means is significant at the less than 0.001 level. The difference of .62 logits means that for an average student in the dictionary group, the odds of getting a question correct was 1.86 times greater than for an average student in the group that did not use dictionaries.[3]

However, not all items functioned the same way with respect to the two treatment groups. In Figure 1, difficulty calibrations for each item by the dictionary group are plotted on the vertical axis, and calibrations for the group that did not use dictionaries are on the horizontal axis. The identity line, and lines indicating a 95% confidence interval also appear on the graph (refer to Wright & Stone, 1990). Note that there are several points that lie outside the 95% confidence interval lines. Those items above the

Table 1
Person Measures Summary

Person Measure (Logits)	Dictionary Group (n=152)	No Dictionary Group (n=145)
Mean	1.52	0.90
Adjusted Standard Deviation	0.76	0.84
Root Mean Squared Error	0.80	0.70
Person Separation	0.95	1.21
Person separation reliability	0.47	.059
Raw Score Percent Correct	75%	65%

Adjusted Standard Deviation is the Standard Deviation adjusted for measurement error: $\text{Adj SD} = \sqrt{SD^2 - RMSE^2}$. Person Separation represents the number of statistically distinct groups into which people can be separated: Person Separation=Adj SD/RMSE. The Person Separation Reliability is the Rasch model equivalent of a conventional reliability coefficient such as Cronbach's α: Person Separation Reliability=(Person Separation)²/(1+Person Separation²).

Table 2
Two-Sample T-Test—Person Measures

Group	M	SD	Difference	Standard Error	t	df	p
Dictionary	1.52	1.18	.62	.127	4.88	296	<0.001
No Dictionary	.90	1.13					

line indicate items that were significantly harder for the group that used dictionaries; the items that are below the line were significantly harder for the group that did not use dictionaries. Table 3 shows the difficulty differential for those items. A positive difference indicates that the item was more difficult for the group that used dictionaries; a negative difference indicates an item that was more difficult for the group that did not use dictionaries. In addition, we investigated the differences in the time taken by the two groups to read the passage. The results are summarized in Table 4. Differences appeared in the number of *I don't know*

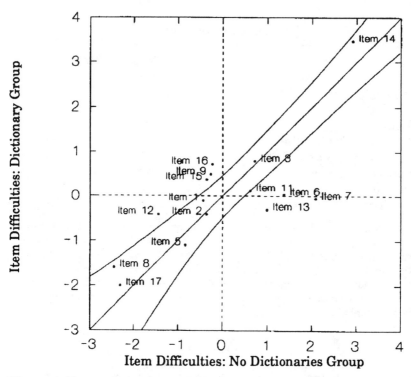

Figure 1. Comparison of item difficulties

Table 3
Differential Item Function

| Item Number | Word Tested | Item Difficulty (Logits) | | Difference |
		Dictionary Group	No Dictionary Group	
7	chant	−0.06	2.08	−2.02
6	sob	0.03	1.37	−1.34
13	faint	−0.31	0.99	−1.30
11	stare	0.12	0.62	−0.50
15	terrible	0.37	−0.36	0.73
9	scare	0.49	−0.27	0.76
8	appear	−1.59	−2.45	0.86
16	strange	0.72	−0.23	0.95
12	happen	−0.42	−1.45	1.03

Table 4
Two-Sample T-Test—Time to Read Passage in Minutes

Group	*M*	*SD*	Diff	*t*	*df*	*p*
Dictionary	21.11	7.24	9.25	−13.81	296	<0.001
No Dictionary	11.86	3.71				

Table 5
Two-Sample T-Test—Number of I Don't Know Responses

Group	*M*	*SD*	Diff	*t*	*df*	*p*
Dictionary	1.07	1.53	.46	4.48	296	<0.001
No Dictionary	1.98	1.97				

responses as well—as presented in Table 5.

Discussion

Overall, using a dictionary apparently had a significant effect on people's performance on the vocabulary test. The mean measures of the group that used dictionaries was about 50% greater than those of the group that did not use dictionaries. This evidence strongly goes against our hypothesis that there would be no difference between the two groups, and provides support for the claim that the use of a bilingual dictionary by EFL students while reading can significantly improve indirect or incidental vocabulary learning.

This finding, however, is not without complications. When we look at the individual items, it is apparent that some items functioned differently from others (cf. Fig. 1 with Table 3). In particular, Items 8, 9, 12, 15, and 16, were significantly more difficult for the group that used dictionaries. Perhaps the use of a dictionary in some cases may be misleading or confusing, that is, if a student is not able to find the appropriate meaning in the dictionary from among all the possible meanings listed. To verify this, we checked the number of meanings listed in a typical

Table 6
Item Calibration Difference and Number of Meanings

Item No.	Word	Difference	Meanings
15	terrible	0.73	9
9	scare	0.76	22
8	appear	0.86	15
16	strange	0.95	24
12	happen	1.03	29

English-Japanese dictionary (Kawamura, 1984) for each of the words in Table 3 that seemed to be more difficult for the group that used dictionaries.[4] These data appear in Table 6.

A Pearson product-moment correlation of the difference in scores with number of meanings gave $r=.81$, with an associated p-value of 0.1. We could not expect a significant difference with only five cases; however, the trend is clear: Dictionaries seemed to have a definite confusing effect on the students in a number of cases, probably because of the large number of entries.

The possibility that using a dictionary might not always be helpful should not be unexpected, for the task of finding the meaning of a word in a dictionary is a complex process. This process may entail looking for a suitable headword, comprehending the entry, locating the appropriate part of the definition, connecting the right sense to the context, and putting the word within the context of the unknown or difficult word in the text. A study by Mitchell (cited in Hartmann, 1987, p. 15), showed that learners may have difficulties with all of the steps in this process. Ard (1982), in a study that involved the use of bilingual dictionaries in writing, found that the use of such dictionaries "often leads to errors" (p. 14).

However, for those who would like their students to use dictionaries, Jacobs (1989) reported that instruction in the use of monolingual learner's dictionaries by foreign language learners of English resulted in significant improvement in the people's ability to use the dictionaries.

. We were surprised that the difference in time that both groups took to read the passage was so great: The students in the group that used dictionaries took nearly twice as long to read the passage as did the other group. For the 1,853 words in the story, the group that used dictionaries read at an average rate of 88 words per minute, whereas the group that did not use dictionaries read at an average rate of 156 words per minute. This finding provides empirical evidence, then, for the belief that using a dictionary while reading causes a decrease in reading speed. It may be argued that the greater amount of time taken to read the passage is what is behind the dictionary group's higher scores, but we found no evidence to support this explanation: The correlation between time taken to read the passage and performance on the test was almost zero (Pearson product moment $r=0.048$).

An unexpected but interesting finding is that students who used dictionaries responded *I don't know* significantly less than did the students who did not use dictionaries. This supports the idea that the text itself was not sufficiently transparent for all students to guess the meaning of all the words. We can imagine the situation in which a student reading the passage encounters an unknown word. The student is able to get a vague idea of what the word means, but may still be unsure of the exact meaning. At this point, a dictionary may be very useful in explicating and focussing the meaning of the word. We have had personal experiences such as this when reading in a foreign language. For words whose meanings could not be inferred completely from the context, using the dictionary to disambiguate the meaning of a word might be very helpful at times.

The major finding of the investigation, that the use of a bilingual dictionary while reading can facilitate the learning of vocabulary by EFL students, was contrary to our hypothesis that using the dictionary would have no effect. Our hypothesis was based on the idea that students would quickly forget the words they looked up in the dictionary, and thus using the dictionary would have no effect on scores on the vocabulary test. Students may in fact quickly forget the words they look up, but the question might be *How quickly?*. The present study suggests that learners did not forget the words in the time between reading the text and taking the test, but what happened after that is not clear. One productive avenue for future research would be a replication of the present study with a longer period of time between reading the text and taking the test.

In a study mentioned at the beginning of this article, Jacobs and Dufon (1990) reported that glossing in the target language had no effect on vocabulary knowledge tested approximately four weeks after students had read a passage. Thus, we might also expect a similar result with vocabulary knowledge gained through the use of a bilingual dictionary while reading.

Because both the group that was permitted to use dictionaries and the one that was not were identical in all respects except for the use of dictionaries, we must conclude that any difference in vocabulary learning, as reflected in performance on the present test, was due to the use of dictionaries. We make this claim even though we did not monitor actual dictionary use. One can argue that nearly any method of monitoring use of the dictionary in this kind of study would be obtrusive and thus would be a threat to the validity of the study. This point was noted by Hulstijn (1993), who devised a method of observing readers' behaviors for looking up words that was as unobtrusive as possible. He provided students with a computerized glossary that recorded which words were looked up without their knowledge. Hulstijn found that students looked up words that they considered relevant but whose meanings they found difficult to guess from the context. He also surmised that even when students could guess meanings from context, they often checked their inferences with the electronic dictionary. We assume that the students in our study used their dictionaries in a similar manner.

We see the issue of dictionary use as extremely important, based simply on the fact that virtually every foreign and second language learner uses one. Considering the ubiquitousness of dictionaries in second language learning, it is rather astounding that more studies have not been done to test the value of their use.

Moreover, many teachers have definite views on whether dictionaries should or should not be used, or what kind of dictionaries (bilingual or monolingual) should be used during pleasure reading. These views are not based on any empirical evidence. Further research in this area should include study of the long-term retention of vocabulary learned through dictionary use.

The present study provides some guidance for teachers in this area. We learn that bilingual dictionaries may have a beneficial effect on vocabulary learning, but there are some trade-offs: Their use results in lower reading speed, and may confuse the learner, especially if there are a large number of entries under the headword from which to choose. Bensoussan et al. (1984) found that teachers believe that their students could not use dictionaries effectively, whereas the students felt they could. At the very least, teachers should not assume that a student knows how to use a dictionary; exercises to familiarize students with the dictionary mat have a beneficial effect. Thompson (1987) provided some useful suggestions in this area. In addition to assessing the longitudinal aspects of vocabulary learning and dictionary use, future research might investigate the effects of teaching students effective strategies to use while consulting bilingual dictionaries.

Notes

[1]Raw test scores are sample dependent, and person scores are test dependent. Moreover, raw scores are nonlinear: The relationship between raw score and implied ability is an *s*-shaped ogive. For this reason, raw scores can be misleading when used in computation of summary statistics such as means and standard deviations, or of test statistics such as *t*-tests. Rasch analysis produces linear, test-free person measures of ability, and linear, person-free test item calibrations of difficulty that are numerically suitable for use in computing statistics. Rasch analysis estimates most probable responses of each person to each test item. The extent that the actual responses differ from these most probable responses is used to construct fit statistics that measure the overall success of the measurement model with the data at hand. See Wright and Stone (1979) for details.

[2]It was clear in retrospect why Item 4 was misfitting. For one thing, the word tested, *shame*, appeared in the text in two different senses. In the beginning of the passage it occurred in the sentence, *What a shame*. Subsequently, it

appeared in the text with the meaning that was tested: *remorse*. Further-more, the correct choice on the test for this item, *wrongness*, is somewhat misleading; that is, wrongness produces a feeling of guilt, not shame. Shame is a feeling resulting from having one's mistake exposed to others. In Japan, shame and saving face are important cultural features. It is no wonder that this item was confusing to the students. It is not as clear why Item 10 was misfitting. The correct choice, *damage*, is not really close to the central meaning of the word, and thus might have been confusing to the students.
[3]A difference of 0.62 logits means the odds of answering correctly are 0.62=1.86 greater.
[4]Because the students were free to choose their own dictionaries, the number of dictionary entries found in Kawamura (1984) that was used in this study may be different from those of other dictionaries used by the participants. Nonetheless, Kawamura is very popular and is likely to be typical of an English-Japanese dictionary used by first-year Japanese college students.

References

Anderson, R. C., & Freebody, P. (1981). Vocabulary knowledge. In J. Guthrie, (Ed.), *Comprehension and teaching: Research reviews* (pp. 77–117). Newark, DE: International Reading Association.

Ard, J. (1982). The use of bilingual dictionaries by ESL students while writing. *ITL Review of Applied Linguistics, 58*, 1–27.

Baxter, J. (1980). The dictionary and vocabulary behavior: A single word or a handful? *TESOL Quarterly, 14*, 325–336.

Bensoussan, M., Sim, D., & Weiss, R. (1984). The effect of dictionary usage on EFL test performance compared with student and teacher attitudes and expectations. *Reading in a Foreign Language, 2*, 262–275.

Day, R. R., Omura, C., & Hiramatsu, M. (1991). Incidental EFL vocabulary learning and reading. *Reading in a Foreign Language, 7*, 541–551.

Day, R. R., Omura, C., & Hiramatsu, M. (to appear). Reading and vocabulary learning. *Reading in a Foreign Language*.

Ha, M. A. (1992). *The role of bilingual dictionaries and reading in foreign language vocabulary learning.* Unpublished master's thesis, University of Hawaii, Honolulu.

Hartmann, R. R. K. (1987). Four perspectives on dictionary use: A critical review of research methods. In A. Cowie (ed.), *The dictionary and the language learner: Papers from the EURALEX Seminar at the University of Leeds, 1–3 April 1985* (pp. 11–28). Tübingen, Germany: Max Niemeyer Verlag.

Hulstijn, J. H. (1993). When do foreign-language learners look up the meaning of unfamiliar words? The influence of task and learner variables. *The Modern Language Journal, 77*, 139–147.

Jacobs, G. (1989). *Dictionaries can help writing—if students know how to use them*. Honolulu, Hawaii: University of Hawaii, Department of Educational Psychology. (ERIC Document Reproduction Service No. ED 316 025)

Jacobs, G., & Dufon, P. (1990, April). *L1 and L2 glosses in L2 reading passages: Their effectiveness for increasing comprehension and vocabulary knowledge*. Paper presented at the annual meeting of the American Education Research Association, Boston.

Just, M. A., & Carpenter, P. A. (1987). *The psychology of reading and language comprehension*. Boston: Allyn and Bacon.

Kawamura, J. (1984). *The new crown English-Japanese* (4th ed.). Tokyo: Sanseido.

Krashen, S. D. (1982). *Principles and practice in second language learning*. Oxford: Pergamon Press.

Laufer, B. (1990). Ease and difficulty in vocabulary learning: Some teaching implication. *Foreign Language Annals, 23*(2), 147–155.

Nutall, C. (1982). *Teaching reading skills in a foreign language*. London, Heinemann Educational Books.

Perfetti, C. A. (1985). *Reading ability*. New York: Oxford University Press.

Pitts, M., White, H., & Krashen, S. D. (1989). Acquiring second language vocabulary through reading: A replication of the *Clockwork Orange* study using second language acquirers. *Reading in a Foreign Language, 5*, 271–275.

Rayner, K., & Pollatsek, A., (1985). *The psychology of reading*. Englewood Cliffs, NJ: Prentice-Hall.

Saragi, T., Nation, I. S. P., & Meister, G. F. (1978). Vocabulary learning and reading, *System, 6*, 72–78.

Stanovich, K. E. (1980). Toward an interactive-compensatory model of individual differences in the development of reading fluency. *Reading Research Quarterly, 16*, 32–71.

Thompson, G. (1987). Using bilingual dictionaries. *ELT Journal, 41*, 282–286.

Wittrock, M., Marks, C., & Doctorow, M. (1975). Reading as a generative process. *Journal of Educational Psychology, 67*, 484–489.

Wright, B. D., Linacre, J. M., & Schulz, M. (1989). *BIGSCALE: A Rasch program for rating scale analysis*. Chicago: Mesa Press.

Wright, B. D., & Stone, M. H. (1979). *Best test design*. Chicago: Mesa Press.

Wright, B. D., & Stone, M. H. (1990). *Control lines for item plots: Rasch measurement practice, research primer No. 13*. Chicago: Mesa Press.

Appendix: The Mystery of an African Mask

Osamu Matsumoto is a doctor. Once he had been a good doctor. For years he had been interested in *medicine*, the study of disease. He had kept up with every idea in *medicine*. Now he almost never read about *medicine*. He read about the dead who returned to life.

One year ago, Dr. Matsumoto had a patient who was very ill. One night, he was called to her home. "She seems *worse*, much *worse*," her nurse said over the telephone. When he got to her apartment, she was dead.

"What a *shame*," Dr. Matsumoto said. "Such a young woman who had most of her life ahead of her. And she had come all the way from Korea to study and become a nurse."

The young patient, Yukiko Shimazaki, lay with her eyes open. She had no heartbeat, no pulse, no breath. Dr. Matsumoto *stared* at her. When he *stared* at her, he thought she moved. He took her wrist again to feel for a pulse. Nothing. But then he felt a *faint* beat. Yukiko began to breathe. Her heart began to beat stronger and stronger. Right before Dr. Matsumoto's eyes, a dead woman came back to life. "Of course she wasn't really dead," he thought. "Her heart must have been beating, but too *faint*ly for me to hear. Her breathing must also have been too *faint* for me to notice." But he believed that she had been dead. From then on, Dr. Matsumoto was a changed man. He still tried to treat his patients. His thoughts were not with them, though. They were on one question: Can the dead come back to life?

When Yukiko Shimazaki became a nurse, Dr. Matsumoto hired her as his assistant in his office. Soon, she would be his wife, as well. He had to *fire* his old assistant to give Yukiko the job.

Masumi Kawasaki was very unhappy. "*Fire* me because of her! How can you *fire* me? I've worked for you for years. What will become of me? And Yukiko . . . she was dead once, and she'll be dead again, soon. With her *faint* heart—"

"Just get out," said Dr. Matsumoto. He didn't care what *happen*ed to Masumi. All he cared about was the dead. Could they come back?

Now, at midnight, Dr. Matsumoto was ready for bed. Fewer and fewer patients came to his office each day, so he was not busy. "Something is *strange* about Dr. Matsumoto," they said. He doesn't pay attention to us anymore." Dr. Matsumoto knew that his life was going wrong. But he could not help himself.

"A doctor should keep patients from dying," he thought. "But what does that mean if the dead can live again?"

Suddenly, he heard a loud knocking on his door. "Osamu, help me, help me!" cried a voice. "Yukiko!" he called. "What's wrong?" He threw the door open, and Yukiko Shimazaki rushed in. She was shivering from cold. And she was also shivering from fear.

"Try to relax, Yukiko. Please calm yourself. What's the matter? Don't *strain* your heart like that," said Dr. Matsumoto.

"The mask, the mask!" *sob*bed Yukiko. "It's come for me. It's after me. It's *terrible*. It's the mask of death!"

"The mask of death? What are you talking about?" asked Dr. Matsumoto.

Yukiko tried to calm herself. "I was in my apartment. I was tired and went to bed early. A little while ago, I heard a *strange* sound, a whirring sound. Then on the wall an old mask *appear*ed. It *appear*ed out of nowhere—an African mask.

"Then I heard the voice *chant*ing:

> Yukiko, Yukiko Shimazaki, hear me.
> I am the face of death.
> From Africa I have come—for you.
> Look at the iron between my eyes;
> Whoever sees my face soon dies.

Then it just went away."

The mask of death! Dr. Matsumoto's head began throbbing. What mysterious thing could this be?

"Yukiko, what did it look like?"

"It was like nothing I have ever seen. The face of the mask was of ivory. It was cracked and old. The dark eyes *stare*d out at me. On the forehead were two iron bars. And around the mask was a band of—of little ivory heads. What could it be?" asked Yukiko.

"I don't know," replied Dr. Matsumoto. "Ever since you came back to life, I have been studying death. But nothing I have read about was like that. Are you sure it was really there?"

"I don't see things that aren't there, Osamu. It was real, and it had come for me," said Yukiko.

"Where did it say it came from?" he asked.

"From Africa. It said it came from Africa."

Yukiko was still shivering. Dr. Matsumoto's hands shook too, as he gave Yukiko some medicine to help calm her.

"Don't worry, Yukiko. It must have been a dream. Some dreams can seem as real as life. I have been talking too much about death. I'll take you home. This medicine will help you relax. You will sleep without dreams."

Soon, Dr. Matsumoto was back in his house, alone. He shook the snow from his coat and went back to the living room. He turned on all the lights. "That was no dream," he said to himself. "Death came for Yukiko once. Now it has come for her again."

The next night was even *worse*. Yukiko heard the whirring sound as soon as she turned out the lights. A bright spot *appear*ed across the room. The spot became *clear*er and *clear*er. It was the *terrible* mask!

The *chant*ing began again:

> Look at the iron between my eyes;
> Whoever sees my face soon dies.

This time there was more:

> See faces around my head;
> They are the faces of the dead.

Yukiko *sob*bed. "Please, please, let me alone. Let me live," she whispered, *sob*bing even more.

Yukiko Shimazaki did not come to work the next morning. Dr. Matsumoto ran to her apartment. She was sitting on her chair, shivering. She told him about the second visit of the ancient mask and the *terrible chant*ing.

"I spent the night reading," Dr. Matsumoto told her. "There is nothing about an old African mask of death in my books. We must have help. I have sent a telegram to the capital of Nigeria, Lagos. The world's greatest expert on African religions is there. I hope that Tejan Kabbah is willing to come. This is vacation time at the University of Nigeria where he teaches."

Soon, a telegram came from Lagos. "Arriving tomorrow morning on Flight 349. Meet me at the airport."

"I hope nothing *happen*s before he arrives," said Yukiko. "I don't know how much more I can stand."

After dinner, Dr. Matsumoto went with Yukiko to her apartment. Night came. They sat up, waiting. Nothing *happen*ed. "Nothing *happen*s when the lights are on," Yukiko said.

"Turn them off, then," said Dr. Matsumoto. "Perhaps it's over. Perhaps it was a dream after all."

As soon as Yukiko switched off the lights, the whirring sound filled the room. Then the spot *appear*ed, fuzzy at first but becoming *clear*er. It was the ancient mask, exactly as Yukiko had described it. And the *chant*ing began. Again, there was more to the *chant* than before.

> Look at the iron between my eyes;
> Whoever sees my face soon dies.
> See faces around my head;
> They are the faces of the dead.
> Look for your face in the ivory;
> When you find it, you're dead like me.

"I have never dreamed of anything like that," whispered Dr. Matsumoto. "Until you came back to life, I believed in science. Now what can I believe? Is there a spirit of death in the shape of an African mask?"

"I hope Tejan Kabbah can help us," Yukiko sighed. "How much longer can I live like this?"

At the airport the next day, they met Tejan Kabbah. They went to Dr. Matsumoto's house. There they looked at pictures of African masks. "Masks are an ancient form of art in African," Mr. Kabbah explained. "There are many types, from many times and places." He turned the page.

"There it is!" Yukiko and Dr. Matsumoto spoke at the same moment. Mr. Kabbah glanced at the page. "Let's wait until tonight," he said.

That night, Yukiko switched off the light. "Where is Mr. Kabbah?" she asked. "What if the mask comes while he is gone?"

Suddenly the mask *appeared*. The singing had two new *terrible* lines:

> This is the night you take your last breath.
> Now is the time of Yukiko Shimazaki's death.

The mask suddenly jumped to the ceiling. Then it was gone as though it had never been there at all. "Turn on the lights!" It was the voice of Tejan Kabbah. He came in through the window. He was holding a *slide projector* and pushing Masumi Kawasaki in front of him.

"As soon as I saw the mask you picked, I knew it was not real, a *fake*," he explained. "That is an ancient African mask, but not a mask of death. It was worn by kings. The faces around it are not the dead. They are the faces of ancient people from Portugal who came to Nigeria four hundred years ago. So the mask was a *fake*," he said.

"When you told me about the sound and the light, I thought of a *slide projector* and the sound of its fan. This woman worked the *slide projector* and spoke from outside the window. She was trying to *scare* Yukiko. Who is she?" asked Mr. Kabbah.

"Masumi," asked Dr. Matsumoto, "why did you do it?"

"My job as your assistant was my whole life. You *fired* me. If I could *scare* her to death, I could get it back. I wanted to *strain* her heart so she would die."

She hung her head in *shame*.

Dr. Matsumoto felt *shame*, too. "I didn't think of you after all those years. Come back. Yukiko really wants a job in the hospital, not in my office as my assistant. And now I know that she was not dead but just in a coma. That means she would seem dead."

"Well," said Mr. Kabbah, "it's time for me to go home."

"Not quite, Mr. Kabbah," said Yukiko. "Please stay for our wedding, as Dr. Matsumoto and I will be married next week. We really want you to attend the wedding."

Vocabulary

I. Circle the answer from a, b, c, or d that best explains the meaning of the italicized word. If you don't know the answer, circle e *I don't know*.

1. *Medicine* is
   a. the study of history
   b. a person who helps a doctor
   c. the study of disease
   d. a person who takes care of children
   e. I don't know

2. A *slide projector*
   a. shows slides
   b. colors slides
   c. copies slides
   d. takes slides
   e. I don't know

3. A *fake* is
   a. something not real
   b. something not clean
   c. something to teach
   d. something to wear
   e. I don't know

4. *Shame* is the feeling of
   a. gentleness
   b. wrongness
   c. happiness
   d. loneliness
   e. I don't know

II. Circle the answer from a, b, c, or d, that best explains or means the same as the italicized word. If you don't know the answer, circle e *I don't know*.

5. To *fire* someone is to
   a. cook someone food
   b. teach someone
   c. help someone
   d. remove someone from a job
   e. I don't know

6. To *sob* is
   a. to spin
   b. to cry
   c. to scream
   d. to laugh
   e. I don't know

7. To *chant* is
   a. to speak
   b. to dance
   c. to win
   d. to sing
   e. I don't know

8. To *appear* is
   a. to refuse
   b. to drink
   c. to some into sight
   d. to go away
   e. I don't know

9. To *scare* is
   a. to frighten
   b. to lose
   c. to boil
   d. to worry
   e. I don't know

10. To *strain* is
    a. to escape
    b. to frustrate
    c. to damage
    d. to tie
    e. I don't know

11. To *stare* is
    a. to walk carefully
    b. to look fixedly
    c. to break roughly
    d. to comb slowly
    e. I don't know

12. To *happen* is
    a. to peel
    b. to lay
    c. to develop
    d. to occur
    e. I don't know

III. Circle the answer from a, b, c, or d that means the *opposite* of the italicized word. If you don't know the answer, circle e *I don't know*.

13. faint
    a. dead
    b. hopeless
    c. strong
    d. weak
    e. I don't know

14. *clear*
    a. bright
    b. vague
    c. dirty
    d. dull
    e. I don't know

15. *terrible*
    a. fearful
    b. delightful
    c. very bad
    d. attractive
    e. I don't know

16. *strange*
    a. dangerous
    b. familiar
    c. smooth
    d. abnormal
    e. I don't know

17. *worse*
    a. strong
    b. darker
    c. better
    d. sleepy
    e. I don't know

Reversed Subtitling and Dual Coding Theory: New Directions for Foreign Language Instruction

Martine Danan
Michigan Technological University

Author's Statement: *Since I conducted the experiments described in my article, some more recent studies have explored the positive effects of subtitled videotapes on foreign/second language learning. For example, a study conducted at the University of Leuven in Belgium (d'Ydewalle & Pavakanum, in press-a), which involved Dutch-speaking students learning Spanish, confirms that lexical acquisition is facilitated to some degree by subtitling, in particular by reversed subtitling (sound track in the native language and subtitles in the foreign language). However, contrary to my earlier findings and those of Lambert, Boehler, and Sidoti (1981), this study also shows that standard subtitling can be beneficial. One particularly important variable that may explain why standard subtitling has been found beneficial is the linguistic environment of those participating in the experiments. It is possible that Belgians, who are accustomed to watching subtitled programs on television, may be able to simultaneously process subtitles and a sound track more easily than North American learners, who receive limited exposure to subtitling. Other variables as to the types of learners and learning conditions should also be studied further: for instance, children versus adult learners, beginning versus advanced students, incidental language acquisition versus intentional learning.*

In addition to assessing the most effective forms of subtitling for different learners, it is essential to conduct further research on the optimal way to incorporate subtitling into instructional materials. A recent study examining the role of subtitling with interactive videodiscs (Borrás & Lafayette, 1994) revealed that language learning is

greatly facilitated by learners being able to selectively access the
subtitles and adapt them to their needs. These conclusions have
obvious implications for lexical acquisition.

Martine Danan, University of Memphis, 1994

The instructional value of video in foreign language classes
is now commonly accepted by most educators, who are aware that
video materials can greatly increase motivation, provide vivid
information about a foreign culture, and build students' confidence in their ability to understand foreign utterances, or at least
the gist of a message, through visual cues. However, little
research has been done about the most effective mode of presentation of foreign language video programs. The present study was
inspired by remarks about the influence of television on foreign
language acquisition in countries in which numerous American
subtitled movies are shown. Many European viewers claim that
their English language skills have improved as a result of watching subtitled programs regularly and, unlike many American
viewers, do not perceive subtitles as a hindrance. Whether such
claims about the role of subtitles could be empirically proven and
applied to foreign language classroom instruction was the purpose of this research project.

Research pertaining to the effects of visual associations on
memory and the mnemonic power of imagery support the belief in
the potential usefulness of video input. In the specific foreign
language learning domain, a number of experiments (e.g., Kellogg
& Howe, 1971) have shown that foreign words associated with
actual objects or imagery techniques are learned more easily.
These findings on the importance of imagery can be explained in
terms of Paivio's dual coding theory (1986, chap. 4) distinguishing
two separate representational systems: the verbal system (V), and
the imagery system (Im) composed of nonverbal objects and
events. According to Paivio's model, the two systems are functionally independent, yet representations in one system can also
activate those in the other because dually coded items (coded
verbally and nonverbally) are linked by referential connections.

Visual traces are remembered better than are verbal components and also have an additive effect when items are encoded dually. Consequently, according to Paivio (1986, chap. 11), in the case of second or foreign language learning, as more foreign words are learned in direct association with appropriate nonverbal referents (objects, but also experiential elements such as events and emotions), the richer and more meaningful are the referential interconnections, thus resulting in better language recall and appropriate use.

A video program providing visual referents and an involving story line could supply some of this nonverbal support. However, considering the complex nature of audiovisual referents, foreign language utterances would initially have to be mapped on the corresponding native language words through the subtitled translation before a connection between the visual referents and the foreign phrases could be established. Whether and how such mapping can occur is central to the issue addressed in this paper.

Current research on subtitling perception supports the view that subtitles are automatically and deeply processed. D'Ydewalle, Van Rensbergen and Pollet (1987) have shown experimentally that the amount of time spent reading subtitles is not significantly different even in extreme cases when the viewers are fluent in the language presented in the soundtrack (and would theoretically not need the subtitles) or when no sound is used (making the reading of the subtitles essential). Because this pattern occurs even in the case of viewers, such as Americans, who have little experience with subtitles, the reading of subtitles is not based on habit. Rather, it appears to be an automatic activity resulting from the priority of visual over verbal input (d'Ydewalle, Praet, Verfaillie, & Van Rensbergen, 1991). Processing subtitles, however, does require more cognitive resources, which explains why spectators who are not used to subtitles have a feeling of difficulty. Dual task methodology experiments have found that the slowest response to an experimental task occurred when both subtitles and sound had to be processed simultaneously (Sohl,[1] cited in d'Ydewalle & Gielen, 1992).

This greater depth of processing, together with the dominance of the visual modality and the less transient nature of
subtitles (compared to sound), might make subtitles a very powerful tool in discourse processing. An experiment that compared
the memory for the exact phrasing of subtitles with that for the
spoken text found that an overwhelming majority of the subtitles
(93%) were correctly identified as opposed to 43% correct identification for sentences without titles (Gielen[2], cited in d'Ydewalle
& Gielen, 1992). These findings suggest that if subtitles are used
in foreign language learning, they should logically contain the
information to be retained, namely the foreign utterances.

A few studies on the effects of subtitling on second or foreign
language learning have already been conducted. A first experiment by Lambert, Boehler, and Sidoti (1981) compared standard
subtitling (subtitles in the native language) with various combinations of audio and visual input. The experimental design
consisted of nine monolingual or bilingual conditions in which no
dialogue, or dialogue in first or second language was combined
with no subtitles or subtitles in either language. An overall
comprehension posttest in first or second language, and three
separate foreign language memory tests for contextual meaning,
spelling and form of phrasing were administered after the students had watched the tapes. The most promising combination for
processing second language information appeared to be reversed
subtitling, in which the soundtrack is in the native language (L1)
and the subtitles in the second language (L2). Students in the
reversed subtitling condition comprehended the foreign input
significantly better than did those in the bimodal L2 input condition (L2 script and dialogue). Surprisingly, standard subtitling
offered little assistance for L2 comprehension and hardly improved performance over L2 script or dialogue alone. Standard
subtitles may even have had a negative effect because they
distracted viewers and prevented them from processing the L2
aural input. The additional contextual meaning and spelling
posttests confirmed the advantage of reversed subtitling over
other forms of subtitling, especially standard subtitling.

A second experiment (Holobow, Lambert, & Sayegh, 1984) focused on three of the most promising conditions—reversed subtitling, bimodal L2 input, and L2 script only—for an extended period of time (11 weeks). Reversed subtitling proved once again to be a significantly more effective tool for second language comprehension than did bimodal L2 input, which in turn allowed for better results than did L2 script. For the combined scores (in the phrase form, contextual meaning, and comprehension tests), reversed subtitling was higher (but not significantly so) than was bimodal L2 input. Moreover, bimodal L2 input scores increased significantly over time, suggesting that this form of subtitling could be a promising alternative with well-trained students.

These two studies involved Grade 5 and 6 pupils who had attended a French immersion program in the Montreal area since Kindergarten. In Canadian immersion programs, French is the only language of instruction in Grades K, 1 and 2, and it amounts to at least 40% of instruction time by Grades 5 and 6. The students in the two studies could therefore be considered functionally bilingual, even though English was their dominant language. In a third experiment (Lambert & Holobow, 1984), the researchers selected seventh-grade pupils whose knowledge of French was significantly lower than in the case of the immersion program pupils, as they had attended only 45 minutes of daily instruction of French as a foreign language since Grade 1. As in the case of the bilingual students, reversed subtitling proved to be the most helpful condition for comprehension and contextual meaning. Bimodal L2 input and L2 script were the least beneficial, which seems to indicate that students with limited foreign language proficiency need to rely on some form of input in their native language to grasp the meaning of a message. Students in the standard subtitling condition performed nearly as well as did those in the L1 script control condition because they relied primarily on the L1 script and bypassed the foreign dialogue.

Lambert et al. (1981) suggested that part of the beneficial effect of reversed subtitling was due to the special interaction of the audio and visual channels. Students were able to process the story line or main information in their dominant language through the more transient audio channel because native language processing is more automatic; and they had more time to focus on the foreign subtitles to learn or review the corresponding foreign utterance. In addition, students might have benefited from the deeper processing of the double modal input because the parallel processing of simultaneous visual and auditory routes should necessitate more resources and cognitive involvement. This deeper processing would also explain why students in the bimodal L2 input condition did better than did those in the L2 script condition (Lambert et al., 1984).

Another interpretation proposed by Lambert et al. (1981), which is not exclusive of the ones just mentioned, is linked to the notion of optimal reading strategy. With reversed subtitling, readers can approach the subtitles with a set of expectations derived from a knowledge of the context and main ideas brought by the L1 dialogue. The importance of contextual knowledge (situation, preceding utterances, structural properties of language, world knowledge) in efficient language processing has been stressed in most current reading theories. Van Dijk and Kintsch (1983), for example, suggest a strategic top-down and bottom-up interaction of all internal and external resources available aiming at "on-line" (p. 5, 25) representation and interpretation. Carpenter and Just (1989) stress that, whenever possible, the preferred strategy is "immediacy of interpretation" (p. 39–40), which favors immediate search in the mental lexicon and integration with the contextual knowledge while a word is fixated. Eye tracking studies during the reading of standard subtitles support the immediacy of interpretation or the strategic views. These studies indicate that the eyes fixate the image briefly before fixating the titles, then might go back and forth between image and titles depending on time left. This pattern suggests that viewers might focus on key words after they use contextual cues and redundant information (derived at least from the image or the speaker's intonation) to guess the meaning of the titles (d'Ydewalle et al., 1991). Processing the audio channel in the dominant language would provide a wealth of contextual cues facilitating efficient reading of the foreign subtitles.

Without the help of translation, beginners are usually unable to benefit from most contextual cues when they read a foreign language text. Experiments conducted by Cziko (1978) have shown that beginning learners of a second language depend mostly on morphological constraints, that is, on an ability to identify parts of speech based on a knowledge of familiar words and the recognition of bound morphemes in unfamiliar words. (For example, a *-tion* ending in English or French serves as a reliable noun marker.) And beginners can often recognize syntactic cues from function words (such as articles, prepositions, and conjunctions), which indicate which parts of speech are likely to follow. (For example, an article will usually be followed by a noun.) Beginners must rely on morphological and syntactic cues because they have difficulties recognizing semantic information provided by the immediate context. Inexperienced language learners are also usually unable to use discourse constraints (i.e., the topic or macrostructure of the text), which require the high level of competence achieved by bilinguals. Therefore, beginning foreign language learners must rely on rigid grammar rules and follow a painstaking bottom-up, step-by-step deciphering process that goes counter to the immediacy of interpretation strategy. On the other hand, with reversed subtitling, the contextual information provided by the dominant audio channel should provide beginners with crucial contextual information likely to facilitate the processing of the foreign discourse.

In addition to facilitating encoding, reversed subtitling could also allow for easier retrieval of information. If the foreign utterance is successfully mapped on the dominant language with the help of the subtitled translation, then an important connection between the two languages is established. This connection could be particularly meaningful in light of the bilingual dual coding theory proposed by Paivio (1986, chap. 11). In bilingualism, according to this model, two separate verbal systems (V_1, V_2) operate in addition to the imagery system (Im). The three independent systems are interconnected, through associative verbal connections (V_1-V_2), or referential connections between verbal and nonverbal elements (V_1-Im, V_2-Im). This theory was supported by experimental data provided by Paivio and Lambert (1981). Their study found that recall was higher for picture labeling than for translation or copying because of the mnemonic superiority of the image code. It also showed that translated words were recalled better than were copied words, presumably because translation engages two separate memory stores. Other studies (Paivio, Clark, & Lambert, 1988; Vaid, 1988) further tested the bilingual dual coding theory by proving that semantic repetition effects were stronger for translation than for synonyms. Unlike translations that draw on memory traces from two systems, synonyms depend on associative connections within a single system. Within-system associations, which are usually based on a wide experiential range, are also more uncertain and less constrained than are translations. Thus, a subtitled video provides a triple connection, between image, sound in one language and text in another, sound and text being linked by translation. Given the additive effects of both image and translation, this combination should be very powerful.

A recent study (d'Ydewalle & Pavakanum, in press-b) tested the effects of the triple connection with these three forms of simultaneous input: image, sound and text. In the earlier experiments by Lambert et al. (1981), Holobow et al. (1984), and Lambert and Holobow (1984), students did not watch an actual video program, but simply listened to an audio script while reading the corresponding word-for-word written translation scrolling up the screen at the speed of the spoken dialogue. In the d'Ydewalle and Pavakanum experiments, on the other hand, students watched a regular TV movie to which subtitles had been added. Normal television viewing conditions were replicated to investigate the potential incidental language acquisition (as opposed to conscious language learning) that occurs when viewers watch foreign language programs. The study was divided into two experiments to compare the incidental language acquisition process with beginning adult learners (Experiment 1) and with beginning adolescent learners (Experiment 2). Both experiments involved a three-by-three design (combining L1 or L2 soundtrack or no sound, with L1 or L2 subtitles or no subtitles) and three posttests measuring vocabulary, sentence construction, and comprehension. Experiment 1 showed some evidence of foreign vocabulary acquisition, especially with reversed and standard subtitling, due to the help of the native language, but did not reveal a significant difference between these two forms of subtitling. The advantage of reversed subtitling was only confirmed on the comprehension test with younger students in Experiment 2, presumably because younger students may have been more likely to ignore the foreign soundtrack in the standard subtitling condition. However, because comprehension was tested entirely in English, these results do not show whether any foreign language acquisition did take place. Further studies are therefore needed to confirm the benefits of reversed subtitling, especially with beginning foreign language learners.

The present study is an extension of the reversed subtitling experiments described above, but it departs from them in its attempt to simulate potential classroom activities and conscious foreign language learning. The experiment was conducted in a normal foreign language class setting and involved students with limited exposure to the foreign language. As in the d'Ydewalle and Pavakanum (in press-b) study, it reproduced a realistic viewing situation, subtitles being added to an actual video program that foreign language students were likely to watch. In addition, testing was aimed at measuring actual production of utterances in a foreign language, which is a closer approximation of instructional goals. In all the studies discussed above, tests consisted of multiple choice items, which involve more passive recognition skills and even possible guessing; none of the measures tested active recall requiring actual foreign language production. As for comprehension, even with L2 testing, it is very difficult to design an accurate measure assessing the actual level of understanding of the foreign utterances because students may have understood the message via the L1 subtitled or dubbed channel and retranslated in their minds before answering the foreign language questionnaire. This is actually the reason that in the Lambert & Holobow (1984) experiment described above, students from the L1 script control group were even able to do quite well on the French comprehension and contextual meaning tests, although they were not exposed to any French input.

For this research project, a pilot test and two subsequent experiments were designed to study how video programs used in foreign language instruction can best assist students in recalling foreign vocabulary. In the pilot study, three conditions were compared: French audio only, standard subtitling, and reversed subtitling. In the following experiments, standard subtitling, which did not appear very promising, was replaced with bimodal L2 input. Based on the experiments conducted by Lambert et al. (1981), it was predicted that students in the reversed subtitling condition would do best. Because reading a foreign script should be easier than simply listening to the transient foreign dialogue, it was also assumed that students in the bimodal L2 input condition would do slightly better than would those in the audio condition.

Experiment 1 (Pilot Study)

Method

Participants. Thirty college students (14 males & 16 females) were selected for this experiment. All were members of two second-year French classes at a small Midwestern university and were requested to participate in the study during regular class time. However, the experimenter was not the students' instructor.

Stimuli/Materials. A five-minute video excerpt combining narration and dialogue was selected and prepared for the experiment. The video excerpt was part of *French in Action*, a 52-part video program specially designed for first- and second-year level French college instruction. The lesson was selected from the second half of the program (Lesson 31), so that presumably no student would have already watched this particular excerpt, which should include new as well as familiar phrases.

French and English subtitles for two of the conditions were produced with a character generator on Beta equipment according to television industry standards. Subtitles cannot be word-for-word translations of the audio version and small deletions often have to be made in the translation because of time, space, and image constraints. Subtitles can have a maximum 30 to 34 character length per line over two lines, and a maximum six-second duration; the minimum length is 1.5 seconds for very short titles (Marleau, 1982; Nootens, personal communication, 19 July 1988). In this study, the lower limit (30 characters/line) was chosen because the students might not have been used to reading subtitles and would have to read foreign sentences in the reversed subtitling condition. In addition, an English voice-over/dubbed version was taped and combined with the French subtitles for the reversed subtitling condition.

Design/Procedure. Students were divided into three groups: Group 1 (11 students) came from one class, and the other two groups (Groups 2 and 3, consisting of 10 and 9 students, respectively) were randomly selected from the second class. Because the experiment took place as a regular class activity, students from the two classes could not be mixed and randomly assigned to the three conditions. However, this drawback should be minor because the two classes had the same instructor and should have benefited from the same methods of instruction.

Although all the students were attending the same course, their actual level of French and prior foreign language experience were very diverse. A language background questionnaire was distributed to the students before the experiment for the purpose of determining their past experience in French. The students' answers indicated that their formal exposure to French in secondary school and/or college ranged from 6 months to 6 years. None had experienced regular.contacts with French speakers or had spent a significant amount of time in French-speaking countries. Most had occasionally watched French-language films and video programs, in particular a few episodes of *French in Action*, which was available in their school language laboratory.

Each group was assigned to one of the following conditions: Group 1 was shown the video program with the French audio track only (the way the original program is normally designed). Group 2 was shown a standard subtitled version of the video (French audio track with English subtitles). Group 3 was shown a reversed subtitled version (English audio track with French subtitles).

The three groups were given an English summary of the scene they were about to see. They were also reminded that they would be tested on the actual wording of the French presented in the soundtrack or the subtitles. Tapes were played on a Beta player connected to a 20-inch television screen. The video segment prepared for each condition was shown twice. Immediately after the second viewing, students were given a French recall test.

The test consisted of a fill-in-the-blank French vocabulary exercise with 20 one-to-three-word items indicated by one to three blanks (see Appendix). Test items chosen for the experiment were not necessarily those emphasized in the original *French in Action* presentation. Instead, the first principle for the selection of each test item was the presence of a clear link with a video image, so that the item would likely be encoded dually during viewing. Thus, five objects that had been foregrounded in the scene were selected. Because the imagery system in the dual coding theory also includes events, unambiguous single actions were chosen in five other cases (such as *crevé* and *repart*, respectively illustrated by the long shot of a flat tire and by the lingering image of the main character driving off again). Because the imagery system includes experiential elements as well, ten items whose meaning should have been made apparent by the situation were picked for the test (e.g., *dois*, in the sense of *owe*, is used by the main character as she pulls out her wallet; or the advice to be *prudente* is given by a concerned-looking character with his finger raised).

In addition to the visual link between verbal and nonverbal elements, test items were also selected according to their estimated degree of complexity and were intended to represent various levels of difficulty for beginning students. Half the items were considered to be at the first-year level (a fact confirmed by the background questionnaires filled out after the test, which showed that half the items were familiar to at least a third of the students). The other ten items were assumed to be unknown to most students and were designed as a measure of new vocabulary acquisition.

A few additional considerations were taken into account in the selection of items. Two- to three-word phrases (12 out of 20 items) were contrasted with single word items. The test also consisted of elements that had been repeated two or more times in the original dialogue (7 items) in addition to single utterance elements. Finally, a variety of grammatical functions were represented in the test (present tense, infinitive, imperative, and gerund verb forms; adjective agreement, and partitive).

Students were given the complete original sentences in which the missing words had to be written in. The video segment was played back a third time without sound or titles and stopped each time the students had to fill in a blank, so that they could be guided through the test sentence by sentence and benefit from visual associations. The image also provided a situational context for the utterance. Thus, a test item that could grammatically take any mass noun or verb, as *vous avez de* ____ or *et Mireille* ____, required a specific answer not only because it was part of a script but, above all, because it was the most meaningful response given the specific situation being shown.

In scoring the tests, the following considerations were taken into account: Only the exact phrases from the original text were acceptable (equivalents and synonyms were not); one- to two-letter variation (depending on the item) was allowed.

After the test items had been corrected, students were asked to check the items that they knew beforehand. Even though this measure is subjective, it provided a form of post-hoc test aimed at assessing students' prior knowledge. Pretesting would not have necessarily given a precise measure of the number of items already known. For example, the excerpt shown contained a number of automobile-related terms that some students had studied in high school and others had not. The post-hoc test, therefore, was a better indication of whether the groups were basically matched for the specific task.

Results and Discussion

The post-hoc test indicated that there was no significant difference in terms of prior knowledge between the three groups. Therefore, result differences between the groups should reflect the effects of the treatment conditions.

ANOVA was applied to study the main effects on the test measure. It showed that the results approached significance: $F(2, 27)=3.07, p=.06$.

The mean and standard deviation for each of the three groups in Table 1 indicate that recall was far greater in the reversed subtitling group than in the other two conditions.

The Fisher Protected Least Significant Difference test did show that the mean differences for Group 1 versus Group 3, and Group 2 versus Group 3 had a .05 level of significance. Students in the reversed subtitling condition were, in fact, able to recall nearly twice as many words as did students in the other conditions.

In an item-by-item comparison, the contrast of the various morphological components did not reveal any clear result pattern. Result differences were due rather to the difficulty level of the items and their degree of connection to contextual clues. One item in particular (repart) led to striking intergroup differences: none

Table 1
Mean Recall as a Function of Viewing Method (Pilot Study)

Viewing Method	n	M	SD
1. French Audio Only	11	3.36	2.87
2. Standard Subtitling	10	3.20	1.93
3. Reversed Subtitling	9	6.33	4.21

$F=3.07, p=.06$

of the students in the French audio group supplied the right answer, and only 10% in the standard subtitling group did; however, 67% of the students in the reversed subtitling group answered correctly. The successful encoding of this item may have been due to a unique combination of reasons. There was a clear one-to-one correspondence between the visual referent and the simple sentence in which the item appeared. Moreover, *repart*, which had already occurred in the script, had a prominent position as the final word of a sentence followed by silent images, which might have given students more time to encode the utterance. In addition, the degree of familiarity with this item (known by nearly 50% of the students) was a good indication of intergroup differences because items that were totally unknown could not usually be activated by any method, and items that were too well known were used correctly by most students, irrespective of the method used.

As an additional measure, a correct/known item ratio (based on the number of items provided correctly on the recall test and those checked for prior knowledge) was compared between the three groups. Again, the difference between the means approached significance, $F(2, 27)=2.91, p=.07$. The respective means for Groups 1, 2, and 3, were .35, .55, and .72, indicating that students in Group 3 were able to recall correctly 72% of the words they knew, and Group 1 correctly recalled only 35%. Thus, reversed subtitling helped activate a large share of the students' prior knowledge.

The results of this experiment suggest that reversed subtitling was by far the most beneficial condition, whereas the standard subtitling group had the worst recall results. Although beginning students were expected to benefit from the help of English in the standard subtitling condition, they commented that the English subtitles distracted them and prevented them from concentrating on the spoken French. As Lambert and Holobow (1984) suggested, English may have been used to comprehend the general message but might also have allowed students to bypass the French completely. Reversed subtitling, on the other hand, may be particularly beneficial because, in accordance with the interpretation given by Lambert et al. (1981), it supplies the assistance of the native language while enabling viewers to focus efficiently on the foreign language utterances once the global meaning is grasped.

The superior performance of beginners in the reversed subtitling condition definitely warranted retesting against other possible input combinations and with larger groups of students. These two considerations were taken into account for the design of the second experiment.

Experiment 2

Method

Participants. Fifty-seven first-year French students from three classes at the same Midwestern university as in the pilot study were requested to participate in the experiment. This experiment took place during regular class time.

Stimuli/Materials. The same video excerpt as in the previous study was used. However, a new tape combining a French audio track and French titles was prepared and replaced the tape with standard subtitling (which had not appeared promising).

Design/Procedure. Each class was assigned to one of the following conditions: Group 1 (21 students) was shown the bimodal French video (French audio with French titles). Group 2 (13 students) was shown the video program with the French audio track only (the way the original program is normally presented). Group 3 (23 students) was shown a reversed subtitled version (English audio track with French subtitles).

As in the pilot study, each group was given an English summary before being shown the video and was informed of the nature of the test that would follow. Tapes were played twice on a Beta player connected to a 20-inch television screen. Immediately after the second viewing, students were given a French recall test.

The test, which consisted of 17 items, was a modified version of the fill-in-the-blank exercise given during the pilot study (see Appendix). Items that appeared too difficult in light of the first results, and most of the two- or three-word phrases were eliminated to simplify the task for first-year students. The association between verbal and visual elements was also made as straightforward as possible. Six of the items represented objects, three were actions, and eight consisted of experiential elements made clear by the situation. Half of the items were familiar to at least a third of the first-year students, as the background questionnaires later confirmed.

Students completed the test while the video was played back a third time and stopped for each missing item, as in the pilot study. Only the exact phrases from the original text were acceptable answers, but one- to two-letter variations were again allowed.

Immediately after the test, students were asked to fill out a background questionnaire indicating the amount of formal French training and informal exposure to French they had had, in particular the number of *French in Action* episodes they had watched. Again, their answers indicated a wide range of experience. Although they all were currently taking their second quarter of college French, some had had no secondary school French instruction and others had had up to four years. They also greatly differed in their exposure to the French video program, some having watched no episodes and others as many as 24.

The questionnaire was handed out before students were asked to perform two additional tasks, which would then reflect longer-term effects. First, they were provided with a list of correct answers and were asked to check the ones they were familiar with prior to the test. Second, they were instructed to give an English translation of all the items, including those they may have learned by watching the video program. The checked and correctly translated items were intended to provide some measure of prior knowledge, while the unchecked and correctly translated items should indicate how much vocabulary learning took place during the experiment.

Table 2
Mean Recall as a Function of Viewing Method (Experiment 2)

Viewing Method	n	M	SD
1. Bimodal Input	21	4.04	2.83
2. French Audio Only	13	1.69	1.43
3. Reversed Subtitling	23	4.56	2.31

F=6.42, p<.005

Results and Discussion

The analysis of variance indicated a highly significant viewing method effect on recall, $F(2, 54)$=6.42, p<.005. The significant effect on the recall measure was due mainly to the large difference between the French audio group and the other two groups. According to the Scheffé F-test, the mean differences for the bimodal group versus the French audio group, and the reversed subtitling group versus the French audio group were highly significant. Table 2 shows that the means for the bimodal and reversed subtitling groups are more than double the mean for the French audio group. Students in the reversed subtitling condition performed best, but the difference between this condition and the bimodal French input condition was not significant.

The item-by-item comparison showed a similar pattern as in the pilot study. Once again, the last test item, *repart*, resulted in the greatest intergroup difference, with 65% of the students answering correctly in the reversed subtitling group, 48% in the bimodal group, and only 15% in the French audio group. The reversed subtitling method seemed to be most beneficial for recall in the case of items already familiar to many students, although some learning did occur with a few unfamiliar items. (In particular, the concrete term *capot* [hood], known by less than 4% of the students, was produced by none of the students in the French audio group, by 14% of those in the bimodal group, and by 26% in the reversed subtitling group. Like *repart*, it appeared at the end of a sentence, followed by a few seconds of silence).

Table 3
Mean Translation Results as a Function of Viewing Method
(Experiment 2)

Viewing Method	n	M	SD
1. Bimodal Input	21	6.33	2.28
2. French Audio Only	13	3.92	1.60
3. Reversed Subtitling	23	7.91	3.19

$F=9.95, p<.0002$

ANOVA showed that the viewing method effect was even more highly significant on the translation test: $F(2, 54)=9.95$, $p<.0002$. Once again, the highest mean was achieved by the reversed subtitling group and the lowest mean by students in the French audio track condition, as illustrated in Table 3. Follow-up analyses with the Scheffé F-test indicated statistically significant differences in mean performance for the three subsets.

The analysis of translated items provides some additional insight into the mechanism at work with subtitling and dual coding. Students in the reversed subtitling group were often able to translate previously unknown items that they could not produce in the recall test. In other words, they were able to learn new vocabulary, especially if they could make a clear connection with a physical object or an action in the video excerpt. For example, *roue de secours* (spare tire) was understood by 22% of the students in the reversed subtitling group but by none in the other two groups; *feu rouge* (traffic light), *capot*, and *cale* (stalls) were translated by none of the students in the French audio version, and by 4–5 times more students in the reversed subtitling group than in the bimodal group.

Although the recall and translation results coincided with the experimental hypothesis, the results of the prior knowledge questionnaire were unexpected. Unlike those in the pilot study, they indicated an overall significant difference of level, $F(2, 54)=4.67, p<.01$. The means greatly differed for the French audio track group (3.84), versus those for the bimodal input group (5.81) and the reversed subtitling group (6.13). The discrepancy between the results of the pilot study and those of the present experiment could be explained by the highly subjective assessment of prior knowledge and the manner in which these particular data were collected. In the pilot study, students checked their prior knowledge as sentences were corrected and answers supplied, which gave students a chance to recall familiar words upon seeing them in context. In this experiment, a list of correct words was given out of context and in random order. One interpretation of the discrepancy between groups is that even if prior knowledge was basically equal among the three groups, words that had not been learned thoroughly enough did not look familiar unless they were activated by the proper method.

To counterbalance this inconclusive assessment of prior knowledge, a second set of analyses was performed with the 20 students who had had no French training before college. Again, the overall recall results were significant, $F(2, 17)=6.39$, $p<.01$, with a significant subset difference between the French audio and the reversed subtitling groups according to the Scheffé F-test. The translation results were highly significant, $F(2, 17)=36.65$, $p<.0001$, and further analyses revealed significant mean differences for all three subsets. Tables 4 and 5 give further information about the means and standard deviations for the three groups in the recall and translation tests.

As a final measure, all the students' prior exposure to the *French in Action* video program was computed to assess whether

Table 4
Mean Recall as a Function of Viewing Method
(Less Experienced Students in Experiment 2)

Viewing Method	n	M	SD
1. Bimodal Input	5	3.20	1.92
2. French Audio Only	7	1.57	1.61
3. Reversed Subtitling	8	5.00	2.00

$F=6.39$, $p<.01$

Table 5
Mean Translation Results as a Function of Viewing Method
(Less Experienced Students in Experiment 2)

Viewing Method	n	M	SD
1. Bimodal Input	5	5.4	1.81
2. French Audio Only	7	3.42	1.27
3. Reversed Subtitling	8	9.62	1.30

$F=36.65, p<.0001$

good performance on recall and translation was the outcome of training and familiarity with audiovisual language instruction. Students' experience with the program was divided into four categories based on the number of episodes they had watched: 0–5, 6–12, 13–19, and 20+. There was no significant difference between the groups on either recall or translation, which confirms that the main effect was indeed due to the viewing methods used during the experiment.

These results confirm previous findings about the usefulness of reversed subtitling for beginning students. They also showed that bimodal input was not quite as effective but was a promising alternative with the added advantage that the spoken and written foreign language could be introduced simultaneously. Given the promising results of bimodal input with beginners, the question arose whether more advanced students would be better able to manage without the native language crutch and derive greater benefits from the bimodal input. Experiment 3 was designed to answer this question.

Experiment 3

Method

Participants. Fifteen college students (6 males & 9 females) attending two third-year French classes at the same Midwestern university as in the previous experiments were requested to participate in the study during regular class time.

Stimuli/Materials. The same materials were used as in Experiment 2, except for the French audio track tape, which was eliminated.

Design/Procedure. Each class was assigned to one of the two following conditions: Group 1 (7 students) was shown the reversed subtitled version. Group 2 (8 students) was shown the bimodal French video.

The same procedure as in Experiment 2 was followed. The only difference resided in the slightly higher difficulty level of the test because these students were more advanced. Although the sentences were identical, a number of single blanks were replaced by double or triple blanks that stood for two- or three- word phrases (see Appendix).

Originally, 14 students in Group 2 took the test, but six students had to be disqualified because two of them had already taken the test in another class and four had spent a year or more in a French-speaking country, according to the information supplied in the background questionnaire.

Results and Discussion

The analysis of variance did not indicate a significant viewing method effect on recall although results were better in the reversed subtitling condition. However, ANOVA showed a significant effect on the translation test: $F(1, 13)=9.48$, $p<.01$. Please refer to Tables 6 and 7 for the means and standard deviations in the recall and translation tests. As with first-year students, the intergroup difference was the greatest for concrete items that were not previously known to the students. (Over half the students in the reversed subtitling group translated the words *cale* and *marguerites* [daisies], whereas no one in the bimodal group understood the first term and only one student translated the second term.)

Based on the self-assessment test, prior knowledge was

Table 6
Mean Recall as a Function of Viewing Method
(Experiment 3)

Viewing Method	n	M	SD
1. Reversed Subtitling	7	8.42	3.95
2. Bimodal Input	8	6.75	2.18

$F=1.07, p=.31$

Table 7
Mean Translation Results as a Function of Viewing Method
(Experiment 3)

Viewing Method	n	M	SD
1. Reversed Subtitling	7	13.85	1.95
2. Bimodal Input	8	9.75	3.01

$F=9.48, p<.01$

about equal in both groups (9.85 in the bimodal group, and 9.00 in the reversed subtitling group). Interestingly enough, the translation scores were very close to the prior knowledge mean for the bimodal group, but much higher for the reversed subtitling group. Thus, students in the reversed subtitling condition could actively recall foreign vocabulary only slightly better than could those in the bimodal condition. However, there was a marked difference at the passive knowledge level. Thanks to the English input, the reversed subtitling group seemed better able to process new words sufficiently well to at least recognize and comprehend them in the translation exercise. It is probable that with some reinforcement and practice they should have the ability to use these new words actively.

General Discussion

The advantages of bimodal input and, above all, reversed

subtitling are clearly revealed in the present study, despite some technical limitations with the production of the dubbed soundtrack for the reversed subtitling tape and imperfect viewing conditions during the experiments.   Ideally, in dubbed productions, lip movements should be perfectly synchronized while sound effects and music remain unchanged, but this was not the case with the video used for these experiments. Also, some students remarked that it was occasionally difficult to read the subtitles because they had to sit too far away from the monitor. These limitations should, in fact, point to the even greater potential of subtitling: If students were to watch a better tape in improved conditions, for example in a language laboratory on an individual basis or in a video room equipped with a very large screen, they should derive even greater benefits from the subtitles.

The comparison of beginning and more advanced students provided somewhat unexpected results. The relatively successful results of the bimodal input for beginning students contradict the findings of Lambert and Holobow (1984), who felt that beginners were unable to process information in the foreign language without relying on their native language. In the present study, even beginners benefited from the bimodal input. Bimodal input may be helpful to beginners only if the material is carefully adapted to their level and contains many already known phrases that can be activated and reinforced by the audiovisual presentation.

In both the bimodal and reversed subtitling conditions, students clearly benefited from processing the written representation of the dialogue. Students often have difficulty recognizing word boundaries in the spoken language, especially if they are not familiar with some of the words. Listening to and reading the text at the same time can at least help students distinguish known from unknown phrases. In addition, the subtitling experiments discussed earlier (e.g., d'Ydewalle & Gielen, 1992) have demonstrated the dominance of the visual modality in efficient encoding and retrieval. Therefore, the modern approach to foreign language teaching, recommending that students learn phrases orally before seeing them in writing, may be questioned by the findings of this study.

The greater beneficial effect of reversed subtitling, even in comparison with the bimodal condition, was confirmed in all the experiments. The overall method effect was highly significant for both the recall and translation measures in the second experiment, which involved the largest number of students, and for the translation measure in the last experiment; also, results approached significance in the pilot study. In the subset analyses, reversed subtitling always led to the best performance. Differences between reversed subtitling and the French audio track condition were significant for recall in the pilot study and in Experiment 2 (the only two studies including the French audio track condition), as well as for translation in Experiment 2. (Translation was not tested in the pilot study.) Compared with the bimodal input condition, reversed subtitling also had a significant effect on translation in both Experiments 2 and 3, but the difference between the two conditions was not very large for the recall measure.

As discussed earlier, reversed subtitling may be particularly beneficial because students have more time to process the foreign discourse and also benefit from the contextual knowledge gained from listening to their native language. In addition, once translation has linked the two verbal systems, students have established more paths for retrieval and can benefit from visual traces as well as from two distinct sets of verbal traces, according to Paivio's (1986) bilingual dual coding theory. This theory and the findings of this study tend to show that translation should play a greater role in foreign language learning than current foreign language theory has allowed.

Reversed subtitling can fulfill two types of educational functions: The results of the fill-in-the blank tests suggest that the reversed subtitling method facilitates the assimilation and active recall of phrases previously introduced. With this method students are reminded of the meaning of semi-familiar foreign phrases through the juxtaposition with their native language equivalents and the associated image. Furthermore, the translation tests demonstrated that reversed subtitling assists students in the passive acquisition of vocabulary, especially when audiovisual referents are simple enough. This method enables students to start memorizing new words when they can establish a direct connection between a term in their native language, the corresponding image of an object or action, and its foreign equivalent. It therefore serves as an efficient way to introduce concrete terms that can be represented visually without any ambiguity.

Although students learned new vocabulary in the context of a script, the translation tests revealed that students, especially in the reversed subtitling condition, were able to comprehend a list of items presented out of context and without any visual support. They are therefore likely to recognize these items in new contexts, but additional experiments are needed to confirm this hypothesis. Further testing should also examine whether students' acquisition of new lexical items through subtitling can facilitate their learning of new morphological and syntactical structures.

Based on the results of this study, a model integrating both reversed subtitling and bimodal input into a complete curriculum can be advocated. First, a video program with reversed subtitling could be presented to students, which should allow them to gain a passive knowledge of a number of new terms. If students were shown the same tape in the bimodal format soon afterwards, they would presumably be better prepared to identify and remember these new terms. The bimodal input would, in turn, enable students to gain exposure to the spoken language and prepare them to comprehend the foreign dialogue without the support of any subtitles in a subsequent stage. With additional practice (repeating the newly learned phrases orally and playacting the script, for instance), students would probably acquire an active knowledge of the items introduced through the subtitling method and could even incorporate them quickly in oral production. Of course, a long-term study is needed to test the efficacy of this proposed model with beginners as well as with more advanced students.

At the very least, the findings of this study confirm that video can be a very valuable tool that helps students process, remember, and actively produce foreign terms. However, immersing students in a flow of foreign utterances without careful preparation may be of little help for their language skills. The pure immersion technique, in which students are expected simply to absorb a foreign language through observation and use of context, may not work unless learners are constantly surrounded with the language for extended periods of time. As more and more video materials are beginning to be commonly used in foreign language classes, it is essential to examine novel ways in which technology may assist the instructor. It is important to conduct new practical experiments, but also to do more theoretical research in second language acquisition and foreign language learning to gain a better understanding of the complex processes involved in these domains.

Notes

[1]Sohl, G. (1989). Het verweken van de vreemdtalige gesproken tekst in een ondertiteld TV-programma [Processing a foreign spoken text in a subtitled television program]. Unpublished master's thesis, University of Leuven, Belgium.

[2]Gielen, M. (1988). Perceptie en ondertitels: De parafoveale en perifere informatieverwerking van ondertitels [Perception and subtitles: Parafoveal and peripheral processing of subtitles]. Unpublished master's thesis, University of Leuven, Belgium.

References

Borrás, I., & Lafayette, R. (1994). Effects of multimedia courseware subtitling on the speaking performance of college students of French. *The Modern Language Journal, 78*, 61–75.

Carpenter, P., & Just, M. (1989). The role of working memory in language comprehension. In D. Khlar & K. Kotovsky (Eds.), *Complex information processing: The impact of Herbert A. Simon* (pp. 31–68). Hillsdale, NJ: Lawrence Erlbaum Associates.

Cziko, G. A. (1978). Differences in first- and second- language reading: The use of syntactic, semantic and discourse constraints. *The Canadian Modern Language Review, 34*, 473–489.

d'Ydewalle, G., & Gielen, I. (1992). Attention allocation with overlapping sound, image, and text. In K. Rayner (Ed.), *Eye movements and visual cognition: Scene perception and reading* (pp. 415–427). New York: Springer.

d'Ydewalle, G., & Pavakanum, U. (in press-a). Does regularly watching subtitled television programs improve language learning. In Y. Gambier (Ed.), *Transferts linguistiques et audiovisuels* [Linguistic and audiovisual transfer]. Lille, France: Presses Universitaires de Lille.

d'Ydewalle, G., & Pavakanum, U. (in press-b). Acquisition of a second/ foreign language by viewing a television program. In P. Winterhoff-Spurk & T. H. A. Van der Voort (Eds.), *Psychology of media in Europe: The state of the part, perspectives for the future*. Leverkusen, Germany: Vieweg/Westdeutscher Verlag.

d'Ydewalle, G., Praet, C., Verfaillie, K., & Van Rensbergen, J. (1991). Watching subtitled television: Automatic reading behavior. *Communication Research, 18*, 650–666.

d'Ydewalle, G., Van Rensbergen, J., & Pollet, J. (1987). Reading a message when the same message is available auditorily in another language: The case of subtitling. In J. K. O'Reagan & A. Lévy-Schoen (Eds.), *Eye movements: From physiology to cognition* (pp. 313–321). Amsterdam: Elsevier Science Publishers/North-Holland.

Holobow, N. E., Lambert, W. E., & Sayegh, L. (1984). Pairing script and dialogue: Combinations that show promise for second or foreign language learning. *Language Learning, 34*(4), 59–76.

Kellogg, G. S., & Howe, M. J. A. (1971). Using words and pictures in foreign language learning. *Alberta Journal of Educational Research, 17*, 87–94.

Lambert, W. E., Boehler, I., & Sidoti, N. (1981). Choosing the languages of subtitles and spoken dialogues for media presentations: Implications for second language education. *Applied Psycholinguistics, 2*, 133–148.

Lambert, W. E., & Holobow, N. E. (1984). Combinations of printed script and spoken dialogues that show promise for beginning students of a foreign language. *Canadian Journal of Behavioural Science, 16*, 1–11.

Marleau, L. (1982). *Les sous-titres: Un mal nécessaire* [Subtitles: A necessary evil]. *Meta, 27*, 271–285.

Paivio, A. (1986). *Mental representation: A dual-coding approach*. New York: Oxford University Press.

Paivio, A., Clark, J., & Lambert, W. (1988). Bilingual dual-coding theory and semantic repetition effects on recall. *Journal of Experimental Psychology: Learning, Memory and Cognition. 14*, 163–172.

Paivio, A., & Lambert, W. Bilingual dual and bilingual memory. (1981). *Journal of Verbal Learning and Verbal Behavior, 20*, 532–539.

Vaid, J. (1988). Bilingual memory representation: A further test of dual coding theory. *Canadian Journal of Psychology, 42*, 84–90.

van Dijk, T. A., & Kintsch, W. (1983). *Strategies of discourse comprehension*. New York: Academic Press.

Appendix: Fill-in-the-Blank Tests

Pilot Study

1. Heureusement, il y avait un <u>frein à main</u>.
2. J'ai été obligée de <u>brûler</u> un feu rouge.
3. <u>Ça marche</u>? Oui, ça va.
4. Je vous <u>dois</u> combien?
5. Au revoir, soyez <u>prudente</u>.
6. A la sortie de Paris, au milieu d'un <u>embouteillage</u>, le moteur cale.
7. Impossible de <u>redémarrer</u>.
8. Deux jeunes gens qui faisaient de l'auto-stop la poussent vers une <u>station-service</u>.
9. Vous êtes <u>en panne</u>? Oui, je ne sais pas ce que c'est.
10. Vous avez <u>de l'essence</u>? Non!
11. Je vous fais <u>le plein</u>? Oui, s'il vous plaît.
12. Je vérifie les niveaux? Oui, je crois qu'il <u>vaut mieux</u>.
13. Elle se prépare à changer la roue, mais la <u>roue de secours</u> est à plat.
14. J'ai <u>crevé</u>. Je vais vous aider.
15. Ne vous <u>en faites</u> pas, je vais envoyer un dépanneur.
16. Mireille attend, en <u>effeuillant</u> des marguerites sur le bord de la route.
17. Il m'aime un peu, beaucoup, passionnément, à la folie, <u>pas du tout</u>.
18. Il va arriver dans une heure, dans une <u>demi-heure</u>, dans un quart d'heure.
19. On répare <u>les deux pneus</u>,
20. et Mireille <u>repart</u>.

Experiment 2

1. Elle brûle le <u>feu</u> rouge.
2. Heureusement, il y avait un <u>frein</u> à main.
3. Voyons ça. Ouvrez votre <u>capot</u>.
4. Ça <u>marche</u>? —Oui, ça va.
5. Je vous <u>dois</u> combien?
6. Au revoir, soyez <u>prudente</u>.
7. A la sortie de Paris, au milieu d'un embouteillage, le moteur <u>cale</u>.
8. Deux jeunes gens qui faisaient de l'auto-stop la poussent vers une station-<u>service</u>.

9. Vous avez de l'essence? —Non!
10. Je vérifie les niveaux? —Oui, je crois qu'il vaut mieux.
11. Le pneu avant gauche crève à la sortie d'un virage.
12. Elle se prépare à changer la roue, mais la roue de secours est à plat.
13. Ne vous en faites pas, je vais vous envoyer un dépanneur. — Oh, c'est gentil, merci.
14. Mireille attend, en effeuillant des marguerites sur le bord de la route.
15. Il m'aime un peu, beaucoup, passionnément, à la folie, pas du tout.
16. Il va arriver dans une heure, dans une demi-heure, dans un quart d'heure.
17. On répare les deux pneus, et Mireille repart.

Experiment 3

1. Elle brûle le feu rouge.
2. Heureusement, il y avait un frein à main.
3. Voyons ça. Ouvrez votre capot.
4. Ça marche? —Oui, ça va.
5. Je vous dois combien?
6. Au revoir, soyez prudente.
7. A la sortie de Paris, au milieu d'un embouteillage, le moteur cale.
8. Deux jeunes gens qui faisaient de l'auto-stop la poussent vers une station-service.
9. Vous avez de l'essence? —Non!
10. Je vérifie les niveaux? —Oui, je crois qu'il vaut mieux.
11. Le pneu avant gauche crève à la sortie d'un virage.
12. Elle se prépare à changer la roue, mais la roue de secours est à plat.
13. Ne vous en faites pas, je vais vous envoyer un dépanneur. — Oh, c'est gentil, merci.
14. Mireille attend, en effeuillant des marguerites sur le bord de la route.
15. Il m'aime un peu, beaucoup, passionnément, à la folie, pas du tout.
16. Il va arriver dans une heure, dans une demi-heure, dans un quart d'heure.
17. On répare les deux pneus, et Mireille repart.

The Influence of Task- and Proficiency-Related Factors on the Use of Compensatory Strategies: A Quantitative Analysis

Nanda Poulisse and Erik Schils
University of Nijmegen

Authors' Statement: *This article reports results with respect to one of the research questions asked in a project on the use of compensatory strategies (CSs) by Dutch learners of English carried out at Nijmegen University between 1983 and 1987. Compensatory strategies in this study can be characterized as strategies used to solve lexical problems. Such strategies are quite frequent in the speech of foreign language (FL) learners, whose knowledge of the FL vocabulary is often limited, and thus constitute an interesting aspect of FL use.*

There are several points to make about this article. First, it was one of the earliest to present quantifiable data on CSs. Until then, most studies in the field had focused on defining the notion of communication strategies and setting up taxonomies. There were only few empirical studies available and most of these were small-scale. The present more substantial study involved 45 participants at three proficiency levels carrying out four tasks. Altogether we analyzed some 35 hours of foreign language speech. On the basis of these data, we were able to answer questions such as "how often do how many people use which strategy in what circumstance?" (Cook, 1993, p. 133). Naturally, the answers to these questions require theoretically based explanation (see below). Thus, the article went beyond the level of description to the level of explanation. Second, the article provides a detailed description of the way in which language-use data like these may be analyzed statistically. Care is taken to describe and explain the various steps in the analysis of variance used, from the global aspects to the more subtle ones of choosing the adequate error terms for testing simple main effects and simple contrasts in a split plot design.

This not only serves to make the analysis more insightful and convincing, if only for statisticians, but also allows other researchers of CSs and related phenomena to follow the same procedures. Third, the findings reported in the article have important methodological implications. The observed task effects on CS use were enormous and bring out the importance of using different elicitation methods in any study of second language use or acquisition that is intended to be generalizable. The differences between superordinate and subordinate CSs (a subordinate CS is embedded within a superordinate CS) are also noteworthy. They demonstrate the effect of the linguistic context in which CSs are used. Clearly, then, it is recommended to analyze super- and subordinate strategies separately. Fourth, the article begins to relate the study of CSs to the study of language use and communication in general. This is achieved both by classifying the data in terms of a taxonomy that reflects the processes underlying CS use and by explaining the results in terms of general communicative principles such as clarity and economy (cf. Grice, 1975; Leech, 1983). By relating the study of CSs to studies in the wider framework of communication, we attempted to remove the study of CSs from the isolated position it had hitherto taken and to place it within a well-developed theoretical framework.

Since publication of this article in Language Learning, *work on CSs has continued in several directions (see, e.g., articles in Kasper and Kellerman, in press). The theoretical framework in particular has been given a great deal of attention (e.g., Bialystok, 1990: Kellerman & Bialystok, 1990; Kellerman & Bialystok, in press; Poulisse, 1990, 1993, in press). Although the positions taken in these articles differ considerably, they do agree on the point that the study of CSs should be incorporated into a framework that also accounts for other aspects of (foreign) language use.*

Nanda Poulisse, University of Amsterdam
Erik Schils, University of Nijmegen, 1994

People who attempt to speak a foreign language are often confronted with lexical problems resulting from an inadequate command of the appropriate vocabulary. Although this occasionally leads to a breakdown in communication, foreign language (FL) learners generally manage to overcome their problems by employing one or more so-called communication strategies (CSs). The following extract illustrates the use of such strategies.[1]

I: mm, where were you last summer?
S: erm 1 in erm 2 Oostenrijk (=Austria) <laughs>, a country uh, near uh Switzerland 1 with uh mountains, too
I: mm
S: with snow   (Austria: 303t4)

Since 1973, when Váradi introduced the topic, CSs have been the focus of increasing interest (see collection of articles in Færch and Kasper, 1983; and the overview given by Poulisse, Bongaerts, & Kellerman, 1984). Most of the initial studies were directed at defining CSs and developing taxonomies that could be used to classify them (e.g., Tarone, Cohen, & Dumas, 1976; Tarone, 1977; Corder, 1978; Færch & Kasper, 1980). The data presented in these studies were generally used to illustrate the definitions of different communication strategy (CS) types, but there were hardly any attempts to analyze them systematically.

Subsequently, a number of empirical studies have sought to answer questions covering the relationship between CS use and learner characteristics such as personality, L1 background, and proficiency level (e.g., Tarone, 1977; Palmberg, 1979; Bialystok & Fröhlich, 1980; Haastrup & Phillipson, 1983). There have also been some attempts to establish the comprehensibility and the effectiveness of learners' CS (e.g., Ervin, 1979; Bialystok & Fröhlich, 1980; Bialystok, 1983). Because most of these studies were exploratory and fairly small scale, the conclusions that could be drawn from them were necessarily tentative. These studies' greatest value, therefore, lies in the practical experience gained in using several experimental tasks. The most important theoretical finding—reported in various studies—is that CS use seems to be task- and item-specific. This implies that to obtain a comprehensive picture of CS use, different tasks with a large variety of items should be used.

So far, there has been only one study in which a serious attempt was made to quantify data to arrive at more substantial conclusions concerning CS use. Paribakht (1982, 1985) compared native and nonnative speakers' CS use in a task that required the participants to describe concrete and abstract concepts. This study involved 60 participants, 20 native speakers of English, and two groups of 20 Persian learners of English at two different proficiency levels. Paribakht concluded that, on the whole, all three groups employed the same types of CSs; however, some groups used certain types of CSs more often than did others. Beginning learners, for instance, were reported to draw more often on their other knowledge sources such as world and paralinguistic knowledge, than were advanced learners. Thus Paribakht's study seems to indicate that CS use and proficiency level are related.

The disadvantage of Paribakht's study is that only one type of task was involved and that one task was not representative of actual communicative situations. This, in addition to the use of a taxonomy that was specifically adapted to her data, has made it difficult to generalize the results of her study.

The Study

The study described in this paper was set up to further investigate some of the factors that are alleged to determine CS use. For reasons of economy we restricted our study to a subset of CSs, namely, compensatory strategies (CpS).[2] These can be characterized as achievement strategies used by the speaker to reach his or her original communicative goal via alternative speech plans (cf. Færch & Kasper, 1980). The factors whose effect on CpS we chose to study were *FL-proficiency level* and *task*.

The FL-learner's proficiency level was frequently mentioned in the earlier studies as a potentially influential factor (cf. Tarone, 1977; Palmberg, 1979; Paribakht, 1982, 1985). This hunch was confirmed in our pilot studies, which revealed that beginning Dutch learners of English used more CpS and used a larger proportion of CpS based on L1 than did advanced learners (cf. Poulisse, 1981; Elsen, de Kleine, de Vries, & Weijnen, 1982). A second reason for concentrating on the factor *FL-proficiency* is Bialystok and Fröhlich's (1980) suggestion that a certain level of proficiency is a prerequisite for effective CS use. It was felt that this was a point that deserved further investigation.

Task was included because previous research had indicated that CS use is probably task-specific. This made it necessary to elicit CpS in a variety of tasks, one of which at least should resemble a realistic communicative situation so that a more generalizable picture of CpS use could be obtained.

Method

The project involved three groups of Dutch learners of English. Group 1 consisted of 15 second-year university students of English, Group 2 consisted of 15 fifth-year VWO pupils,[3] and Group 3 consisted of 15 third-year VWO pupils. The three groups had been learning English for just over seven, four, and two years, respectively. The students in the three groups may be characterized as advanced, intermediate, and beginning learners of English.

The students were tested individually on three tasks.[4] The first task was a picture description task. The students were given 40 colored photographs of familiar objects such as *a bib, an abacus*, and *a car*. Pretests involving a group of third-year university students of English had shown that the English words for 20 of these objects are generally unknown to Dutch learners of English. The other 20 items were objects whose names the students were likely to know. They were included as fillers to encourage the students. The students were asked to look at the photographs one by one and to make it clear in English which object they saw, either by naming it, or in any other way. They were asked to do this in such a way so as to allow an Englishman, who would later listen to the recordings of the session, to identify the objects. During this task the students were not given any feedback so as to ensure that none would be helped more than others.

The second task was a story retell task. It consisted of five ten-line stories, the first of which served as a practice run. The students were asked to listen to recordings of these stories read in Dutch by an experienced reader. After each story they were asked to retell it in English. Pictures had been drawn to accompany the stories to make sure that the students would not omit too many essential details. The students could look at these pictures while listening to the stories and while retelling them. Again, no feedback was given, but because stories are naturally monologues, this did not affect the naturalness of the task.

The third task was a 20-minute interview with a native speaker of English, during which discussions ensued on everyday topics such as school, holidays, cooking, and sports. The native speaker was a 29-year-old woman from Ireland who knew scarcely any Dutch. The first five minutes of the interview were not analyzed because they had served as a warm-up period.

The tasks were administered in two sessions which each lasted approximately 90 minutes. All data were recorded on video and subsequently transcribed.

The Identification[5] and Classification of CpS

The CpS in Task I were identified on the basis of problem indicators such as pauses, repetitions, false starts, a rising intonation, sighs, laughs, and comments such as "oh dear" and "what's it called again". Because we ourselves had determined the problems in this task and hence the occasions for CpS use, this was thought to be a reasonably adequate method of identification.

The CpS in Tasks II and III were not as easy to identify. In Task II it was not always clear whether the students had had *lexical* problems for which they had compensated by means of CpS or if their problems had been more general: for example, that they had forgotten elements of the story. In Task III the students had been relatively free to determine the speech topic and thus to hide their problems or to avoid them. For this reason two identification methods were combined to identify the CpS in these tasks. First, two independent judges determined where CpS had occurred on the basis of problem indicators in the data. And second, we based the identification on a third person's interpretation of retrospective data, namely, comments that the students themselves had given on their performance immediately after having completed the task. Eventually, the criterion for a *clear case* of CpS use in Tasks II and III was set up as *identified by both of the judges and / or on the basis of the retrospective comments*. There was one exception to this rule: irrespective of the judges' decisions, utterances were not identified as CpS if the retrospective comments clearly indicated that they did not qualify as such.

All clear cases of CpS were classified by means of a process-oriented taxonomy that distinguished between *conceptual* and *linguistic* strategies. In the case of a conceptual strategy, the speaker manipulates the concept and refers to it either by listing (some of) its defining and/or characteristic features, or by using the word for a related concept that shares a number of these features. In the first case the approach is analytic; in the second case it is *holistic*. Often analytic strategies include a reference to a related concept that is subsequently modified to enable the listener to identify the intended concept uniquely.

Linguistic strategies result from the speaker's manipulation of his or her linguistic knowledge. In the case of an FL or L2 learner, this will be knowledge of the syntactic, morphological, or phonological rules that apply in the L1, some knowledge of these rules in the L2 (and possibly the L3), and knowledge of the similarities and dissimilarities between the L1 and the L2 (and the L3). Two main types of linguistic strategies can be distinguished. One is the use of L2 rules of morphological derivation to create what the speaker assumes to be comprehensible L2 lexis. This strategy will be referred to as *morphological creativity*. The other linguistic strategy is a *transfer strategy*, operating on the basis of supposed similarities between languages (cf. Kellerman, 1977). Utterances resulting from this strategy may or may not be morphologically and/or phonologically adapted.

Figure 1 gives an overview of the CpS types discussed in this section together with some illustrative examples. For ease of reference they will from now on be referred to as ANCO (ANalytic COnceptual), HOCO (HOlistic COnceptual), LIMO (LInguistic MOrphological creativity), and LITRA (LInguistic TRAnsfer). It will be noted that this taxonomy is much more parsimonious than

conceptual	analytic	this you use for a baby so uh, that it can't uh make uh, his clothes erm 3 uh dirty (bib: 114t1)	
		big uh 1 big uh, cars, they're not uh really cars but big and high (truck: 304t4)	
	holistic	vegetables (peas: 301t4)	
		table (desk: 303t4)	
linguistic	morphological creativity	representator (representative: 214t3)	
		to ironize (to iron: 209t3)	
	transfer	middle (waist, Du: middel: 309t1)	
		cuffer (hairdresser, Fr: coiffeur: 314t3)	

Figure 1. An overview of CpS types

are most of the early taxonomies of CS. It is also more general, and for this reason it is applicable to a large variety of data. Its most important advantage, though, is that it enables one to focus one's attention on the processes that supposedly underlie CpS use, rather than on the linguistic forms of the resulting utterances. (For a more elaborate discussion of our reasons for developing a new taxonomy of CpS, see Bialystok & Kellerman, 1987; Kellerman, Bongaerts & Poulisse, 1987; Poulisse, 1987.)

Analyses and Results

Compensatory strategies can occur at two levels. Apart from strategies that directly compensate for the missing word, there are CpS that are embedded within other CpS. These occur when the speaker runs into a second lexical problem before he or she has solved the first one. We will refer to the former as *superordinate* CpS and to the latter as *subordinate* CpS. An example of a subordinate CpS (for flies) embedded in a superordinate CpS (for flyswat) is given below.

If there are uh little animals erm and you want to make them, dead, you can 3 uh hit them with the thing
(flyswat: 310t1)

Table 1
The Number of Superordinate and Subordinate CpS per Task

Group	Task I Pictures		Task II Story Retell		Task III Interview		Totals	
	Super	Sub	Super	Sub	Super	Sub	Super	Sub
1	293	54	165	16	221	9	679	79
2	302	176	298	32	321	23	921	231
3	302	157	339	61	392	42	1,033	260
Totals	897	387	802	109	934	74	2,633	570

Group 1: University students; Group 2: Fifth-year VWO pupils; Group 3: Third-year VWO pupils

Separate analyses were carried out for superordinate and subordinate CpS.

All in all, we elicited 3,203 clear cases of CpS. Of these 2,633 were superordinate CpS and 570 were subordinate. Table 1 shows how they were divided across proficiency groups and tasks.

The numbers of CpS elicited per student in each of the tasks were placed in a 45×3 matrix and analyzed as a two-factor ANOVA with one intersubject factor (Proficiency Groups 1, 2, & 3) and one intrasubject factor (tasks). Of course, the task factor was not interesting per se, as possible differences would at most reflect their noncomparability. However, what was interesting, was that *tasks* interacted significantly with groups, both for the superordinate date, $F(4, 84=5.83, p<.001$ and for the subordinate data, $F(4, 84)=6.70, p<.001$. Therefore, we contrasted the group means at the separate task-levels in two ways, namely (a) university students versus VWO pupils and (b) fifth-year VWO pupils versus third-year VWO pupils. The results of these contrasts are given in Table 2 (superordinate data) and Table 3 (subordinate data).

The comparison of university students (Group 1) and VWO pupils (Groups 2 & 3) in general confirms our prediction of an inverse relationship between the absolute number of CpS used by

Table 2
Group Contrasts per Task (Superordinate Data)

Contrast	Task	Ss	df	M	F	p
Group 1 vs. Groups 2 and 3						
	I	3.60	1	3.60	0.11	.746
	II	1152.04	1	1152.04	33.61	.000
	III	822.04	1	822.04	23.99	.000
Group 2 vs. Group 3						
	I	0.00	1	0.00	0.00	1.000
	II	58.80	1	58.80	1.72	.193
	III	172.80	1	172.80	5.04	.026
Error[a]		4318.40	126	34.27		

[a]Ss w groups and tasks *Ss w groups pooled

Table 3
Group Contrasts per Task (Subordinate Data)

Contrast	Task	Ss	df	M	F	p
Group 1 vs. Groups 2 and 3						
	I	547.60	1	547.60	49.56	.000
	II	41.34	1	41.34	3.74	.055
	III	23.51	1	23.51	2.13	.147
Group 2 vs. Group 3						
	I	10.80	1	10.80	0.98	.325
	II	28.03	1	28.03	2.54	.114
	III	13.33	1	13.33	1.21	.274
Error[a]		1392.13	126	11.05		

[a]Ss w groups and tasks *Ss w groups pooled

the students and their proficiency level. The university students produced fewer superordinate CpS than did the VWO pupils, except in Task I. This is not surprising though, because the number of superordinate CpS to be used in this task was largely predetermined by the number of problems included in it. Twenty pictures of difficult objects generally resulted in the use of 20 superordinate CpS. University students also produce fewer

Table 4
The Number of Superordinate CpS by Task, Group, and CpS Type

	Task I	Task II	Task III	Totals
Group 1				
ANCO	279	94	93	466
HOCO	2	59	77	138
LIMO	1	3	1	5
LITRA	6	4	43	53
Group 2				
ANCO	296	173	161	630
HOCO	0	85	86	171
LIMO	0	6	3	9
LITRA	2	24	67	93
Group 3				
ANCO	291	215	201	707
HOCO	3	78	101	182
LIMO	1	5	1	7
LITRA	3	32	87	122
Totals	884	778	921	2,583

subordinate CpS than do VWO pupils, although the difference in the interview condition reflects only a tendency in the predicted direction.

The differences between the VWO groups are smaller: the global tendency only reaches significance for superordinate CpS in the interview.

Table 4 gives some more detailed information about superordinate CpS. It specifies how often each type of CpS was used by each group. It will be noted that the number of CpS included in this and the following table is somewhat smaller than that reported in Table 1 (the differences are 50 and 4, respectively). This is because not all CpS could be unequivocally interpreted as instances of a particular CpS type. For instance, an utterance such as *clothes-maker* (for tailor) can be interpreted as ANCO—a tailor makes clothes—or as LITRA on the basis of

Table 5
The Number of Subordinate CpS by Task, Group, and CpS Type

	Task I	Task II	Task III	Totals
Group 1				
ANCO	18	5	2	25
HOCO	27	5	5	37
LIMO	3	2	0	5
LITRA	6	4	2	12
Group 2				
ANCO	62	10	4	76
HOCO	61	11	8	80
LIMO	1	0	0	
LITRA	50	11	10	71
Group 3				
ANCO	49	20	12	81
HOCO	55	21	21	97
LIMO	5	2	0	7
LITRA	47	18	9	74
Totals	384	109	73	566

Dutch *kleermaker*. Because of their ambiguity, utterances such as these were not included in the analyses. Table 4 shows that most of the CpS used by the students were ANCO. The use of HOCO is clearly task-dependent: whereas there are hardly any CpS of this type in Task I, they occur quite frequently in Tasks II and III. This is also true for LITRA, which is quite frequent in Task III but rare in Task I. The use of LIMO is virtually negligible for all tasks and proficiency levels.

Table 5 gives the same information for subordinate CpS. Compared with Table 4, the differences in preferred CpS type are striking. ANCO is by no means predominant in the case of subordinate CpS: it is outnumbered by HOCO whereas LITRA is also relatively frequent. Again there are hardly any instances of LIMO at the subordinate level so that we must conclude that this CpS type played a very minor role indeed.[6]

For the statistical analyses the frequencies reported in Tables 4 and 5 were converted into proportions. Like Paribakht (1982, 1985) we felt this would give a more realistic picture of the effect of *task* and *proficiency level* on the students' preference for particular CpS types. Consider, for instance, the use of superordinate HOCO in Task II (cf. Table 4). If one were to go by frequencies alone, one would have to conclude that Group 1 uses fewer CpS of this type than do Groups 2 and 3 (59 vs. 85 vs. 78). However, a comparison of the proportions would lead to a markedly different conclusion. Group 1 students solve their lexical problems in this task by means of HOCO in 36.8% of the cases (59 out of 160), Group 2 in 29.5% of the cases (85 out of 288), and Group 3 in 23.6% (78 out of 330). Hence, one could conclude that, relatively, Group 1 uses more HOCO in Task II than do Groups 2 and 3. The same argument applies at the level of a single student's frequencies pattern where a student using 12 instances of HOCO out of a total of 15 CpS (80%) can be said to respond more holistically conceptually than a person with 20 instances of this strategy out of a total of 40 CpS (50%).

In view of the above, every single student's frequencies pattern on each of the tasks was converted in the corresponding relative frequencies pattern, yielding three such patterns per student (i.e., one per task). Subsequently, for each of the four CpS types in turn, a 45×3 (Ss by task) matrix was constructed with entries indicating the student's relative use of the particular CpS type in each of the tasks. This was done separately for superordinate and subordinate CpS so that a total of eight matrices was created. The tables listed in Appendix 1 contain the cell, row, column, and grand means of the proportions in these matrices. Each matrix was then analyzed as a two-way ANOVA with one intersubject factor (proficiency level) and one intrasubject factor (task). Because we are dealing with proportions, an arcsine (inverse sine) transformation was applied to the data before the ANOVA was run. The effect of the procedure, which has been recommended by Winer (1971), is to stabilize the intracell variances.

The first step in the analyses of the above-mentioned design

Table 6
Preliminary Interaction Tests
(df=[4, 84]; error term: tasks * participants within groups)

	Superordinate		Subordinate	
	F	p	F	p
ANCO	1.31	.272	0.53	.711
HOCO	2.46	.051	0.62	.649
LIMO	0.20	.936	0.41	.800
LITRA	2.27	.069	0.96	.433

is to determine whether the group and task factors interact in their possible effect on the dependent variables ANCO, HOCO, LIMO, and LITRA. If they do not, this leads to a simplification of the subsequent analytical steps: only main effects for groups and tasks will need to be considered. In the case of interaction, however, separate group analyses of task differences and task analyses of group differences must be carried out. The results of the preliminary interaction tests, that is, the obtained F ratios and the corresponding significance values, are given in Table 6.

It appears that groups and tasks hardly interact in their effect on the various dependent variables. Only for superordinate HOCO and LITRA do the interaction effects border on significance. With respect to the analyses of these two CpS types we shall therefore proceed with caution and concentrate on group comparisons of task and task comparisons of group. For the remaining analyses only main effects will need to be considered.

The results of the eight ANOVAs are listed in Tables 7 and 8, which relate superordinate and subordinate CpS, respectively. Where appropriate, simple effects are reported instead of main effects. All significant effects are followed by the results of Newman-Keuls range tests in the columns labelled 1–2, 1–3, and 2–3. In these columns the symbols –, <, and > are used to indicate if the comparison is nonsignificant or significant in the indicated direction. The symbols are doubled (<< or >>) when the comparison is significant at the .01 level rather than at the .05 level. The

Table 7
Summary of Tests of Main or Simple Main Effects and, Where
Applicable, Newman-Keuls Comparisons (Superordinate Data)

Source:	Groups	1–2	1–3	2–3	Tasks	1–2	1–3	2–3
Error Term:	Ss w Gr[a]				Tasks * Ss w Gr			
df:	(2, 42)				(2, 84)			
ANCO	*F* 2.91	–	–	–	425.31	>>	>>	>>
	p .066				.000			
	MSerr .084				.049			
HOCO Task I	*F* 0.21	–	–	–	125.66	<<	<<	–
	p .812				Gr 1 .000			
	MSerr .047				.049			
Task II	*F* 5.95	–	>>	–	90.66	<<	<<	–
	p .003				Gr 2 .000			
	MSerr .047				.045			
Task III	*F* 6.98	>>	>>	–	67.55	<<	<<	–
	p .001				Gr 3 .000			
	MSerr .047				.045			
LIMO	*F* 0.15	–	–	–	6.46	<<	–	>>
	p .859				.002			
	MSerr .010				.012			
LITRA Task I	*F* 0.25	–	–	–	24.60	–	<<	<<
	p .776				Gr 1 .000			
	MSerr .067				.061			
Task II	*F* 4.80	<	<<	–	20.22	<<	<<	<<
	p .010				Gr 2 .000			
	MSerr .067				.061			
Task III	*F* 1.48	–	–	–	31.53	<<	<<	<<
	p .230				Gr 3 .000			
	MSerr .067				.061			

[a]The error term for groups in the test of simple main effects is Ss w Gr pooled with tasks * Ss w Gr

Table 8
Summary of Tests of Main Effects and, Where Applicable, Newman-Keuls Comparisons (Subordinate Data)

Source:	Groups	1–2	1–3	2–3	Tasks	1–2	1–3	2–3
Error Term:	Ss w Gr				Tasks * Ss w Gr			
df:	(2, 42)				(2, 84)			
ANCO	F 1.00 p .375 MSerr .469	–	–	–	9.00 .000 .530	>	>>	>
HOCO	F 1.80 p .178 MSerr .701	–	–	–	3.22 .045 .660	–	>	>
LIMO	F 1.46 p .243 MSerr .029	–	–	–	3.06 .052 .028	–	>	–
LITRA MSerr	F 3.22 p .050 .740	<?	<?	–	1.53 .233 .489	–	–	–

error terms and degrees of freedom used in the F ratios are given at the top of the table. For groups, the error term in the test of *simple main effects* is Ss w Gr pooled with tasks * Ss w Gr (cf. Kirk, 1968, pp. 263–265). For tasks, the error term is the same for main effects and simple main effects. From Table 7 it appears that proficiency level plays only a minor role in the selection of superordinate CpS. The only significant differences are the greater use of HOCO by Group 1 in Tasks II and III, and the less frequent use of LITRA by that same group in Task II. None of the differences between Groups 2 and 3 (third-year and fifth year VWO pupils) is significant.

Task effects, however, are considerable in the case of superordinate CpS. For ANCO, all Newman-Keuls comparisons are significant: the proportion of ANCO is greatest in Task I, less in Task II, and least in Task III. HOCO is less frequent in Task I than in Tasks II and III. This is true for all three proficiency groups; however, none of the differences between Tasks II and III with respect to this CpS type is significant. LIMO occurs most often in Task II. The difference is significant, both in comparison with Task I and with Task III. This result should be considered with some skepticism because the proportions for this CpS type were based upon very low frequencies (cf. Tables 4 and 6). Finally, the use of LITRA proved to be greatest in Task III and, with the exception of the university students, greater in Task II than in Task I.

Table 8 reveals that for subordinate CpS, too, there are hardly any proficiency level effects. The only difference that approaches significance is that between Group 1 and Groups 2 and 3 in the case of LITRA, which is used less often by the university students.

Again, we find that there are a number of task effects, but here they are less strong than in the case of superordinate CpS. The differences in the proportional use of ANCO are similar to those observed for superordinate CpS. ANCO occurs more often in Task I, less often in Task II, and least often in Task III. Subordinate HOCO occurs more often in Task I than in Task III. This is also the case for subordinate LIMO, but for reasons mentioned above, this result is rather dubious. These last two task effects, it should be noted, are inverted in comparison with those for superordinate CpS. Finally, it appears that there are no significant task-related differences at all with respect to LITRA as a subordinate CpS.

Two general conclusions to be drawn from Tables 7 and 8 are that task effects are much larger than are proficiency level effects and that many of the effects observed with superordinate CpS disappear with subordinate CpS.

The different effects of the factors task and proficiency level can be visualized by means of an analytic technique called correspondence analysis (Benzécri, 1976). This technique, which can be applied by means of the ANACOR program (Bettonvil, 1981), makes a multidimensional representation of row categories (here: nine task-proficiency level combinations) and column categories (here: four different CpS types).

This is structured so that the distance between the two categories expresses the *popularity* of a particular column category with a particular row category. Popularity, here, can be defined as the extent to which the observed frequency of a particular column category exceeds its expected frequency. Thus, in our study a CpS type is popular, and its distance to a task-proficiency level combination is small, if this CpS type was used more often in this particular task-proficiency level combination than one would expect on the assumption of independence. (For a detailed account of correspondence analysis, and for a description of the arithmetic procedures employed in it, see Gifi, 1981.)

Figures 2 and 3 depict the ANACOR plots for super- and subordinate CpS in our study. The first plot reveals a distinct task-related pattern. Numbers 1, 4, and 7 (Task I); 2, 5, and 8 (Task II); and 3, 6, and 9 (Task III) clearly cluster together. The A, denoting ANCO, is right in the center of the plot, indicating its frequent occurrence in each of the three tasks. The positions of the other letters indicate that HOCO (B) is more or less equally popular in Tasks II and III, that LIMO (C) is relatively popular in Task II, and that LITRA (D) is most popular in Task III.

If we now look at Figure 3, we see that there is no such clear pattern in the case of subordinate CpS. The task-related clusters are not distinct and tend to overlap. The distances between numbers relating to any one of the tasks are often larger than are those between numbers relating to different tasks. As in Figure 2, it is not possible to discern any distinct proficiency level-related clusters either.

The two ANACOR plots visually support the findings reported earlier on the basis of ANOVA: that task is a more dominant factor than is proficiency level in determining the choice of CpS and that any effects to be observed are stronger for superordinate than they are for subordinate CpS.

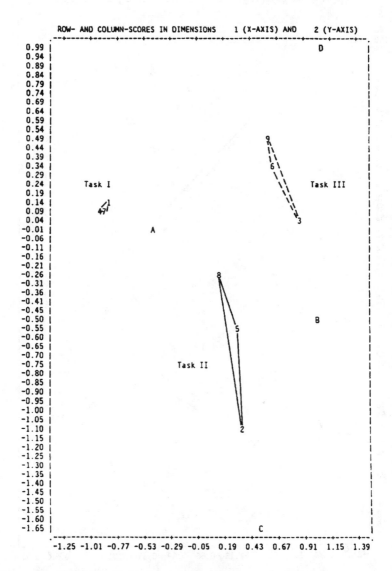

ROW- AND COLUMN-SCORES IN DIMENSIONS   1 (X-AXIS) AND   2 (Y-AXIS)

Figure 2. ANACOR plot for superordinate compensatory strategies. (A=ANCO; B=HOCO; C=LIMO; D=LITRA; 1=Group 1, Task I; 2=Group 1, Task II; 3=Group 1, Task III; 4=Group 2, Task I; 5=Group 2, Task II; 6=Group 2, Task III; 7=Group 3, Task I; 8=Group 3, Task II; 9=Group 3, Task III.)

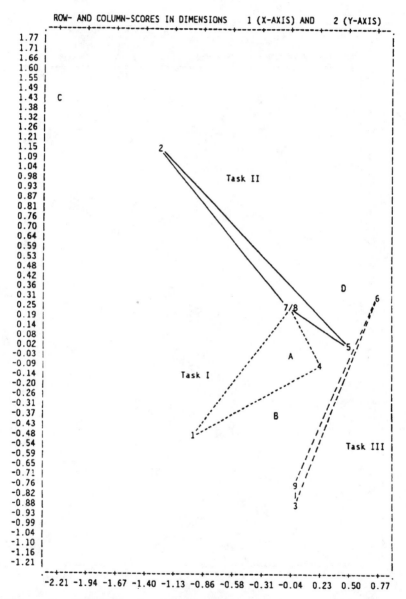

Figure 3. ANACOR plot for subordinate compensatory strategies. (A=ANCO; B=HOCO; C=LIMO; D=LITRA; 1=Group 1, Task I; 2=Group 1, Task II; 3=Group 1, Task III; 4=Group 2, Task I; 5=Group 2, Task II; 6=Group 2, Task III; 7=Group 3, Task I; 8=Group 3, Task II; 9=Group 3, Task III.)

Discussion

The first result reported in the preceding section concerned the inverse relationship between the absolute number of CpS used and the students' proficiency level. The less-proficient students (VWO pupils) produced a higher number of CpS than did those who were more proficient (university students). This can be explained as an obvious consequence of the VWO pupils' more limited command of the FL vocabulary. They encounter more lexical problems and therefore need to resort to CpS more often. The lack of many significant differences in the number of CpS used by third-year VWO and fifth-year VWO pupils is noteworthy. Despite differences in proficiency, these two groups need to resort to CpS equally often.

In the remainder of this section we will discuss the observed differences in the choice of particular CpS types. This discussion will be divided into three parts: (a) we will suggest an explanation for the large role played by the factor *task*; (b) we will briefly go into the few proficiency-related differences we found after which we will attempt to explain why we did not find any more; and (c) we will try to account for the reduced effects of both *task* and *proficiency level* in the case of subordinate CpS.

Task Effects

To explain the enormous effect of the factor *task* it is useful to first determine how the tasks differed and the effects these differences had on CpS choice. As will be recalled, Task I was a picture naming/description task, Task II was a story retell task, and Task III was an oral interview. These tasks differ in a number of respects. The following are the most relevant to our study.

Task Demands: The instruction for Task I required the students to solve all lexical problems (posed by the photographs). In Tasks II and III, however, it was possible to leave some problems unresolved and yet successfully complete the task as a whole. Particularly in Task III, the interview, the students could decide to risk misunderstanding on the part of the interlocutor if they judged a message to be of little relevance. Thus Task I required a higher level of clarity than did Tasks II and III.

Context: The tasks differed in the possibility they provided to make use of the context. In Task I this possibility was practically nonexistent. The problems were not embedded within a context as the photographs were presented in isolation, but in Tasks II and III the stories and the interview *did* provide contextual information. Consequently, in Task I all information had to be contained in the CpS themselves, whereas in Tasks II and III the speaker could rely on the context to provide some information too.

Time Constraints: There were no time constraints in Task I. Strictly speaking, there were no time constraints in Tasks II and III either; however, after having carried out Task II, some students reported they had abstained from using elaborate CpS for recurring problems because they felt it was awkward to keep repeating the same lengthy utterances. In Task III conversational rules may have presented a time constraint. As Beattie (1980) reports, pauses longer than five or six seconds may cause the speaker to lose his or her turn. Thus, whereas in Task I the students could spend as much time on their CpS as they thought fit, they probably felt they could not do so in Tasks II and III.

The Presence of an Interlocutor: There was no interlocutor present in Tasks I and II, whereas in Task III there was. The possibility of obtaining feedback in Task III enabled students to check whether a CpS had been sufficiently well understood and to apply a second one only if necessary.

Considering that ANCO is generally most informative, certainly when many properties are mentioned, but also most time-consuming, it is not surprising that this CpS type abounds in Task I, which required informative strategies, but did not impose any time constraints. The use of ANCO in this task may have been further increased because no interlocutor was present. As they could not obtain feedback, the students may have overcompensated to make sure that their CpS were understood (cf. Krauss & Weinheimer, 1966, for a similar effect of the absence of feedback).

Because HOCO is a CpS that tends to be less informative, whereas LITRA is only comprehensible if there is shared linguistic knowledge, these CpS types are less appropriate in Task I. In Tasks II and III, however, they could be used effectively, because these tasks do not always demand a high level of clarity. Moreover, Task III allows one to check whether comprehension has occurred. Another possible reason for the increased use of HOCO and LITRA in Tasks II and III is that these CpS types tend to be short, which makes them particularly suitable for use in situations in which time is limited.

The important role played by factors such as *task demands, context, time available,* and *presence of an interlocutor* is not surprising. These factors are among those that govern communication in general (see Clark & Clark, 1977, pp. 225–226). Because CpS are, in effect, part of the communication process, albeit only in case of lexical problems, it would, in fact, be decidedly odd if they were not affected by the same factors.

Proficiency Level Effects

It was observed that there were only few proficiency level effects. The ones we found concerned the greater use of superordinate HOCO by university students in Tasks II and III and the larger use of LITRA by VWO pupils in Task II for superordinate CpS and in all tasks for subordinate CpS. The most plausible explanation for the differences in the use of HOCO is that learners of a lower proficiency level do not have a sufficiently large FL vocabulary at their disposal to come up with suitable approximations. The greater use of LITRA by low-proficiency students is in accordance with our expectations, which were based upon previous research. Because of their limited command of the FL, the students have to resort to the L1 more often. In view of this it is remarkable that we did not find more proficiency-related differences. For instance, one would have expected high-proficiency students to use fewer LITRA in Task III (the interview) because, at their level, there should be no need to make use of the

L1. A possible explanation is that the task effects were so powerful that they overruled any proficiency effects that might have occurred. In this particular case, the presence of the interlocutor and the need to carry on with the conversation may have induced the university students to use a fast LITRA first and add another CpS only if the interlocutor failed to understand it.

However, one should be careful not to overlook the possibility that the proficiency level of Group 3 may not have been low enough to bring the expected differences to light. In this respect it is worth noting that the three proficiency groups all seem to meet the minimal proficiency requirements for effective CpS use (cf. Bialystok & Fröhlich, 1980). It is not inconceivable that once this level has been reached, proficiency-related differences only reflect themselves in the linguistic realization of CpS and not in the distribution of CpS types.

Differences Between Superordinate and Subordinate CpS

Both task and proficiency effects proved to be stronger for superordinate than for subordinate CpS. For task effects in particular the differences were striking. This can be explained if one considers that subordinate CpS are, by definition, always embedded within the context of a superordinate CpS. This particular position of subordinate CpS has certain consequences. On the one hand, it means that subordinate CpS must not be too long, because lengthy strategies embedded within other strategies are likely to cause processing problems to both the speaker and the listener. On the other hand, it suggests that there is relatively little need for subordinate CpS to be fully informative. After all, the context (i.e., the superordinate CpS) provides some information too, which may facilitate the interpretation of the subordinate CpS. The need to be brief and the absence of the need to be fully informative apparently overrule the usual task effects. This may well explain why HOCO and LITRA—which are typically short but not necessarily very informative—occurred frequently as subordinate CpS in all three tasks, including Task I.

Conclusion

The project described in this paper is one of the first empirical studies of CpS—or for that matter CS—that allows a quantitative analysis of the data. This enabled us to determine the effect of the factors *task* and *proficiency level* on the use of CpS. It appeared proficiency level is inversely related to the number of CpS used by the students, although the differences between third-year VWO and fifth-year VWO pupils are small.

Contrary to our expectations, proficiency level proved to have only a limited effect on the choice of CpS. The data indicate that task-related factors are much more dominant in this respect. The students generally estimated how much information they needed to give—considering task demands, the context, and the interlocutor—and selected a CpS that was appropriately informative. Although the students did not as a rule expend more effort than was necessary, they did attempt to produce clear and comprehensible speech—within the time available. This suggests that in selecting CpS the students observed the same conversational principles that affect communication in general (cf. Grice, 1975; Leech, 1983).

It was more difficult to explain the lack of substantial proficiency-related differences. Two possible explanations were offered: (a) that the *proficiency level* factor is overruled by the more powerful *task* factor and (b) that our lowest proficiency level was not low enough. At present there is no way to decide whether any of these explanations is correct. Evidently more research, with students of a lower proficiency level, will need to be done first.

Notes

[1]This extract is taken from the data collected in the project *The Use of Compensatory Strategies by Dutch Learners of English*. The project is being carried out at The University of Nijmegen (Holland), and financed by the university's research pool. It is supervised by Theo Bongaerts and Eric Kellerman, whose contribution to the project and to this paper we hereby acknowledge. In this and subsequent extracts "S" stands for student and "I" stands for interviewer. Pauses are indicated by numbers, "1" being a one-

second pause, "2" being a two-second pause, and so on. Pauses of less than one second are marked by a comma. Relevant information on the students' or the interviewer's behavior is given between angular brackets (< >).

[2]In the remainder of this article we will use the abbreviation CS to refer to the more general notion of communication strategy when discussing previous research. We will use CpS whenever reference is made to compensatory strategies as studied in the Nijmegen project.

[3]VWO is a type of Dutch secondary school that prepares pupils for entrance into a university. It lasts six years during which time English is generally taught as a main subject for three 50-minute periods a week.

[4]A fourth task was included in the project to permit comparison of the use of referential strategies in L1 and L2. This task, an abstract picture description task comparable to Task 1, will not be reported on here (but see Bongaerts & Poulisse, 1989).

[5]A much more detailed account of our identification procedures and, in particular, of our use of retrospective methods for this purpose, is given in Poulisse, Bongaerts, and Kellerman (1987).

[6]In our **oral** data there are very few instances of LIMO (34, a mere 1%). It should be noted, however, that Zimmerman (1987) in a study of **written** data elicited from advanced German learners of English by means of a translation task, quotes many errors that he classifies as *form-oriented approximations*. Many of these errors closely resemble what we have called morphological "creations" (e.g., "illucitation" for 'illustration/illumination' and "incitement" for 'incentive').

References

Beattie, G. (1980). Encoding units in spontaneous speech: Some implications for the dynamics of conversation. In H. Dechert & M. Raupach (Eds.), *Temporal variables in speech: Studies in honour of Frieda Goldman Eisler* (pp. 132–143). The Hague, Holland: Mouton.

Benzécri, J. P. (1976). *L'analyse des données: Part 2. L'analyse des correspondences*. Paris: Dunod.

Bettonvil, B. (1981). *ANACOR: Correspondence analysis of contingency tables*. Leiden, Holland: Leiden University, Department of Data Theory.

Bialystok, E. (1990). *Communication strategies: A psychological analysis of second-language use*. Oxford: Basil Blackwell.

Cook, V. J. (1993). *Linguistics and second language teaching*. Basingstoke, Hants: Macmillan.

Grice, H. P. (1975). Logic and conversation. *Syntax and Semantics, 3*, 41–58.

Kasper, G., & Kellerman, E. (Eds.). (in press). *Advances in communication strategy research*. London: Longman.

Kellerman, E. (1977). Towards a characterization of the strategy of transfer in second language learning. *Interlanguage Studies Bulletin, 2*, 58–145.

Kellerman, E., & Bialystok, E. (in press). On psychological plausibility in the study of communication strategies. In G. Kasper & E. Kellerman (Eds.), *Advances in communication strategy research*. London: Longman.

Kellerman, E., Bongaerts, T., & Poulisse, N. (1987). Strategy and system in L2 referential communication. In R. Ellis (Ed.), *Second language acquisition in context* (pp. 100–112). Englewood Cliffs, NJ: Prentice-Hall.

Kirk, R. (1968). *Experimental design: Procedures for the behavioral sciences*. Belmont, CA: Brooks/Cole Publishing Company.

Krauss, R., & Weinheimer, S. (1966). Concurrent feedback, confirmation, and the encoding of referents in verbal communication. *Journal of Personality and Social Psychology, 4,* 343–346.

Leech, G. (1983). *Principles of pragmatics*. London: Longman.

Palmberg, R. (1979). Investigating communication strategies. In R. Palmberg (Ed.), *Perception and production of English: Papers on interlanguage* (pp. 33–75). Turku, Finland: Åbo University.

Paribakht, T. (1982). *The relationship between the use of communication strategies and aspects of target language proficiency: A study of Persian ESL students*. Unpublished doctoral dissertation, University of Toronto, Ontario, Canada.

Paribakht, T. (1985). Strategic competence and language proficiency. *Applied Linguistics, 6,* 132–146.

Poulisse, N. (1981). *Communication strategies: A comparative analysis*. Unpublished manuscript, University of Nijmegen, Department of Applied Linguistics, Nijmegen, Holland.

Poulisse, N. (1987). Problems and solutions in the classification of compensatory strategies. *Second Language Research, 3,* 141–153.

Poulisse, N. (1990). *The use of compensatory strategies by Dutch learners of English*. Dordrecht, Holland: Foris.

Poulisse, N. (1993). A theoretical account of lexical communication strategies. In R. Schreuder & B. Weltens (Eds), *The bilingual lexicon* (pp. 157–189). Amsterdam: John Benjamins.

Poulisse, N. (in press). Compensatory strategies and the principles of clarity and economy. In G. Kasper & E. Kellerman (Eds.), *Advances in communication strategy research*. London: Longman.

Poulisse, N., Bongaerts, T., & Kellerman, E. (1984). On the use of compensatory strategies in second language performance. *Interlanguage Studies Bulletin, 8,* 70–105.

Poulisse, N., Bongaerts, T., & Kellerman, E. (1987). The use of retrospective verbal reports in the analysis of compensatory strategies. In C. Færch & G. Kasper (Eds.), *Introspection in second language research* (pp. 213–229). Clevedon, Avon: Multilingual Matters.

Tarone, E. (1977). Conscious communication strategies in interlanguage: A progress report. In H. Brown, C. Yorio, & R. Crymes (Eds.), *On TESOL '77: Teaching and learning English as a second language* (pp. 194–203). Washington, DC: TESOL.

Tarone, E., Cohen, A., & Dumas, G. (1983). A closer look at some interlanguage terminology: A framework for communication strategies. In C. Færch & G. Kasper (Eds.), *Strategies in interlanguage communication* (pp. 4–14). London: Longman.

Váradi, T. (1983). Strategies of target language communication: Message adjustment. In C. Færch & G. Kasper (Eds.), *Strategies in interlanguage communication* (pp. 79–99). London: Longman.

Winer, B. (1971). *Statistical principles in experimental design* (2nd ed.). New York: McGraw-Hill.

Zimmerman, R. (1987). Form-oriented and content-oriented lexical errors in L2 learners. *International Review of Applied Linguistics in Language Teaching, 25,* 55–67.

Appendix 1:
The Relative Use of Each CpS Type/Task/Group

Table A–1
Means for Cells, Rows, Columns, and Grand Mean for ANCO (Superordinate Data)

	Task I	Task II	Task III	Rows
Group 1	.970	.583	.425	.659
Group 2	.993	.608	.542	.714
Group 3	.977	.645	.523	.715
Columns	.980	.612	.497	.696

Table A–2
Means for Cells, Rows, Columns, and Grand Mean for HOCO (Superordinate Data)

	Task I	Task II	Task III	Rows
Group 1	.007	.367	.380	.251
Group 2	.000	.290	.272	.187
Group 3	.010	.238	.258	.168
Columns	.005	.298	.303	.202

Table A–3
Means for Cells, Rows, Columns, and Grand Mean for LIMO
(Superordinate Data)

	Task I	Task II	Task III	Rows
Group 1	.003	.023	.003	.010
Group 2	.000	.019	.007	.009
Group 3	.003	.015	.002	.007
Columns	.002	.019	.004	.008

Table A–4
Means for Cells, Rows, Columns, and Grand Mean for LITRA
(Superordinate Data)

	Task I	Task II	Task III	Rows
Group 1	.020	.027	.193	.080
Group 2	.006	.083	.179	.090
Group 3	.010	.102	.218	.110
Columns	.012	.071	.196	.093

Table A–5
Means for Cells, Rows, Columns, and Grand Mean for ANCO
(Subordinate Data)

	Task I	Task II	Task III	Rows
Group 1	.378	.193	.055	.209
Group 2	.348	.236	.136	.240
Group 3	.327	.298	.193	.273
Columns	.351	.242	.128	.241

Table A–6
Means for Cells, Rows, Columns, and Grand Mean for HOCO
(Subordinate Data)

	Task I	Task II	Task III	Rows
Group 1	.384	.191	.156	.243
Group 2	.393	.380	.229	.334
Group 3	.363	.361	.322	.349
Columns	.380	.311	.234	.309

Table A–7
Means for Cells, Rows, Columns, and Grand Mean for LIMO
(Subordinate Data)

	Task I	Task II	Task III	Rows
Group 1	.032	.027	.000	.020
Group 2	.007	.000	.000	.002
Group 3	.023	.021	.000	.014
Columns	.021	.016	.000	.012

Table A–8
Means for Cells, Rows, Columns, and Grand Mean for LITRA
(Subordinate Data)

	Task I	Task II	Task III	Rows
Group 1	.139	.189	.056	.128
Group 2	.252	.251	.302	.268
Group 3	.288	.320	.151	.253
Columns	.226	.254	. 170	.216

Index

abstract
  concepts 158, 285
  words 8, 62, 114, 120, 217
acoustic similarity 10, 107, 143, 146
adjective 113, 217, 265
adverb 113
alphabetic writing system 116
aphasics 113
approximation 129, 131, 261, 305, 308
articulatory
  assembly 147, 151
  features 109, 110, 149–150
associative connections 260
attention 83, 94, 193, 219, 290
attentional processing 83, 91
auditory image 216, 219
automaticity 5–6, 81–82, 84, 86, 90–91, 95–96, 99–101

bilingual lexicon 2, 36
bilingualism 32, 34, 36, 60–64, 259
  additive 61–62, 66, 75, 77
  sequential 61, 63, 66, 74
  simultaneous 4–5, 31, 33, 35, 61–62, 66, 73–75, 77
  subtractive 61, 66, 75
bilinguality 59, 61, 75
bimodal input 256–258, 262, 268, 270–273, 275–278

causal path analyses 156
Chinese ideographs 18, 173, 175, 179–180
cognate 8–10, 18, 71, 149, 157
comprehensible input 188–189, 192–194, 215, 219
comprehensible output 194
concrete
  noun 16, 120, 158, 217, 220, 270, 274
  words 8, 114, 278
consciousness 16
context-reduced task 62
controlled processing 6, 90–91, 97, 100–101
conversational modifications 188
interactionally modified input 190–192, 196, 204, 206, 210, 212–219
premodified input 190, 192, 196, 198, 201, 204, 206, 210, 212, 215–216, 219
crosslinguistic influence 6, 8–9
cues 14–15, 117, 168, 181, 193
  contextual 171, 180, 258, 259
  syntactic 259
  temporal 171, 180
  visual 254

decontextualized language 62
depth of processing 17, 256